The Ruins, or, Meditation on the Revolutions of Empires: and The Law of Nature

by C. F. Volney

BLACK CLASSIC PRESS
P.O. Box 13414
Baltimore, MD 21203
A Young Press With Some Very Old Ideas

C. F. VOLNEY.

The Ruins, or, Meditation on the Revolutions of
Empires: and The Law of Nature

by C. F. Volney

Published 1991

by

BLACK CLASSIC PRESS

Published from the Peter Eckler edition 1890

Cover design by Tony Browder

Library of Congress Card Catalog Number 90- 082691

ISBN:0- 933121- 52- 0

Founded in 1978 Black Classic Press specializes in bringing to light
obscure and significant works by and about people of African descent. If our books are not available in your area ask your local
bookseller to order them. Our current list of titles can be obtained by
writing:

BLACK CLASSIC PRESS
c/o List
P.O. Box 13414
Baltimore, MD 21203
A Young Press With Some Very Old Ideas

PUBLISHER'S PREFACE.

HAVING recently purchased a set of stereotyped plates of *Volney's Ruins*, with a view of reprinting the same, I found, on examination, that they were considerably worn by the many editions that had been printed from them, and that they greatly needed both repairs and corrections. A careful estimate showed that the amount necessary for this purpose would go far towards reproducing this standard work in modern type and in an improved form. After due reflection this course was at length decided upon, and all the more readily, as by discarding the old plates and resetting the entire work, the publisher was enabled to greatly enhance its value, by inserting the translator's preface as it appeared in the original edition, and also to restore many notes and other valuable material which had been carelessly omitted in the American reprint.

An example of an important omission of this kind may be found on the fifteenth, sixteenth, and seventeenth pages of this volume, which may be appropriately referred to in this connection. It is there stated, in describing the ancient kingdom of Ethiopia, and the ruins of Thebes, her opulent metropolis, that "There a people, now forgotten, discovered, while others were yet barbarians, the elements of the arts and sciences. A race of men, now rejected from society for their sable skin and frizzled hair, founded on the study of the laws of nature, those civil and religious systems which still govern the universe."

A voluminous note, in which standard authorities are cited, seems to prove that this statement is substantially correct, and that we are in reality indebted to the ancient Ethiopians, to the fervid imagination of the persecuted and despised negro, for the various religious systems now so highly revered by the different branches of both the Semitic and Aryan races. This fact, which is so frequently referred to in Mr. Volney's writings, may perhaps solve the question as to the origin of all religions, and may even suggest a solution to the secret so long concealed beneath the flat nose, thick lips, and negro features of the Egyptian Sphinx. It may also confirm the statement of Dioderus, that "the Ethiopians conceive themselves as the inventors of divine worship, of festivals, of solemn assemblies, of sacrifices, and of every other religious practice."

That an imaginative and superstitious race of black men should have invented and founded, in the dim obscurity of past ages, a system of religious belief that still enthralls the minds and clouds the intellects of the leading representatives of modern theology,— that still clings to the thoughts, and tinges with its potential influence the literature and faith of the civilized and cultured nations of Europe and America, is indeed a strange illustration of the mad caprice of destiny, of the insignificant and apparently trivial causes that oft produce the most grave and momentous results.

The translation here given closely follows that published in Paris by Levrault, Quai Malaquais, in 1802, which was under the direction and careful supervision of the talented author; and whatever notes Count Volney then thought necessary to insert in his work, are here carefully reproduced without abridgment or modification.

The portrait, maps and illustrations are from a French edition of Volney's complete works, published by Bossange Frères at No. 12 Rue de Seine, Paris, in 1821,—one year after the death of Mr. Volney. It is a presentation copy "on the part of Madame, the Countess de Volney, and of the nephew of the author," and it may therefore be taken for granted that Mr. Volney's portrait, as here given, is correct, and was satisfactory to his family.

An explanation of the figures and diagrams shown on the map of the *Astrological Heaven of the Ancients* has been added in the appendix by the publisher.

PETER ECKLER.

New York, January 3, 1890.

TRANSLATOR'S PREFACE

OF THE ENGLISH EDITION PUBLISHED IN PARIS.

TO offer the public a new translation of *Volney's Ruins* may require some apology in the view of those who are acquainted with the work only in the English version which already exists, and which has had a general circulation. But those who are conversant with the book in the author's own language, and have taken pains to compare it with that version, must have been struck with the errors with which the English performance abounds. They must have regretted the loss of many original beauties, some of which go far in composing the essential merits of the work.

The energy and dignity of the author's manner, the unaffected elevation of his style, the conciseness, perspicuity and simplicity of his diction, are everywhere suited to his subject, which is ᴈmn, novel, luminous, affecting,—a subject perhaps the most universally interesting to the human race that has ever been presented to their contemplation. It takes the most liberal and comprehensive view of the social state of man, develops the sources of his errors in the most perspicuous and convincing manner, overturns his prejudices with the greatest delicacy and moderation, sets the wrongs he has suffered, and the rights he ought to cherish, in the clearest point of view, and lays before him the true foundation of morals—his only means of happiness.

As the work has already become a classical one, even in English, and as it must become and continue to be so regarded in all languages in which it shall be faithfully rendered, we wish it to suffer as little as possible from a change of country;—that as much of the spirit of the original be transfused and preserved as is consistent with the nature of translation.

How far we have succeeded in performing this service for the English reader we must not pretend to determine. We believe, however, that we have made an improved translation, and this without claiming any particular merit on our part, since we have had advantages which our predecessor had not. We have been aided by his labors; and, what is of still more importance, our work has been done under the inspection of the author, whose critical knowledge of both languages has given us a great facility in avoiding such errors as might arise from hurry or mistake.

Paris, November 1, 1802.

PREFACE OF THE LONDON EDITION.*

THE plan of this publication was formed nearly ten years ago; and allusions to it may be seen in the preface to *Travels in Syria and Egypt,* as well as at the end of that work, (published in 1787). The performance was in some forwardness when the events of 1788 in France interrupted it. Persuaded that a development of the theory of political truth could not sufficiently acquit a citizen of his debt to society, the author wished to add practice; and that particularly at a time when a single arm was of consequence in the defence of the general cause.

The same desire of public benefit which induced him to suspend his work, has since engaged him to resume it, and though it may not possess the same merit as if it had appeared under the circumstances that gave rise to it, yet he imagines that at a time when new passions are bursting forth,—passions that must communicate their activity to the religious opinions of men,—it is of importance to disseminate such moral truths as are calculated to operate as a curb and restraint. It is with this view he has endeavored to give to these truths, hitherto treated as abstract, a form likely to gain them a reception.

It was found impossible not to shock the violent prejudices of some readers; but the work, so far from being the fruit of a disorderly and perturbed spirit, has been dictated by a sincere love of order and humanity.

After reading this performance it will be asked, how it was possible in 1784 to have had an idea of what did not take place till the year 1790? The solution is simple. In the original plan the legislator was a fictitious and hypothetical being: in the present, the author has substituted an existing legislator; and the reality has only made the subject additionally interesting.

* Published by T. Allman, 42 Holborn Hill, London, 1851.

PREFACE OF THE AMERICAN EDITION.*

—

I F books were to be judged of by their volume, the following
would have but little value; if appraised by their contents,
it will perhaps be reckoned among the most instructive.

In general, nothing is more important than a good elementary book; but, also, nothing is more difficult to compose and
even to read: and why? Because, as every thing in it should
be analysis and definition, all should be expressed with truth
and precision. If truth and precision are wanting, the object
has not been attained; if they exist, its very force renders it
abstract.

The first of these defects has been hitherto evident in all
books of morality. We find in them only a chaos of incoherent
maxims, precepts without causes, and actions without a motive. The pedants of the human race have treated it like a
little child: they have prescribed to it good behavior by
frightening it with spirits and hobgoblins. Now that the
growth of the human race is rapid, it is time to speak reason
to it; it is time to prove to men that the springs of their improvement are to be found in their very organization, in the
interest of their passions, and in all that composes their ex-

* The copy from which this preface is reprinted was published in Boston by
Charles Gaylord, in 1833. It was given to the writer, when a mere lad, by a lady
— almost a stranger — who was traveling through the little hamlet on the banks
of the Hudson where he then resided. This lady assured me that the book was
of great value, containing noble and sublime truths; and the only condition she
attached to the gift was, that I should read it carefully and endeavor to understand its meaning. This I willingly promised and faithfully performed; and all
who have " climbed the heights," and escaped from the thraldom of superstitious
faith, will concede the inestimable value of such a gift — rich with the peace and
consolation that the truth imparts.—*Pub.*

istence.   It is time to demonstrate that morality is a physical
and geometrical science, subject to the rules and calculations of the other mathematical sciences: and such is the
advantage of the system expounded in this book, that the
basis of morality being laid in it on the very nature of things,
it is both constant and immutable; whereas, in all other theological systems, morality being built upon arbritary opinions,
not demonstrable and often absurd, it changes, decays, expires
with them, and leaves men in an absolute depravation.   It is
true that because our system is founded on facts and not on
reveries, it will with much greater difficulty be extended and
adopted: but it will derive strength from this very struggle,
and sooner or later the eternal religion of Nature must overturn the transient religions of the human mind.

This book was published for the first time in 1793, under
the title of *The French Citizen's Catechism.*   It was at first
intended for a national work, but as it may be equally well
entitled the Catechism of men of sense and honor, it is to be
hoped that it will become a book common to all Europe.   It
is possible that its brevity may prevent it from attaining the
object of a popular classical work, but the author will be satisfied if he has at least the merit of pointing out the way to
make a better.

VOLNEY'S RUINS;

OR, MEDITATION ON THE REVOLUTIONS OF EMPIRES.

THE superior merits of this work are too well known to require commendation; but as it is not generally known that there are in circulation three English translations of it, varying materially in regard to faithfulness and elegance of diction, the publisher of the present edition inserts the following extracts for the information of purchasers and readers:

PARIS TRANSLATION,
First published in this Country by Dixon and Sickels.

INVOCATION.

HAIL, solitary ruins! holy sepulchres, and silent walls! you I invoke; to you I address my prayer. While your aspect averts, with secret terror, the vulgar regard, it excites in my heart the charm of delicious sentiments — sublime contemplations. What useful lessons! what affecting and profound reflections you suggest to him who knows how to consult you. When the whole earth, in chains and silence, bowed the neck before its tyrants, you had already proclaimed the truths which they abhor, and confounding the dust of the king with that of the meanest slave, had announced to man the sacred dogma of Equality! Within your pale, in solitary adoration of Liberty, I saw her Genius arise from the mansions of the dead; not such as she is painted by the impassioned multitude, armed with fire and sword, but under the august aspect of Justice, poising in her hand the sacred balance, wherein are weighed the actions of men at the gates of eternity.

O Tombs! what virtues are yours! you appal the tyrant's heart, and poison with secret alarm his impious joys; he flies, with coward step, your incorruptible aspect, and erects afar his throne of insolence.

LONDON TRANSLATION.

INVOCATION.

Solitary ruins, sacred tombs, ye mouldering and silent walls, all hail! To you I address my invocation. While the vulgar shrink from your aspect with secret terror, my heart finds in the contemplation a thousand delicious sentiments, a thousand admirable recollections. Pregnant, I may truly call you, with useful lessons, with pathetic and irresistible advice to the man who knows how to consult you. Awhile ago the whole world bowed the neck in silence before the tyrants that oppressed it; and yet in that hopeless moment you already proclaimed the truths that tyrants hold in abhorrence: mixing the dust of the proudest kings with that of the meanest slaves, you called upon us to contemplate this example of Equality. From your caverns, whither the musing and anxious love of Liberty led me, I saw escape its venerable shade, and with unexpected felicity, direct its flight and marshal my steps the way to renovated France.

Tombs! what virtues and potency do you exhibit! **Tyrants tremble at your aspect**—you poison with secret alarm their impious pleasures—they turn from you with impatience, and, coward like, endeavor to forget you amid the sumptuousness of their palaces.

PHILADELPHIA TRANSLATION.

INVOCATION.

Hail, ye solitary ruins, ye sacred tombs, and silent walls! 'Tis your auspicious aid that I invoke; 'tis to you my soul, wrapt in meditation, pours forth its prayers! What though the profane and vulgar mind shrinks with dismay from your august and awe-inspiring aspect; to me you unfold the sublimest charms of contemplation and sentiment, and offer to my senses the luxury of a thousand delicious and enchanting thoughts! How sumptuous the feast to a being that has a taste to relish, and an understanding to consult you! What rich and noble admonitions; what exquisite and pathetic lessons do you read to a heart that is susceptible of exalted feelings! When oppressed humanity bent in timid silence throughout the globe beneath the galling yoke of slavery, it was you that proclaimed aloud the birthright of those truths which tyrants tremble at while they detect, and which, by sinking the loftiest head of the proudest potentate, with all his boasted pageantry, to the level of mortality with his meanest slave, confirmed and ratified by your unerring testimony the sacred and immortal doctrine of Equality.

Musing within the precincts of your inviting scenes of philosophic solitude, whither the insatiate love of true-born Liberty had led me, I beheld her Genius ascending, not in the spurious character and habit of a blood-thirsty Fury, armed with daggers and instruments of murder, and followed by a frantic and intoxicated multitude, but under the placid and chaste aspect of Justice, holding with a pure and unsullied hand the sacred scales in which the actions of mortals are weighed on the brink of eternity.

The first translation was made and published in London soon after the appearance of the work in French, and, by a late edition, is still adopted without alteration. Mr. Volney, when in this country in 1797, expressed his disapprobation of this translation, alleging that the translator must have been overawed by the government or clergy from rendering his ideas faithfully ; and, accordingly, an English gentleman, then in Philadelphia, volunteered to correct this edition. But by his endeavors to give the true and full meaning of the author with great precision, he has so overloaded his composition with an exuberance of words, as in a great measure to dissipate the simple elegance and sublimity of the original. Mr. Volney, when he became better acquainted with the English language, perceived this defect; and with the aid of our countryman, Joel Barlow, made and published in Paris a new, correct, and elegant translation, of which the present edition is a faithful and correct copy.

CONTENTS.

THE LAW OF NATURE.

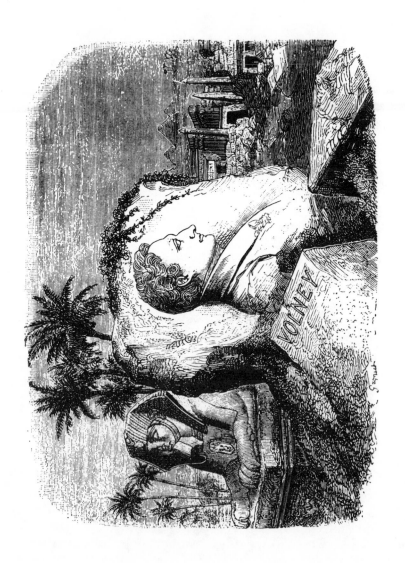

LIFE OF VOLNEY.

BY COUNT DARU.

————

CONSTANTINE FRANCIS CHASSEBEUF DE VOLNEY was
born in 1757 at Craon, in that intermediate condition
of life, which is of all the happiest, since it is deprived
only of fortune's too dangerous favors, and can aspire to the
social and intellectual advantages reserved for a laudable
ambition.

From his earliest youth, he devoted himself to the search
after truth, without being disheartened by the serious studies
which alone can initiate us into her secrets. After having
become acquainted with the ancient languages, the natural
sciences and history, and being admitted into the society of
the most eminent literary characters, he submitted, at the age
of twenty, to an illustrious academy, the solution of one of the
most difficult problems that the history of antiquity has left
open for discussion. This attempt received no encouragement from the learned men who were appointed his judges;
and the author's only appeal from their sentence was to his
courage and his efforts.

Soon after, a small inheritance having fallen to his lot, the
difficulty was how to spend it (these are his own words.) He
resolved to employ it in acquiring, by a long voyage, a new
fund of information, and determined to visit Egypt and Syria.
But these countries could not be explored to advantage without a knowledge of the language. Our young traveller was
not to be discouraged by this difficulty. Instead of learning
Arabic in Europe, he withdrew to a convent of Copts, until he
had made himself master of an idiom that is spoken by so
many nations of the East. This resolution showed one of those
undaunted spirits that remain unshaken amid the trials of life.

Although, like other travellers, he might have amused us
with an account of his hardships and the perils surmounted
by his courage, he overcame the temptation of interrupting
his narrative by personal adventures. He disdained the

beaten track. He does not tell us the road he took, the accidents he met with, or the impressions he received. He carefully avoids appearing upon the stage ; he is an inhabitant of the country, who has long and well observed it, and who describes its physical, political, and moral state. The allusion would be entire if an old Arab could be supposed to possess all the erudition, all the European philosophy, which are found united and in their maturity in a traveller of twenty-five.

But though a master in all those artifices by which a narration is rendered interesting, the young man is not to be discerned in the pomp of labored descriptions. Although possessed of a lively and brilliant imagination, he is never found unwarily explaining by conjectural systems the physical or moral phenomena he describes. In his observations he unites prudence with science. With these two guides he judges with circumspection, and sometimes confesses himself unable to account for the effects he has made known to us.

Thus his account has all the qualities that persuade — accuracy and candor. And when, ten years later, a vast military enterprise transported forty thousand travellers to the classic ground, which he had trod unattended, unarmed and unprotected, they all recognized a sure guide and an enlightened observer in the writer who had, as it seemed, only preceded them to remove or point out a part of the difficulties of the way.

The unanimous testimony of all parties proved the accuracy of his account and the justness of his observations ; and his *Travels in Egypt and Syria* were, by universal suffrage, recommended to the gratitude and the confidence of the public.

Before the work had undergone this trial it had obtained in the learned world such a rapid and general success, that it found its way into Russia. The empress, then (in 1787) upon the throne, sent the author a medal, which he received with respect, as a mark of esteem for his talents, and with gratitude, as a proof of the approbation given to his principles. But when the empress declared against France, Volney sent back the honorable present, saying : " If I obtained it from her esteem, I can only preserve her esteem by returning it."

The revolution of 1789, which had drawn upon France the menaces of Catharine, had opened to Volney a political career. As deputy in the assembly of the states-general, the first words he uttered there were in favor of the publicity of their deliberations. He also supported the organization of the national guards, and that of the communes and departments.

At the period when the question of the sale of the domain lands was agitated (in 1790,) he published an essay in which he lays down the following principles: "The force of a State is in proportion to its population; population is in proportion to plenty; plenty is in proportion to tillage; and tillage, to personal and immediate interest, that is to the spirit of property. Whence it follows, that the nearer the cultivator approaches the passive condition of a mercenary, the less industry and activity are to be expected from him; and, on the other hand, the nearer he is to the condition of a free and entire proprietor, the more extension he gives to his own forces, to the produce of his lands, and the general prosperity of the State."

The author draws this conclusion, that a State is so much the more powerful as it includes a greater number of proprietors,—that is, a greater division of property.

Conducted into Corsica by that spirit of observation which belongs only to men whose information is varied and extensive, he perceived at the first glance all that could be done for the improvement of agriculture in that country: but he knew that, for a people firmly attached to ancient customs, there can exist no other demonstration or means of persuasion than example. He purchased a considerable estate, and made experiments on those kinds of tillage that he hoped to naturalize in that climate. The sugar-cane, cotton, indigo and coffee soon demonstrated the success of his efforts. This success drew upon him the notice of the government. He was appointed director of agriculture and commerce in that island, where, through ignorance, all new methods are introduced with such difficulty.

It is impossible to calculate all the good that might have resulted from this peaceable magistracy; and we know that neither instruction, zeal, nor a persevering courage was wanting to him who had undertaken it. Of this he had given convincing proofs. It was in obedience to another sentiment, no less respectable, that he voluntarily interrupted the course of his labors. When his fellow citizens of Angers appointed him their deputy in the constituent assembly, he resigned the

employment he held under government, upon the principle
that no man can represent the nation and be dependent for a
salary upon those by whom it is administered.

Through respect for the independence of his legislative
functions, he had ceased to occupy the place he possessed in
Corsica before his election, but he had not ceased to be a bene-
factor of that country. He returned thither after the session
of the constituent assembly. Invited into that island by the
principal inhabitants, who were anxious to put into practice
his lessons, he spent there a part of the years 1792 and 1793.

On his return he published a work entitled: *An Account
of the Present State of Corsica.* This was an act of courage;
for it was not a physical description, but a political review of
the condition of a population divided into several factions and
distracted by violent animosities. Volney unreservedly revealed the abuses, solicited the interest of France in favor of
the Corsicans, without flattering them, and boldly denounced
their defects and vices ; so that the philosopher obtained the
only recompense he could expect from his sincerity—he was
accused by the Corsicans of heresy.

To prove that he had not merited this reproach, he published soon after a short treatise entitled: *The Law of Nature,
or Physical Principles of Morality.*

He was soon exposed to a much more dangerous charge,
and this, it must be confessed, he did merit. This philosopher, this worthy citizen, who in our first National assembly
had seconded with his wishes and his talents the establishment of an order of things which he considered favorable to
the happiness of his country, was accused of not being sin-
cerely attached to that liberty for which he had contended;
that is to say, of being averse to anarchy. An imprisonment
of ten months, which only ended after the 9th of Thermidor,
was a new trial reserved for his courage.

The moment at which he recovered his liberty, was when the
horror inspired by criminal excesses had recalled men to
those noble sentiments which fortunately are one of the first
necessaries of civilized life. They sought for consolations in
study and literature after so many misfortunes, and organized a plan of public instruction.

It was in the first place necessary to insure the aptitude of those to whom education should be confided; but as the systems were various, the best methods and a unity of doctrine were to be determined. It was not enough to interrogate the masters, they were to be formed, new ones were to be created, and for that purpose a school was opened in 1794, wherein the celebrity of the professors promised new instruction even to the best informed. This was not, as was objected, beginning the edifice at the roof, but creating architects, who were to superintend all the arts requisite for constructing the building.

The more difficult their functions were, the greater care was to be taken in the choice of the professors; but France, though then accused of being plunged in barbarism, possessed men of transcendent talents, already enjoying the esteem of all Europe, and we may be bold to say, that by their labors, our literary glory had likewise extended its conquests. Their names were proclaimed by the public voice, and Volney's was associated with those of the men most illustrious in science and in literature.*

This institution, however, did not answer the expectations that had been formed of it, because the two thousand students that assembled from all parts of France were not equally prepared to receive these transcendent lessons, and because it had not been sufficiently ascertained how far the theory of education should be kept distinct from education itself.

Volney's *Lectures on History*, which were attended by an immense concourse of auditors, became one of his chief claims to literary glory. When forced to interrupt them, by the suppression of the Normal school, he might have reasonably expected to enjoy in his retirement that consideration which his recent functions had added to his name. But, disgusted with the scenes he had witnessed in his native land, he felt that passion revive within him which, in his youth, had led him to visit Africa and Asia. America, civilized within a century, and free only within a few years, fixed his attention. There every thing was new,—the inhabitants, the constitution, the earth itself. These were objects worthy of his observation. When embarking for this voyage, however, he felt emotions very different from those which formerly accompanied him

*Lagrange, Laplace, Berthollet, Garat, Bernardin de Saint-Pierre, Daubenton, Hauy, Volney, Sicard, Monge, Thouin, La Harpe, Buache Mentelle,

into **Turkey.** Then in the prime of life, he joyfully bid adieu to a land where peace and plenty reigned, to travel amongst barbarians; now, mature in years, but dismayed at the spectacle and experience of injustice and persecution, it was with diffidence, as we learn from himself, that he went to implore from a free people an asylum for a sincere friend of that liberty that had been so profaned.

Our traveller had gone to seek for repose beyond the seas. He there found himself exposed to aggression from a celebrated philosopher, Dr. Priestley. Although the subject of this discussion was confined to the investigation of some speculative opinions, published by the French writer in his work entitled *The Ruins*, the naturalist in this attack employed a degree of violence which added nothing to the force of his arguments, and an acrimony of expression not to be expected from a philosopher. M. Volney, though accused of Hottentotism and ignorance, preserved in his defence, all the advantages that the scurrility of his adversary gave over him. He replied in English, and Priestley's countrymen could only recognize the Frenchman in the refinement and politeness of his answer.

Whilst M. Volney was travelling in America, there had been formed in France a literary body which, under the name of Institute, had attained in a very few years a distinguished rank amongst the learned societies of Europe. The name of the illustrious traveller was inscribed in it at its formation, and he acquired new rights to the academical honors conferred on him during his absence, by the publication of his observations *On the Climate and Soil of the United States*.

These rights were further augmented by the historical and physiological labors of the Academician. An examination and justification of *The Chronology of Herodotus*, with numerous and profound researches on *The History of the most Ancient Nations*, occupied for a long time him who had observed their monuments and traces in the countries they inhabited. The trial he had made of the utility of the Oriental languages inspired him with an ardent desire to propagate the knowledge of them; and to be propagated, he felt how necessary it was to render it less difficult. In this view he conceived the project of applying to the study of the idioms of

Asia, a part of the grammatical notions we possess concerning the languages of Europe. It only appertains to those conversant with their relations of dissimilitude or conformity to appreciate the possibility of realizing this system. The author has, however, already received the most flattering encouragement and the most unequivocal appreciation, by the inscription of his name amongst the members of the learned and illustrious society founded by English commerce in the Indian peninsula.

M. Volney developed his system in three works,* which prove that this idea of uniting nations separated by immense distances and such various idioms, had never ceased to occupy him for twenty-five years. Lest those essays, of the utility of which he was persuaded, should be interrupted by his death, with the clay-cold hand that corrected his last work, he drew up a will which institutes a premium for the prosecution of his labors. Thus he prolonged, beyond the term of a life entirely devoted to letters, the glorious services he had rendered to them.

This is not the place, nor does it belong to me to appreciate the merit of the writings which render Volney's name illustrious. His name had been inscribed in the list of the Senate, and afterwards of the House of Peers. The philosopher who had travelled in the four quarters of the world, and observed their social state, had other titles to his admission into this body, than his literary glory. His public life, his conduct in the constituent assembly, his independent principles, the nobleness of his sentiments, the wisdom and fixity of his opinions, had gained him the esteem of those who can be depended upon, and with whom it is so agreeable to discuss political interests.

Although no man had a better right to have an opinion, no one was more tolerant for the opinions of others. In State assemblies as well as in Academical meetings, the man whose counsels were so wise, voted according to his conscience, which nothing could bias ; but the philosopher forgot his superiority to hear, to oppose with moderation, and sometimes

---

* *On the Simplification of Oriental Languages, 1795.*
The European Alphabet Applied to the Languages of Asia, 1819.
Hebrew Simplified, 1820.

to doubt. The extent and variety of his information, the force
of his reason, the austerity of his manners, and the noble simplicity of his character, had procured him illustrious friends
in both hemispheres ; and now that this erudition is extinct in
the tomb,* we may be allowed at least to predict that he was
one of the very few whose memory shall never die.

———

A list of the Works Published by Count Volney.

TRAVELS IN EGYPT AND SYRIA during the years 1783, 1784,
and 1785: 2 vols. 8vo. — 1787.

CHRONOLOGY OF THE TWELVE CENTURIES that preceded
the entrance of Xerxes into Greece.

CONSIDERATIONS ON THE TURKISH WAR, in 1788.

THE RUINS, or Meditations on the Revolutions of Empires —
1791.

ACCOUNT OF THE PRESENT STATE OF CORSICA — 1793.

THE LAW OF NATURE, or Physical Principles of Morality —
1793.

ON THE SIMPLIFICATION OF ORIENTAL LANGUAGES — 1795.

A LETTER TO DR. PRIESTLEY — 1797.

LECTURES ON HISTORY, delivered at the Normal School in
the year 3 — 1800.

ON THE CLIMATE AND SOIL OF THE UNITED STATES OF
AMERICA, to which is added an account of Florida, of the
French colony of Scioto, of some Canadian Colonies, and
of the Savages. — 1803.

REPORT MADE TO THE CELTIC ACADEMY ON THE RUSSIAN
WORK OF PROFESSOR PALLAS, entitled "A Comparative
Vocabulary of all the Languages in the World."

THE CHRONOLOGY OF HERODOTUS conformable with his
Text — 1808 and 1809.

NEW RESEARCHES ON ANCIENT HISTORY, 3 vols. 8vo. —1814

THE EUROPEAN ALPHABET Applied to the Languages of
Asia — 1819.

A HISTORY OF SAMUEL — 1819.

HEBREW SIMPLIFIED — 1820.

* He died in Paris on the 20th of April, 1820.

INVOCATION.

HAIL solitary ruins, holy sepulchres and silent walls! you I invoke; to you I address my prayer. While your aspect averts, with secret terror, the vulgar regard, it excites in my heart the charm of delicious sentiments—sublime contemplations. What useful lessons, what affecting and profound reflections you suggest to him who knows how to consult you! When the whole earth, in chains and silence, bowed the neck before its tyrants, you had already proclaimed the truths which they abhor; and confounding the dust of the king with that of the meanest slave, had announced to man the sacred dogma of Equality. Within your pale, in solitary adoration of Liberty, I saw her Genius arise from the mansions of the dead; not such as she is painted by the impassioned multitude, armed with fire and sword, but under the august aspect of Justice, poising in her hand the sacred balance wherein are weighed the actions of men at the gates of eternity!

O Tombs! what virtues are yours! You appal the tyrant's heart, and poison with secret alarm his impious joys. He flies, with coward step, your incorruptible aspect, and erects afar his throne of insolence.* You punish the powerful oppressor; you wrest from avarice and extortion their ill-gotten gold, and you avenge the feeble whom they have despoiled;

---

* The cathedral of St. Denis is the tomb of the kings of France; and it was because the towers of that edifice are seen from the Castle of St. Germain, that Louis XIV. quitted that admirable residence, and established a new one in the savage forests of Versailles.

(This note, like many others, has been omitted from the American editions. It seems pertinent to the subject, and is explanatory of the text.—*Pub.*)

you compensate the miseries of the poor by the anxieties of
the rich ; you console the wretched, by opening to him a last
asylum from distress ; and you give to the soul that just
equipoise of strength and sensibility which constitutes wisdom — the true science of life. Aware that all must return to
you, the wise man loadeth not himself with the burdens of
grandeur and of useless wealth : he restrains his desires
within the limits of justice ; yet, knowing that he must
run his destined course of life, he fills with employment all
its hours, and enjoys the comforts that fortune has allotted
him. You thus impose on the impetuous sallies of cupidity a
salutary rein! you calm the feverish ardor of enjoyments
which disturb the senses ; you free the soul from the fatiguing
conflict of the passions ; elevate it above the paltry interests
which torment the crowd; and surveying, from your com-
manding position, the expanse of ages and nations, the mind
is only accessible to the great affections—to the solid ideas
of virtue and of glory.

Ah! when the dream of life is over, what will then avail
all its agitations, if not one trace of utility remains behind ?

O Ruins! to your school I will return! I will seek again
the calm of your solitudes ; and there, far from the afflicting
spectacle of the passions, I will cherish in remembrance the
love of man, I will employ myself on the means of effecting
good for him, and build my own happiness on the promotion
of his.

THE RUINS OF EMPIRES.

CHAPTER I.

THE JOURNEY.

IN the eleventh year of the reign of. Abd-ul-Hamid, son of
Ahmid, emperor of the Turks ; when the Nogais-Tartars
were driven from the Crimea, and a Mussulman prince of
the blood of Gengis-Kahn became the vassal and guard of a
Christian woman and queen,* I was travelling in the Ottoman
dominions, and through those provinces which were anciently
the kingdoms of Egypt and Syria.

My whole attention bent on whatever concerns the happiness of man in a social state, I visited cities, and studied the
manners of their inhabitants ; entered palaces, and observed
the conduct of those who govern ; wandered over fields, and
examined the condition of those who cultivated them : and
nowhere perceiving aught but robbery and devastation,
tyranny and wretchedness, my heart was oppressed with sorrow and indignation.

I saw daily on my road fields abandoned, villages deserted,
and cities in ruin. Often I met with ancient monuments,
wrecks of temples, palaces and fortresses, columns, aqueducts
and tombs. This spectacle led me to meditate on times past,
and filled my mind with contemplations the most serious and
profound.

Arrived at the city of Hems, on the border of the Orontes,
and being in the neighborhood of Palmyra of the desert, I

* In the eleventh year of Abd-ul-Hamid, that is 1784 of the Christian era, and
1198 of the Hegira. The emigration of the Tartars took place in March, immediately on the manifesto of the empress, declaring the Crimea to be incorporated
with Russia. The Mussulman prince of the blood of Gengis-Khan was Chahin-
Guerai. Gengis-Khan was borne and served by the kings whom he conquered :
Chahin, on the contrary, after selling his country for a pension of eighty thousand
roubles, accepted the commission of captain of guards to Catherine II. He afterwards returned home, and according to custom was strangled by the Turks.

resolved to visit its celebrated ruins. After three days jour-
neying through arid deserts, having traversed the Valley of
Caves and Sepulchres, on issuing into the plain, I was suddenly struck with a scene of the most stupendous ruins — a
countless multitude of superb columns, stretching in avenues
beyond the reach of sight. Among them were magnificent
edifices, some entire, others in ruins; the earth every where
strewed with fragments of cornices, capitals, shafts, entabla-
tures, pilasters, all of white marble, and of the most exquisite
workmanship. After a walk of three-quarters of an hour
along these ruins, I entered the enclosure of a vast edifice,
formerly a temple dedicated to the Sun; and accepting the
hospitality of some poor Arabian peasants, who had built
their hovels on the area of the temple, I determined to devote
some days to contemplate at leisure the beauty of these stupendous ruins.

Daily I visited the monuments which covered the plain;
and one evening, absorbed in reflection, I had advanced to
the Valley of Sepulchres. I ascended the heights which surround it from whence the eye commands the whole group of
ruins and the immensity of the desert. The sun had sunk
below the horizon: a red border of light still marked his track
behind the distant mountains of Syria; the full-orbed moon
was rising in the east, on a blue ground, over the plains of
the Euphrates; the sky was clear, the air calm and serene;
the dying lamp of day still softened the horrors of approaching darkness; the refreshing night breezes attempered the
sultry emanations from the heated earth; the herdsmen had
given their camels to repose, the eye perceived no motion on
the dusky and uniform plain; profound silence rested on the
desert; the howlings only of the jackal,* and the solemn notes
of the bird of night, were heard at distant intervals. Darkness now increased, and through the dusk could only be
discerned the pale phantasms of columns and walls. The
solitude of the place, the tranquillity of the hour, the majesty
of the scene, impressed on my mind a religious pensiveness.
The aspect of a great city deserted, the memory of times past,

---

* An animal resembling a dog and a fox. It preys on other small animals, and
upon the bodies of the dead on the field of battle. It is the Canis aureus of
Linnæus.

"Here said I, here once flourished an opulent city, here was the seat of a powerful empire."—Page 5.

compared with its present state, all elevated my mind to high contemplations. I sat on the shaft of a column, my elbow reposing on my knee, and head reclining on my hand, my eyes fixed, sometimes on the desert, sometimes on the ruins, and fell into a profound reverie.

CHAPTER II.

THE REVERIE.

HERE, said I, once flourished an opulent city; here was the seat of a powerful empire. Yes! these places now so wild and desolate, were once animated by a living multitude; a busy crowd thronged in these streets, now so solitary. Within these walls, where now reigns the silence of death, the noise of the arts, and the shouts of joy and festivity incessantly resounded; these piles of marble were regular palaces; these fallen columns adorned the majesty of temples; these ruined galleries surrounded public places. Here assembled a numerous people for the sacred duties of their religion, and the anxious cares of their subsistence; here industry, parent of enjoyments, collected the riches of all climes, and the purple of Tyre was exchanged for the precious thread of Serica;* the soft tissues of Cassimere for the sumptuous tapestry of Lydia; the amber of the Baltic for the pearls and perfumes of Arabia; the gold of Ophir for the tin of Thule.

* *The precious thread of Serica.*—That is, the silk originally derived from the mountainous country where the *great wall* terminates, and which appears to have been the cradle of the Chinese empire. *The tissues of Cassimere.*—The shawls which Ezekiel seems to have described under the appellation of Choudchoud. *The gold of Ophir.*—This country, which was one of the twelve Arab cantons, and which has so much and so unsuccessfully been sought for by the antiquarians, has left, however, some trace of itself in Ofor, in the province of Oman, upon the Persian Gulf, neighboring on one side to the Sabeans, who are celebrated by Strabo for their abundance of gold, and on the other to Aula or Hevila, where the pearl fishery was carried on. See the 27th chapter of Ezekiel, which gives a very curious and extensive picture of the commerce of Asia at that period.

And now behold what remains of this powerful city : a miserable skeleton! What of its vast domination: a doubtful and obscure remembrance! To the noisy concourse which thronged under these porticoes, succeeds the solitude of death. The silence of the grave is substituted for the busy hum of public places; the affluence of a commercial city is changed into wretched poverty; the palaces of kings have become a den of wild beasts; flocks repose in the area of temples, and savage reptiles inhabit the sanctuary of the gods. Ah! how has so much glory been eclipsed? how have so many labors been annihilated? Do thus perish then the works of men — thus vanish empires and nations?

And the history of former times revived in my mind; I remembered those ancient ages when many illustrious nations inhabited these countries; I figured to myself the Assyrian on the banks of the Tygris, the Chaldean on the banks of the Euphrates, the Persian reigning from the Indus to the Mediterranean. I enumerated the kingdoms of Damascus and Idumea, of Jerusalem and Samaria, the warlike states of the Philistines, and the commercial republics of Phœnicia. This Syria, said I, now so depopulated, then contained a hundred flourishing cities, and abounded with towns, villages, and hamlets.* In all parts were seen cultivated fields, frequented roads, and crowded habitations. Ah! whither have flown those ages of life and abundance? — whither vanished those brilliant creations of human industry? Where are those ramparts of Nineveh, those walls of Babylon, those palaces of Persepolis, those temples of Balbec and of Jerusalem? Where are those fleets of Tyre, those dock-yards of Arad, those work-shops of Sidon, and that multitude of sailors, of pilots, of merchants, and of soldiers? Where those husbandmen, harvests, flocks, and all the creation of living beings in which the face of the earth rejoiced? Alas! I have passed over this desolate land! I have visited the palaces, once the scene of so much splendor, and I beheld nothing but solitude and desolation. I sought the ancient inhabitants and their works, and found nothing but a trace, like the foot-prints of a traveller over the sand. The temples are fallen, the palaces

---

* According to Josephus and Strabo, there were in Syria twelve millions of souls, and the traces that remain of culture and habitation confirm the calculation

overthrown, the ports filled up, the cities destroyed; and the earth, stripped of inhabitants, has become a place of sepulchres. Great God! whence proceed such fatal revolutions? What causes have so changed the fortunes of these countries? Wherefore are so many cities destroyed? Why has not this ancient population been reproduced and perpetuated?

Thus absorbed in meditation, a crowd of new reflections continually poured in upon my mind. Every thing, continued I, bewilders my judgment, and fills my heart with trouble and uncertainty. When these countries enjoyed what constitutes the glory and happiness of man, they were inhabited by infidel nations: It was the Phœnician, offering human sacrifices to Moloch, who gathered into his stores the riches of all climates; it was the Chaldean, prostrate before his serpent-god,* who subjugated opulent cities, laid waste the palaces of kings, and despoiled the temples of the gods; it was the Persian, worshipper of fire, who received the tribute of a hundred nations; they were the inhabitants of this very city, adorers of the sun and stars, who erected so many monuments of prosperity and luxury. Numerous herds, fertile fields, abundant harvests—whatsoever should be the reward of piety—was in the hands of these idolaters. And now, when a people of saints and believers occupy these fields, all is become sterility and solitude. The earth, under these holy hands, produces only thorns and briers. Man soweth in anguish, and reapeth tears and cares. War, famine, pestilence, assail him by turns. And yet, are not these the children of the prophets? The Mussulman, Christian, Jew, are they not the elect children of God, loaded with favors and miracles? Why, then, do these privileged races no longer enjoy the same advantages? Why are these fields, sanctified by the blood of martyrs, deprived of their ancient fertility? Why have those blessings been banished hence, and transferred for so many ages to other nations and different climes?

At these words, revolving in my mind the vicissitudes which have transmitted the sceptre of the world to people so different in religion and manners from those in ancient Asia to the most recent of Europe, this name of a natal land revived in me the sentiment of my country; and turning my eyes

* The dragon Bell.

towards France, I began to reflect on the situation in which I had left her.*

I recalled her fields so richly cultivated, her roads so admirably constructed, her cities inhabited by a countless people, her fleets spread over every sea, her ports filled with the produce of both the Indies: and then comparing the activity of her commerce, the extent of her navigation, the magnificence of her buildings, the arts and industry of her inhabitants, with what Egypt and Syria had once possessed, I was gratified to find in modern Europe the departed splendor of Asia; but the charm of my reverie was soon dissolved by a last term of comparison. Reflecting that such had once been the activity of the places I was then contemplating, who knows, said I, but such may one day be the abandonment of our countries? Who knows if on the banks of the Seine, the Thames, the Zuyder-Zee, where now, in the tumult of so many enjoyments, the heart and the eye suffice not for the multitude of sensations,—who knows if some traveller, like myself, shall not one day sit on their silent ruins, and weep in solitude over the ashes of their inhabitants, and the memory of their former greatness.

At these words, my eyes filled with tears: and covering my head with the fold of my mantle, I sank into gloomy meditations on all human affairs. Ah! hapless man, said I in my grief, a blind fatality sports with thy destiny!† A fatal necessity rules with the hand of chance the lot of mortals! But no: it is the justice of heaven fulfilling its decrees!—a God of mystery exercising his incomprehensible judgments! Doubtless he has pronounced a secret anathema against this land: blasting with maledictions the present, for the sins of past generations. Oh! who shall dare to fathom the depths of the Omnipotent?

And sunk in profound melancholy, I remained motionless.

* In the year 1782, at the close of the American war.

† Fatality is the universal and rooted prejudice of the East. "It was written," is there the answer to every thing. Hence result an unconcern and apathy, the most powerful impediments to instruction and civilization.

" Suddenly on my left, by the glimmering light of the moon, through the columns and ruins of a neighboring temple, I thought I saw an apparition, pale, clothed in large flowing robes, such as spectres are painted rising from their tombs."—Page 9.

CHAPTER III.

THE APPARITION.

WHILE thus absorbed, a sound struck my ear, like the agitation of a flowing robe, or that of slow footsteps on dry and rustling grass. Startled, I opened my mantle, and looking about with fear and trembling, suddenly, on my left, by the glimmering light of the moon, through the columns and ruins of a neighboring temple, I thought I saw an apparition, pale, clothed in large and flowing robes, such as spectres are painted rising from their tombs. I shuddered: and while agitated and hesitating whether to fly or to advance toward the object, a distinct voice, in solemn tones, pronounced these words:

How long will man importune heaven with unjust complaint? How long, with vain clamors, will he accuse Fate as the author of his calamities? Will he forever shut his eyes to the light, and his heart to the admonitions of truth and reason? The light of truth meets him everywhere; yet he sees it not! The voice of reason strikes his ear; and he hears it not! Unjust man! if for a moment thou canst suspend the delusion which fascinates thy senses, if thy heart can comprehend the language of reason, interrogate these ruins! Read the lessons which they present to thee! And you, evidences of twenty centuries, holy temples! venerable tombs! walls once so glorious, appear in the cause of nature herself! Approach the tribunal of sound reason, and bear testimony against unjust accusations! Come and confound the declamations of a false wisdom or hypocritical piety, and avenge the heavens and the earth of man who calumniates them both!

What is that blind fatality, which without order and without law, sports with the destiny of mortals? What is that unjust necessity, which confounds the effect of actions, whether of wisdom or of folly? In what consist the anathemas of heaven over this land? Where is that divine malediction which per-

petuates the abandonment of these fields? Say, monuments
of past ages! have the heavens changed their laws and the
earth its motion? Are the fires of the sun extinct in the
regions of space? Do the seas no longer emit their vapors?
Are the rains and the dews suspended in the air? Do the
mountains withhold their springs? Are the streams dried up?
And do the plants no longer bear fruit and seed? Answer,
generation of falsehood and iniquity, hath God deranged
the primitive and settled order of things which he himself
assigned to nature? Hath heaven denied to earth, and earth
to its inhabitants, the blessings they formerly dispensed?
If nothing hath changed in the creation, if the same means
now exist which before existed, why then are not the present
what former generations were? Ah! it is falsely that you
accuse fate and heaven! it is unjustly that you accuse God
as the cause of your evils! Say, perverse and hypocritical
race! if these places are desolate, if these powerful cities are
reduced to solitude, is it God who has caused their ruin?
Is it his hand which has overthrown these walls, destroyed
these temples, mutilated these columns, or is it the hand of
man? Is it the arm of God which has carried the sword into
your cities, and fire into your fields, which has slaughtered
the people, burned the harvests, rooted up trees, and ravaged
the pastures, or is it the hand of man? And when, after the
destruction of crops, famine has ensued, is it the vengeance
of God which has produced it, or the mad fury of mortals?
When, sinking under famine, the people have fed on impure
aliments, if pestilence ensues, is it the wrath of God which
sends it, or the folly of man? When war, famine and pestilence, have swept away the inhabitants, if the earth remains
a desert, is it God who has depopulated it? Is it his rapacity
which robs the husbandman, ravages· the fruitful fields, and
wastes the earth, or is it the rapacity of those who govern?
Is it his pride which excites murderous wars, or the pride of
kings and their ministers? Is it the venality of his decisions
which overthrows the fortunes of families, or the corruption
of the organs of the law? Are they his passions which, under
a thousand forms, torment individuals and nations, or are
they the passions of man? And if, in the anguish of their
miseries, they see not the remedies, is it the ignorance of God

which is to blame, or their ignorance? Cease then, mortals, to accuse the decrees of Fate, or the judgments of the Divinity! If God is good, will he be the author of your misery? If he is just, will he be the accomplice of your crimes? No, the caprice of which man complains is not the caprice of fate; the darkness that misleads his reason is not the darkness of God; the source of his calamities is not in the distant heavens, it is beside him on the earth; it is not concealed in the bosom of the divinity; it dwells within himself, he bears it in his own heart.

Thou murmurest and sayest: What! have an infidel people then enjoyed the blessings of heaven and earth? Are the holy people of God less fortunate than the races of impiety? Deluded man! where then is the contradiction which offends thee? Where is the inconsistency which thou imputest to the justice of heaven? Take into thine own hands the balance of rewards and punishments, of causes and effects. Say: when these infidels observed the laws of the heavens and the earth, when they regulated well-planned labors by the order of the seasons and the course of the stars, should the Almighty have disturbed the equilibrium of the universe to defeat their prudence? When their hands cultivated these fields with toil and care, should he have diverted the course of the rains, suspended the refreshing dews, and planted crops of thorns? When, to render these arid fields productive, their industry constructed aqueducts, dug canals, and led the distant waters across the desert, should he have dried up their sources in the mountains? Should he have blasted the harvests which art had nourished, wasted the plains which peace had peopled, overthrown cities which labor had created, or disturbed the order established by the wisdom of man? And what is that infidelity which founded empires by its prudence, defended them by its valor, and strengthened them by its justice — which built powerful cities, formed capacious ports, drained pestilential marshes, covered the ocean with ships, the earth with inhabitants; and, like the creative spirit, spread life and motion throughout the world? If such be infidelity, what then is the true faith? Doth sanctity consist in destruction? The God who peoples the air with birds, the earth with animals, the waters with fishes — the God who animates all nature—is he then a God of ruins and tombs? **Demands he** devastation for homage, and conflagration for sacrifice? **Re-** quires he groans for hymns, murderers for votaries, a ravaged and desolate earth for his temple? Behold then, holy and believing people, what are your works! behold the fruits of your piety! You have massacred the people, burned their cities, destroyed cultivation, reduced the earth to a solitude; and you ask the reward of your works! Miracles then must be performed! The people whom you extirpated must be recalled to life, the walls rebuilt which you have overthrown, the harvests reproduced which you have destroyed, the waters regathered which you have dispersed; the laws, in fine, of heaven and earth reversed; those laws, established by God himself, in demonstration of his magnificence and wisdom; those eternal laws, anterior to all codes, to all the prophets; those immutable laws, which neither the passions nor the ignorance of man can pervert. But that passion which mis- taketh, that ignorance which observeth neither causes nor effects, hath said in its folly: "All things flow from chance; a blind fatality poureth out good and evil upon the earth; success is not to the prudent, nor felicity to the wise;" or, assuming the language of hypocrisy, she hath said, "all things are from God; he taketh pleasure in deceiving wisdom and confounding reason." And Ignorance, applauding herself in her malice, hath said, "thus will I place myself on a par with that science which confounds me—thus will I excel that pru- dence which fatigues and torments me." And Avarice hath added: "I will oppress the weak, and devour the fruits of his labors; and I will say, it is fate which hath so ordained." But I! I swear by the laws of heaven and earth, and by the law which is written in the heart of man, that the hypocrite shall be deceived in his cunning—the oppressor in his ra- pacity! The sun shall change his course, before folly shall prevail over wisdom and knowledge, or ignorance surpass prudence, in the noble and sublime art of procuring to man his true enjoyments, **and of building his happiness on an enduring foundation.**

CHAPTER IV.

THE EXPOSITION.

THUS spoke the Phantom. Confused with this discourse, and my heart agitated with different reflections, I remained long in silence. At length, taking courage, I thus addressed him: Oh, Genius of tombs and ruins! Thy presence, thy severity, hath disordered my senses; but the justice of thy discourse restoreth confidence to my soul. Pardon my ignorance. Alas, if man is blind, shall his misfortune be also his crime? I may have mistaken the voice of reason; but never, knowingly, have I rejected its authority. Ah! if thou readest my heart, thou knowest with what enthusiasm it seeketh truth. Is it not in its pursuit that thou seest me in this sequestered spot? Alas! I have wandered over the earth, I have visited cities and countries; and seeing everywhere misery and desolation, a sense of the evils which afflict my fellow men hath deeply oppressed my soul. I have said, with a sigh: is man then born but for sorrow and anguish? And I have meditated upon human misery that I might discover a remedy. I have said, I will separate myself from the corruption of society; I will retire far from palaces where the mind is depraved by satiety, and from the hovel where it is debased by misery. I will go into the desert and dwell among ruins; I will interrogate ancient monuments on the wisdom of past ages; I will invoke from the bosom of the tombs the spirit which once in Asia gave splendor to states, and glory to nations; I will ask of the ashes of legislators, *by what secret causes do empires rise and fall; from what sources spring the prosperity and misfortunes of nations; on what principles can the peace of society, and the happiness of man be established?*

I ceased, and with submissive look awaited the answer of the Genius.

Peace and happiness, said he, attend those who practice justice! Since thy heart, O mortal, with sincerity seeketh truth; since thine eyes can still recognize her through the mist of prejudice, thy prayer shall not be in vain. I will unfold to thy view that truth thou invokest; I will teach thy reason that knowledge thou seekest; I will reveal to thee the science of ages and the wisdom of the tombs.

Then approaching and laying his hand on my head, he said: Rise, mortal, and extricate thy senses from the dust in which thou movest.

Suddenly a celestial flame seemed to dissolve the bands which held us to the earth ; and, like a light vapor, borne on the wings of the Genius, I felt myself wafted to the regions above. Thence, from the aerial heights, looking down upon the earth, I perceived a scene altogether new. Under my feet, floating in the void, a globe like that of the moon, but smaller and less luminous, presented to me one of its phases; and that phase * had the aspect of a disk varigated with large spots, some white and nebulous, others brown, green or gray, and while I strained my sight to distinguish what they were, the Genius exclaimed:

Disciple of Truth, knowest thou that object?

O Genius, answered I, if I did not see the moon in another quarter of the heavens, I should have supposed that to be her globe. It has the appearance of that planet seen through the telescope during the obscuration of an eclipse. These varigated spots might be mistaken for seas and continents.

They are seas and continents, said he, and those of the very hemisphere which you inhabit.

What! said I, is that the earth—the habitation of man ?

Yes, replied he, that brown space which occupies irregularly a great portion of the disk, and envelops it almost on every side, is what you call the great ocean, which advancing from the south pole towards the equator, forms first the great gulf of India and Africa, then extends eastward across the Malay islands to the confines of Tartary, while towards the west it encircles the continents of Africa and of Europe, even to the north of Asia.

That square peninsula under our feet is the arid country of the Arabs ; the great continent on its left, almost as naked in its interior, with a little verdure only towards its borders,

* See Plate representing half the terrestrial globe, opposite page 10.

is the parched soil inhabited by black-men.* To the north, beyond a long, narrow and irregular sea,† are the countries of Europe, rich in meadows and cultivated fields. On its right, from the Caspian Sea, extend the snowy and naked plains of Tartary. Returning in this direction, that white space is the vast and barren desert of Cobi, which separates China from the rest of the world. You see that empire in the furrowed plain which obliquely rounds itself off from our sight. On yonder coasts, those ragged tongues of land and scattered points are the peninsulas and islands of the Malays, the wretched possessors of the spices and perfumes. That triangle which advances so far into the sea, is the too famous peninsula of India.‡ You see the winding course of the Ganges, the rough mountains of Thibet, the lovely valley of Cachemere, the briny deserts of Persia, the banks of the Euphrates and Tygris, the deep bed of the Jordan and the canals of the solitary Nile.

O Genius, said I, interrupting him, the sight of a mortal reaches not to objects at such a distance. He touched my eyes, and immediately they became piercing as those of an eagle; nevertheless the rivers still appeared like waving lines, the mountains winding furrows, and the cities little compartments, like the squares of a chess-board.

And the Genius proceeded to enumerate and point out the objects to me: Those piles of ruins, said he, which you see in that narrow valley watered by the Nile, are the remains of opulent cities, the pride of the ancient kingdom of Ethiopia. § Behold the wrecks of her metropolis, of Thebes with her

---

* Africa.   † The Mediterranean.

‡ Of what real good has been the commerce of India to the mass of the people? On the contrary, how great the evil occasioned by the superstition of this country having been added to the general superstition !

§ In the new *Encyclopedia* 3rd vol. Antiquities, is published a memoir, respecting the chronology of the twelve ages anterior to the passing of Xerxes into Greece, in which I conceive myself to have proved that Upper Egypt formerly composed a distinct kingdom, known to the Hebrews by the name of *Kous*, and to which the appellation of Ethiopia was specially given. This kingdom preserved its independence to the time of Psammeticus ; at which period, being united to the Lower Egypt, it lost its name of Ethiopia, which thenceforth was bestowed upon the nations of Nubia, and upon the different tribes of blacks, including Thebes, their metropolis.

hundred palaces,* the parent of cities, and monument of the caprice of destiny. There a people, now forgotten, discovered, while others were yet barbarians, the elements of the

*The idea of a city with a hundred gates, in the common acceptation of the word, is so absurd, that I am astonished the equivoque has not before been felt.

It has ever been the custom of the East to call palaces and houses of the great by the name of gates, because the principal luxury of these buildings consists in the singular gate leading from the street into the court, at the farthest extremity of which the palace is situated. It is under the vestibule of this gate that conversation is held with passengers, and a sort of audience and hospitality given. All this was doubtless known to Homer; but poets make no commentaries, and readers love the marvellous.

This city of Thebes, now Lougsor, reduced to the condition of a miserable village, has left astonishing monuments of its magnificence. Particulars of this may be seen in the plates of Norden, in Pocock, and in the recent travels of Bruce. These monuments give credibility to all that Homer has related of its splendor, and lead us to infer its political power and external commerce.

Its geographical position was favorable to this twofold object. For, on one side, the valley of the Nile, singularly fertile, must have early occasioned a numerous population ; and, on the other, the Red Sea, giving communication with Arabia and India, and the Nile with Abyssinia and the Mediterranean, Thebes was thus naturally allied to the richest countries on the globe ; an alliance that procured it an activity so much the greater, as Lower Egypt, at first a swamp, was nearly, if not totally, uninhabited. But when at length this country had been drained by the canals and dikes which Sesostris constructed, population was introduced there, and wars arose which proved fatal to the power of Thebes. Commerce then took another route, and descended to the point of the Red Sea, to the canals of Sesostris (see Strabo), and wealth and activity were transferred to Memphis. This is manifestly what Diodorus means when he tells us (lib. i. sect. 2), that as soon as Memphis was established and made a wholesome and delicious abode, kings abandoned Thebes to fix themselves there. Thus Thebes continued to decline, and Memphis to flourish, till the time of Alexander, who, building Alexandria on the border of the sea, caused Memphis to fall in its turn ; so that prosperity and power seem to have descended historically step by step along the Nile; whence it results, both physically and historically, that the existence of Thebes was prior to that of the other cities. The testimony of writers is very positive in this respect. "The Thebans," says Diodorus, " consider themselves as the most ancient people of the earth, and assert, that with them originated philosophy and the science of the stars. Their situation, it is true, is infinitely favorable to astronomical observation, and they have a more accurate division of time into months and years than other nations," etc.

What Diodorus says of the Thebans, every author, and himself elsewhere, repeat of the Ethiopians, which tends more firmly to establish the identity of this place of which I have spoken. " The Ethiopians conceive themselves," says he, lib. iii., "to be of greater antiquity than any other nation : and it is probable that, born under the sun's path, its warmth may have ripened them earlier than other men. They suppose themselves also to be the inventors of divine worship, of festivals, of solemn assemblies, of sacrifices, and every other religious practice. They affirm that the Egyptians are one of their colonies, and that the Delta, which was formerly sea, became land by the conglomeration of the earth of the higher country which was washed down by the Nile. They have, like the Egyptians, two species

arts and sciences. A race of men now rejected from society for their *sable skin and frizzled hair*, founded on the study of the laws of nature, those civil and religious systems which still govern the universe. Lower down, those dusky points are the pyramids whose masses have astonished you. Beyond that, the coast, hemmed in between the sea and a narrow ridge of mountains, was the habitation of the Phœnicians. These were the famous cities of Tyre, of Sidon, of Ascalon, of Gaza, and of Berytus. That thread of water with no outlet, is the river Jordan ; and those naked rocks were once the theatre of events that have resounded throughout the world. Behold that desert of Horeb, and that Mount Sinai ; where, by means beyond vulgar reach, a genius, profound and bold, established institutions which have weighed on the whole human race. On that dry shore which borders it, you perceive no longer any trace of splendor ; yet there was an emporium of riches. There were those famous Ports of Idumea, whence the fleets of Phœnicia and Judea, coasting the Arabian peninsula, went

of letters, hieroglyphics, and the alphabet ; but among the Egyptians the first was known only to the priests, and by them transmitted from father to son, whereas both species were common among the Ethiopians."

"The Ethiopians," says Lucian, page 985, "were the first who invented the science of the stars, and gave names to the planets, not at random and without meaning, but descriptive of the qualities which they conceived them to possess ; and it was from them that this art passed, still in an imperfect state, to the Egyptians."

It would be easy to multiply citations upon this subject ; from all which it follows, that we have the strongest reasons to believe that the country neighboring to the tropic was the cradle of the sciences, and of consequence that the first learned nation was a nation of Blacks ; for it is incontrovertible, that, by the term Ethiopians, the ancients meant to represent a people of black complexion, thick lips, and woolly hair. I am therefore inclined to believe, that the inhabitants of Lower Egypt were originally a foreign colony imported from Syria and Arabia, a medley of different tribes of savages, originally shepherds and fishermen, who, by degrees formed themselves into a nation, and who, by nature and descent, were enemies of the Thebans, by whom they were no doubt despised and treated as barbarians.

I have suggested the same ideas in my *Travels into Syria*, founded upon the black complexion of the Sphinx. I have since ascertained that the antique images of Thebias have the same characteristic ; and Mr. Bruce has offered a multitude of analogous facts ; but this traveller, of whom I heard some mention at Cairo, has so interwoven these facts with certain systematic opinions, that we should have recourse to his narratives with caution.

It is singular that Africa, situated so near us, should be the least known country on the earth. The English are at this moment making explorations, the success of which ought to excite our emulation.

into the Persian gulf, to seek there the pearls of Hevila, the
gold of Saba and of Ophir.   Yes, there on that coast of Oman
and of Barhain was the seat of that commerce of luxuries,
which, by its movements and revolutions, fixed the destinies
of ancient nations.* Thither came the spices and precious
stones of Ceylon, the shawls of Cassimere, the diamonds of
Golconda, the amber of Maldivia, the musk of Thibet, the
aloes of Cochin, the apes and peacocks of the continent of

* Ailah (Eloth), and Atsiom-Gaber (Hesion-Geber.) The name of the first of
these towns still subsists in its ruins, at the point of the gulf of the Red Sea, and
in the route which the pilgrims take to Mecca.   Hesion has at present no trace,
any more than Quolzoum and Faran : it was, however, the harbor for the fleets of
Solomon.   The vessels of this prince conducted by the Tyrians, sailed along the
coast of Arabia to Ophir, in the Persian Gulf, thus opening a communication with
the merchants of India and Ceylon.   That this navigation was entirely of Tyrian
invention, appears both from the pilots and shipbuilders employed by the Jews,
and the names that were given to the trading islands, viz. Tyrus and Aradus, now
Barhain.   The voyage was performed in two different modes, either in canoes of
osier and rushes, covered on the outside with skins done over with pitch : (these
vessels were unable to quit the Red Sea, or so much as to leave the shore.)   The
second mode of carrying on the trade was by means of vessels with decks of the
size of our river boats, which were able to pass the strait and to weather the
dangers of the ocean ; but for this purpose it was necessary to bring the wood from
Mount Libanus and Cilicia, where it is very fine and in great abundance.   This
wood was first conveyed in floats from Tarsus to Phœnicia, for which reason the
vessels were called ships of Tarsus ; from whence it has been ridiculously inferred,
that they went round the promontory of Africa as far as Tortosa in Spain.   From
Phœnicia it was transported on the backs of camels to the Red Sea, which practice
still continues, because the shores of this sea are absolutely unprovided with wood
even for fuel.   These vessels spent a complete year in their voyage, that is, sailed
one year, sojourned another, and did not return till the third.   This tediousness
was owing first to their cruising from port to port, as they do at present ; secondly,
to their being detained by the Monsoon currents; and thirdly, because, according
to the calculations of Pliny and Strabo, it was the ordinary practice among the
ancients to spend three years in a voyage of twelve hundred leagues.   Such a
commerce must have been very expensive, particularly as they were obliged to
carry with them their provisions, and even fresh water.   For this reason Solomon
made himself master of Palmyra, which was at that time inhabited, and was
already the magazine and high road of merchants by the way of the Euphrates.
This conquest brought Solomon much nearer to the country of gold and pearls.
This alternative of a route either by the Red Sea or by the river Euphrates was
to the ancients, what in later times has been the alternative in a voyage to the
Indies, either by crossing the Isthmus of Suez or doubling the Cape of Good
Hope.   It appears that till the time of Moses, this trade was carried on across
the desert of Syria and Thebais; that afterwards it fell into the hands of the
Phœnicians, who fixed its site upon the Red Sea ; and that it was mutual jealousy
that induced the kings of Nineveh and Babylon to undertake the destruction of
Tyre and Jerusalem.   I insist the more upon these facts, because I have never
seen any thing reasonable upon the subject.

India, the incense of Hadramaut, the myrrh, the silver, the gold dust and ivory of Africa; thence passing, sometimes by the Red Sea on the vessels of Egypt and Syria, these luxuries nourished successively the wealth of Thebes, of Sidon, of Memphis and of Jerusalem; sometimes, ascending the Tygris and Euphrates, they awakened the activity of the Assyrians, Medes, Chaldeans, and Persians; and that wealth, according to the use or abuse of it, raised or reversed by turns their domination. Hence sprung the magnificence of Persepolis, whose columns you still perceive; of Ecbatana, whose seven-fold wall is destroyed; of Babylon,* now leveled with the earth; of Nineveh, of which scarce the name remains; of Thapsacus, of Anatho, of Gerra, and of desolated Palmyra. O names for ever glorious! fields of renown! countries of never-dying memory! what sublime lessons doth your aspect offer! what profound truths are written on the surface of your soil! remembrances of times past, return into my mind! places, witnesses of the life of man in so many different ages, retrace for me the revolutions of his fortune! say, what were their springs and secret causes! say, from what sources he derived success and disgrace! unveil to himself the causes of his evils! correct him by the spectacle of his errors! teach him the wisdom which belongeth to him, and let the experience of past ages become a means of instruction, and a germ of happiness to present and future generations.

* It appears that Babylon occupied on the eastern banks of the Euphrates a space of ground six leagues in length. Throughout this space bricks are found by means of which daily additions are made to the town of Hellè. Upon many of these are characters written with a nail similar to those of Persepolis. I am indebted for these facts to M. de Beauchamp, grand vicar of Babylon, a traveller equally distinguished for his knowledge of astronomy and for his veracity.

CHAPTER V.

CONDITION OF MAN IN THE UNIVERSE.

THE Genius, after some moments of silence, resumed in these words:

I have told thee already, O friend of truth! that man vainly ascribes his misfortunes to obscure and imaginary agents; in vain he seeks as the source of his evils mysterious and remote causes. In the general order of the universe his condition is, doubtless, subject to inconveniences, and his existence governed by superior powers; but those powers are neither the decrees of a blind fatality, nor the caprices of whimsical and fantastic beings. Like the world of which he forms a part, man is governed by natural laws, regular in their course, uniform in their effects, immutable in their essence; and those laws,—the common source of good and evil,—are not written among the distant stars, nor hidden in codes of mystery; inherent in the nature of terrestrial beings, interwoven with their existence, at all times and in all places, they are present to man; they act upon his senses, they warn his understanding, and give to every action its reward or punishment. Let man then know these laws! let him comprehend the nature of the elements which surround him, and also his own nature, and he will know the regulators of his destiny; he will know the causes of his evils and the remedies he should apply.

When the hidden power which animates the universe, formed the globe which man inhabits, he implanted in the beings composing it, essential properties which became the law of their individual motion, the bond of their reciprocal relations, the cause of the harmony of the whole; he thereby established a regular order of causes and effects, of principles and consequences, which, under an appearance of chance, governs the universe, and maintains the equilibrium of the world. Thus, he gave to fire, motion and activity; to air, elasticity; weight and density to matter; he made air lighter than water, metal heavier than earth, wood less cohesive than steel; he decreed flame to ascend, stones to fall, plants to vegetate; to man, who was to be exposed to the action of so many different beings, and still to preserve his frail life, he gave the faculty of sensation. By this faculty all action hurtful to his existence gives him a feeling of pain and evil, and all which is salutary, of pleasure and happiness. By these sensations, man, sometimes averted from that which wounds his senses, sometimes allured towards that which soothes them, has been obliged to cherish and preserve his own life; thus, self-love, the desire of happiness, aversion to pain, become the essential and primary laws imposed on man by nature herself—the laws which the directing power, whatever it be, has established for his government—and which laws, like those of motion in the physical world, are the simple and fruitful principle of whatever happens in the moral world.

Such, then, is the condition of man: on one side, exposed to the action of the elements which surround him, he is subject to many inevitable evils; and if, in this decree, nature has been severe, on the other hand, just and even indulgent, she has not only tempered the evils with equivalent good, she has also enabled him to increase the good and alleviate the evil. She seems to say:

"Feeble work of my hands, I owe thee nothing, and I give thee life; the world wherein I placed thee was not made for thee, yet I give thee the use of it; thou wilt find in it a mixture of good and evil; it is for thee to distinguish them; for thee to guide thy footsteps in a path containing thorns as well as roses. Be the arbiter of thine own fate; I put thy destiny into thine own hands!"

Yes, man is made the architect of his own destiny; he, himself, hath been the cause of the successes or reverses of his own fortune; and if, on a review of all the pains with which he has tormented his own life, he finds reason to weep over his own weakness or imprudence, yet, considering the beginnings from which he sat out, and the height attained, he has, perhaps, still reason to presume on his strength, and to pride himself on his genius.

CHAPTER VI.

THE PRIMITIVE STATE OF MAN.

FORMED naked in body and in mind, man at first found himself thrown, as it were by chance, on a rough and savage land: an orphan, abandoned by the unknown power which had produced him, he saw not by his side beings descended from heaven to warn him of those wants which arise only from his senses, nor to instruct him in those duties which spring only from his wants. Like to other animals, without experience of the past, without foresight of the future, he wandered in the bosom of the forest, guided only and governed by the affections of his nature. By the pain of hunger, he was led to seek food and provide for his subsistence; by the inclemency of the air, he was urged to cover his body, and he made him clothes; by the attraction of a powerful pleasure, he approached a being like himself, and he perpetuated his kind.

Thus the impressions which he received from every object, awakening his faculties, developed by degrees his understanding, and began to instruct his profound ignorance: his wants excited industry, dangers formed his courage; he learned to distinguish useful from noxious plants, to combat the elements, to seize his prey, to defend his life; and thus he alleviated its miseries.

Thus self-love, aversion to pain, the desire of happiness, were the simple and powerful excitements which drew man from the savage and barbarous condition in which nature had placed him. And now, when his life is replete with enjoyments, when he may count each day by the comforts it brings, he may applaud himself and say:

" It is I who have produced the comforts which surround me; it is I who am the author of my own happiness; a safe dwelling, convenient clothing, abundant and wholesome nourishment, smiling fields, fertile hills, populous empires, all is my work; without me this earth, given up to disorder, would have been but a filthy fen, a wild wood, a dreary desert."

Yes, creative man, receive my homage! Thou hast measured the span of the heavens, calculated the volume of the stars, arrested the lightning in its clouds, subdued seas and storms, subjected all the elements. Ah! how are so many sublime energies allied to so many errors?

CHAPTER VII.

PRINCIPLES OF SOCIETY.

WANDERING in the woods and on the banks of rivers in pursuit of game and fish, the first men, beset with dangers, assailed by enemies, tormented by hunger, by reptiles, by ravenous beasts, felt their own individual weakness; and, urged by a common need of safety, and a reciprocal sentiment of like evils, they united their resources and their strength; and when one incurred a danger, many aided and succored him; when one wanted subsistence, another shared his food with him. Thus men associated to secure their existence, to augment their powers, to protect their enjoyments; and self-love thus became the principle of society.

Instructed afterwards by the experience of various and repeated accidents, by the fatigues of a wandering life, by the distress of frequent scarcity, men reasoned with themselves and said:

" Why consume our days in seeking scattered fruits from a parsimonious soil? why exhaust ourselves in pursuing prey which eludes us in the woods or waters? why not collect under our hands the animals that nourish us? why not apply our cares in multiplying and preserving them? We will feed on their increase, be clothed in their skins, and live exempt from the fatigues of the day and solicitude for the morrow."

And men, aiding one another, seized the nimble goat, the timid sheep; they tamed the patient camel, the fierce bull, the impetuous horse; and, applauding their own industry, they sat down in the joy of their souls, and began to taste repose and comfort: and self-love, the principle of all reasoning, became the incitement to every art, and every enjoyment.

When, therefore, men could pass long days in leisure, and in communication of their thoughts, they began to contemplate the earth, the heavens, and their own existence, as objects of curiosity and reflection; they remarked the course of the seasons, the action of the elements, the properties of fruits and plants; and applied their thoughts to the multiplication of their enjoyments. And in some countries, having observed that certain seeds contained a wholesome nourishment in a small volume, convenient for transportation and preservation, they imitated the process of nature; they confided to the earth rice, barley, and corn, which multiplied to the full measure of their hope; and having found the means of obtaining within a small compass and without removal, plentiful subsistence and durable stores, they established themselves in fixed habitations; they built houses, villages, and towns; formed societies and nations; and self-love produced all the developments of genius and of power.

Thus by the aid of his own faculties, man has raised himself to the astonishing height of his present fortune. Too happy if, observing scrupulously the law of his being, he had faithfully fulfilled its only and true object! But, by a fatal imprudence, sometimes mistaking, sometimes transgressing its limits, he has launched forth into a labyrinth of errors and misfortunes; and self-love, sometimes unruly, sometimes blind, became a principle fruitful in calamities.

CHAPTER VIII.

SOURCES OF THE EVILS OF SOCIETY.

IN truth, scarcely were the faculties of men developed, when, inveigled by objects which gratify the senses, they gave themselves up to unbridled desires. The sweet sensations which nature had attached to their real wants, to endear to them their existence, no longer satisfied them. Not content with the abundance offered by the earth or produced by industry, they wished to accumulate enjoyments, and coveted those possessed by their fellow men. The strong man rose up against the feeble, to take from him the fruit of his labor; the feeble invoked another feeble one to repel the violence. Two strong ones then said:

"Why fatigue ourselves to produce enjoyments which we may find in the hands of the weak? Let us join and despoil them; they shall labor for us, and we will enjoy without labor."

And the strong associating for oppression, and the weak for resistance, men mutually afflicted each other; and a general and fatal discord spread over the earth, in which the passions, assuming a thousand new forms, have generated a continued chain of misfortunes.

Thus the same self-love which, moderate and prudent, was a principle of happiness and perfection, becoming blind and disordered, was transformed into a corrupting poison; and cupidity, offspring and companion of ignorance, became the cause of all the evils that have desolated the earth.

Yes, ignorance and cupidity! these are the twin sources of all the torments of man! Biased by these into false ideas of happiness, he has mistaken or broken the laws of nature in his own relation with external objects; and injuring his own existence, has violated individual morality; shutting through these his heart to compassion, and his mind to justice, he has injured and afflicted his equal, and violated social morality. From ignorance and cupidity, man has armed against man, family against family, tribe against tribe; and the earth is become a theatre of blood, of discord, and of rapine. By ignorance and cupidity, a secret war, fermenting in the bosom of every state, has separated citizen from citizen; and the same society has divided itself into oppressors and oppressed, into masters and slaves; by these, the heads of a nation, sometimes insolent and audacious, have forged its chains within its own bowels; and mercenary avarice has founded political despotism. Sometimes, hypocritical and cunning, they have called from heaven a lying power, and a sacrilegious yoke; and credulous cupidity has founded religious despotism. By these have been perverted the ideas of good and evil, just and unjust, vice and virtue; and nations have wandered in a labyrinth of errors and calamities.

The cupidity of man and his ignorance,—these are the evil genii which have wasted the earth! These are the decrees of fate which have overthrown empires! These are the celestial anathemas which have smitten these walls once so glorious, and converted the splendor of a populous city into a solitude of mourning and of ruins! But as in the bosom of man have sprung all the evils which have afflicted his life, there he also is to seek and to find their remedies.

CHAPTER IX.

ORIGIN OF GOVERNMENT AND LAWS.

IN fact, it soon happened that men, fatigued with the evils they reciprocally inflicted, began to sigh for peace; and reflecting on their misfortunes and the causes of them, they said:

"We are mutually injuring each other by our passions; and, aiming to grasp every thing, we hold nothing. What one seizes to-day, another takes to-morrow, and our cupidity reacts upon ourselves. Let us establish judges, who shall arbitrate our rights, and settle our differences. When the strong shall rise against the weak, the judge shall restrain him, and dispose of our force to suppress violence; and the life and property of each shall be under the guarantee and protection of all ; and all shall enjoy the good things of nature."

Conventions were thus formed in society, sometimes express, sometimes tacit, which became the rule for the action of individuals, the measure of their rights, the law of their reciprocal relations ; and persons were appointed to superintend their observance, to whom the people confided the balance to weigh rights, and the sword to punish transgressions.

Thus was established among individuals a happy equilibrium of force and action, which constituted the common security. The name of equity and of justice was recognized and revered over the earth ; every one, assured of enjoying in peace, the fruits of his toil, pursued with energy the objects of his attention ; and industry, excited and maintained by the reality or the hope of enjoyment, developed all the riches of art and of nature. The fields were covered with harvests, the valleys with flocks, the hills with fruits, the sea with vessels, and man became happy and powerful on the earth. Thus did his own wisdom repair the disorder which his imprudence had occasioned; and that wisdom was only the effect of his own organization. He respected the enjoyments of others in order to secure his own; and cupidity found its corrective in the enlightened love of self.

Thus the love of self, the moving principle of every individual, becomes the necessary foundation of every association ; and on the observance of that law of our nature has depended the fate of nations. Have the factitious and conventional laws tended to that object and accomplished that aim ? Every one, urged by a powerful instinct, has displayed all the faculties of his being ; and the sum of individual felicities has constituted the general felicity. Have these laws, on the contrary, restrained the effort of man toward his own happiness ? His heart, deprived of its exciting principle, has languished in inactivity, and from the oppression of individuals has resulted the weakness of the state.

As self-love, impetuous and improvident, is ever urging man against his equal, and consequently tends to dissolve

society, the art of legislation and the merit of administrators
consists in attempering the conflict of individual cupidities,
in maintaining an equilibrium of powers, and securing to
every one his happiness, in order that, in the shock of society
against society, all the members may have a common interest
in the preservation and defence of the public welfare.

The internal splendor and prosperity of empires then, have
had for their efficient cause the equity of their laws and government; and their respective external powers have been in
proportion to the number of persons interested, and their
degree of interest in the public welfare.

On the other hand, the multiplication of men, by complica-
ting their relations, having rendered the precise limitation of
their rights difficult, the perpetual play of the passions having
produced incidents not foreseen—their conventions having
been vicious, inadequate, or nugatory—in fine, the authors of
the laws having sometimes mistaken, sometimes disguised
their objects; and their ministers, instead of restraining the
cupidity of others, having given themselves up to their own;
all these causes have introduced disorder and trouble into
societies; and the viciousness of laws and the injustice of
governments, flowing from cupidity and ignorance, have
become the causes of the misfortunes of nations, and the sub-
version of states.

———

CHAPTER X.

GENERAL CAUSES OF THE PROSPERITY OF ANCIENT STATES.

SUCH, O man who seekest wisdom, such have been the
causes of revolution in the ancient states of which thou
contemplatest the ruins! To whatever spot I direct my
view, to whatever period my thoughts recur, the same principles of growth or destruction, of rise or fall, present themselves to my mind. Wherever a people is powerful, or an
empire prosperous, there the conventional laws are conformable with the laws of nature—the government there procures

for its citizens a free use of their faculties, equal security for their persons and property. If, on the contrary, an empire goes to ruin, or dissolves, it is because its laws have been vicious, or imperfect, or trodden under foot by a corrupt government. If the laws and government, at first wise and just, become afterwards depraved, it is because the alternation of good and evil is inherent to the heart of man, to a change in his propensities, to his progress in knowledge, to a combination of circumstances and events; as is proved by the history of the species.

In the infancy of nations, when men yet lived in the forest, subject to the same wants, endowed with the same faculties, all were nearly equal in strength; and that equality was a circumstance highly advantageous in the composition of society: as every individual, thus feeling himself sufficiently independent of every other, no one was the slave, none thought of being the master of another. Man, then a novice, knew neither servitude nor tyranny; furnished with resources sufficient for his existence, he thought not of borrowing from others; owning nothing, requiring nothing, he judged the rights of others by his own, and formed ideas of justice sufficiently exact. Ignorant, moreover, in the art of enjoyments, unable to produce more than his necessaries, possessing nothing superfluous, cupidity remained dormant; or if excited, man, attacked in his real wants, resisted it with energy, and the foresight of such resistance ensured a happy balance.

Thus original equality, in default of compact, maintained freedom of person, security of property, good manners, and order. Every one labored by himself and for himself; and the mind of man, being occupied, wandered not to culpable desires. He had few enjoyments, but his wants were satisfied; and as indulgent nature had made them less than his resources, the labor of his hands soon produced abundance—abundance, population; the arts unfolded, culture extended, and the earth, covered with numerous inhabitants, was divided into different dominions.

The relations of man becoming complicated, the internal order of societies became more difficult to maintain. Time and industry having generated riches, cupidity became more active; and because equality, practicable among individuals, could not subsist among families, the natural equilibrium was broken; it became necessary to supply it by a factitious equilibrium; to set up chiefs, to establish laws; and in the primitive inexperience, it necessarily happened that these laws, occasioned by cupidity, assumed its character. But different circumstances concurred to correct the disorder, and oblige governments to be just.

States, in fact, being weak at first, and having foreign enemies to fear, the chiefs found it their interest not to oppress their subjects; for, by lessening the confidence of the citizens in their government, they would diminish their means of resistance—they would facilitate foreign invasion, and by exercising arbitrary power, have endangered their very existence.

In the interior, the firmness of the people repelled tyranny; men had contracted too long habits of independence; they had too few wants, and too much consciousness of their own strength.

States being of a moderate size, it was difficult to divide their citizens so as to make use of some for the oppression of others. Their communications were too easy, their interest too clear and simple: besides, every one being a proprietor and cultivator, no one needed to sell himself, and the despot could find no mercenaries.

If, then, dissensions arose, they were between family and family, faction and faction, and they interested a great number. The troubles, indeed, were warmer; but fears from abroad pacified discord at home. If the oppression of a party prevailed, the earth being still unoccupied, and man, still in a state of simplicity, finding every where the same advantages, the oppressed party emigrated, and carried elsewhere their independence.

The ancient states then enjoyed within themselves numerous means of prosperity and power. Every one finding his own well-being in the constitution of his country, took a lively interest in its preservation. If a stranger attacked it, having to defend his own field, his own house, he carried into combat all the passions of a personal quarrel; and, devoted to his own interests, he was devoted to his country.

As every action useful to the public attracted its esteem and gratitude, every one became eager to be useful ; and self-love multiplied talents and civic virtues.

Every citizen contributing equally by his talents and person, armies and funds were inexhaustible, and nations displayed formidable masses of power.

The earth being free, and its possession secure and easy, every one was a proprietor; and the division of property preserved morals, and rendered luxury impossible.

Every one cultivating for himself, culture was more active, produce more abundant; and individual riches became public wealth.

The abundance of produce rendering subsistence easy, population was rapid and numerous, and states attained quickly the term of their plenitude.

Productions increasing beyond consumption, the necessity of commerce arose ; and exchanges took place between people and people ; which augmented their activity and reciprocal advantages.

In fine, certain countries, at certain times, uniting the advantages of good government with a position on the route of the most active circulation, they became emporiums of flourishing commerce and seats of powerful domination. And on the shores of the Nile and Mediterranean, of the Tygris and Euphrates, the accumulated riches of India and of Europe raised in successive splendor a hundred different cities.

The people, growing rich, applied their superfluity to works of common and public use ; and this was in every state, the epoch of those works whose grandeur astonishes the mind; of those wells of Tyre, of those dykes of the Euphrates, of those subterranean conduits of Media,* of those

---

* See respecting these monuments my *Travels into Syria*, vol. ii. p. 214.

From the town or village of Samouât the course of the Euphrates is accompanied with a double bank, which descends as far as its junction with the Tygris, and from thence to the sea, being a length of about a hundred leagues, French measure. The height of these artificial banks is not uniform, but increases as you advance from the sea ; it may be estimated at from twelve to fifteen feet. But for them, the inundation of the river would bury the country around, which is flat, to an extent of twenty or twenty-five leagues ; and even notwithstanding these banks, there has been in modern times an overflow, which has covered the whole triangle formed by the junction of this river to the Tygris, being a space of country of one hundred and thirty square leagues. By the stagnation of these waters an epidemical disease of the most fatal nature was occasioned. It follows

fortresses of the desert, of those aqueducts of Palmyra, of those temples, of those porticoes. And such labors might be immense, without oppressing the nations ; because they were the effect of an equal and common contribution of the force of individuals animated and free.

Thus ancient states prospered, because their social institutions conformed to the true laws of nature ; and because men, enjoying liberty and security for their persons and their property, might display all the extent of their faculties,—all the energies of their self-love.

CHAPTER XI.

GENERAL CAUSES OF THE REVOLUTIONS AND RUIN OF ANCIENT STATES.

CUPIDITY had nevertheless excited among men a constant and universal conflict, which incessantly prompting individuals and societies to reciprocal invasions, occasioned successive revolutions, and returning agitations.

from hence, 1. That all the flat country bordering upon these rivers, was originally a marsh; 2. That this marsh could not have been inhabited previously to the construction of the banks in question ; 3. That these banks could not have been the work but of a population prior as to date ; and the elevation of Babylon, therefore, must have been posterior to that of Nineveh, as I think I have chronologically demonstrated in the memoir above cited. See *Encyclopedia*, vol. xiii, of *Antiquities*.

The modern Aderbidjân, which was a part of Medea, the mountains of Koulderstan, and those of Diarbekr, abound with subterranean canals, by means of which the ancient inhabitants conveyed water to their parched soil in order to fertilize it. It was regarded as a meritorious act and a religious duty prescribed by Zoroaster, who, instead of preaching celibacy, mortifications, and other pretended virtues of the monkish sort, repeats continually in the passages that are preserved respecting him in the Sad-der and the Zend-avesta :

" That the action most pleasing to God is to plough and cultivate the earth, to water it with running streams, to multiply vegetation and living beings, to have numerous flocks, young and fruitful virgins, a multitude of children," etc., etc.

Among the aqueducts of Palmyra it appears certain, that, besides those which conducted water from the neighboring hills, there was one which brought it even from the mountains of Syria. It is to be traced a long way into the Desert where it escapes our search by going under ground.

And first, in the savage and barbarous state of the first men, this audacious and fierce cupidity produced rapine, violence, and murder, and retarded for a long time the progress of civilization.

When afterwards societies began to be formed, the effect of bad habits, communicated to laws and governments, corrupted their institutions and objects, and established arbitrary and factitious rights, which depraved the ideas of justice, and the morality of the people.

Thus one man being stronger than another, their inequality —an accident of nature—was taken for her law ; * and the strong being able to take the life of the weak, and yet sparing him, arrogated over his person an abusive right of property ; and the slavery of individuals prepared the way for the slavery of nations.

Because the head of a family could be absolute in his house, he made his own affections and desires the rule of his conduct; he gave or resumed his goods without equality, without justice ; and paternal despotism laid the foundation of despotism in government.†

* Almost all the ancient philosophers and politicians have laid it down as a principle that men are born unequal, that nature his created some to be free, and others to be slaves. Expressions of this kind are to be found in Aristotle, and even in Plato, called the divine, doubtless in the same sense as the mythological reveries which he promulgated. With all the people of antiquity, the Gauls, the Romans, the Athenians, the right of the strongest was the right of nations ; and from the same principle are derived all the political disorders and public national crimes that at present exist.

† Upon this single expression it would be easy to write a long and important chapter. We might prove in it, beyond contradiction, that all the abuses of national governments, have sprung from those of domestic government, from that government called patriarchal, which superficial minds have extolled without having analyzed it. Numberless facts demonstrate, that with every infant people, in every savage and barbarous state, the father, the chief of the family, is a despot, and a cruel and insolent despot. The wife is his slave, the children his servants. This king sleeps or smokes his pipe, while his wife and daughters perform all the drudgery of the house, and even that of tillage and cultivation, as far as occupations of this nature are practised in such societies ; and no sooner have the boys acquired strength then they are allowed to beat the females, and make them serve and wait upon them as they do upon their fathers. Similar to this is the state of our own uncivilized peasants. In proportion as civilization spreads, the manners become milder, and the condition of the women improves, till, by a contrary excess, they arrive at dominion, and then a nation becomes effeminate and corrupt. It is remarkable that parental authority is great in proportion as the government is despotic. China, India, and Turkey are striking

In societies formed on such foundations, when time and labor had developed riches, cupidity restrained by the laws, became more artful, but not less active. Under the mask of union and civil peace, it fomented in the bosom of every state an intestine war, in which the citizens, divided into contending corps of orders, classes, families, unremittingly struggled to appropriate to themselves, under the name of *supreme power*, the ability to plunder every thing, and render every thing subservient to the dictates of their passions; and this spirit of encroachment, disguised under all possible forms, but always the same in its object and motives, has never ceased to torment the nations.

Sometimes, opposing itself to all social compact, or breaking that which already existed, it committed the inhabitants of a country to the tumultuous shock of all their discords; and states thus dissolved, and reduced to the condition of anarchy, were tormented by the passions of all their members.

Sometimes a nation, jealous of its liberty, having appointed agents to administer its government, these agents appropriated the powers of which they had only the guardianship: they employed the public treasures in corrupting elections, gaining partisans, in dividing the people among themselves. By these means, from being temporary they became perpetual; from elective, hereditary; and the state, agitated by the intrigues of the ambitious, by largesses from the rich and factious, by the venality of the poor and idle, by the influence of orators, by the boldness of the wicked, and the weakness of the virtuous, was convulsed with all the inconveniences of democracy.

The chiefs of some countries, equal in strength and mutually fearing each other, formed impious pacts, nefarious associations; and, apportioning among themselves all power, rank, and honor, unjustly arrogated privileges and immunities; erected themselves into separate orders and distinct classes; reduced the people to their control; and, under the

examples of this. One would suppose that tyrants gave themselve accomplices and interested subaltern despots to maintain their authority. In opposition to this the Romans will be cited, but it remains to be proved that the Romans were men truly free; and their quick passage from their republican despotism to their abject servility under the emperors, gives room at least for considerable doubt as to that freedom.

name of *aristocracy*, the state was tormented by the passions of the wealthy and the great.

Sacred impostors, in other countries, tending by other means to the same object, abused the credulity of the ignorant. In the gloom of their temples, behind the curtain of the altar, they made their gods act and speak ; gave forth oracles, worked miracles, ordered sacrifices, levied offerings, prescribed endowments ; and, under the names of theocracy and of religion, the state became tormented by the passions of the priests.

Sometimes a nation, weary of its dissensions or of its tyrants, to lessen the sources of evil, submitted to a single master ; but if it limited his powers, his sole aim was to enlarge them ; if it left them indefinite, he abused the trust confided to him ; and, under the name of monarchy, the state was tormented by the passions of kings and princes.

Then the factions, availing themselves of the general discontent, flattered the people with the hope of a better master ; dealt out gifts and promises, deposed the despot to take his place ; and their contests for the succession, or its partition, tormented the state with the disorders and devastations of civil war.

In fine, among these rivals, one more adroit, or more fortunate, gained the ascendency, and concentrated all power within himself. By a strange phenomenon, a single individual mastered millions of his equals, against their will and without their consent ; and the art of tyranny sprung also from cupidity.

In fact, observing the spirit of egotism which incessantly divides mankind, the ambitious man fomented it with dexterity, flattered the vanity of one, excited the jealousy of another, favored the avarice of this, inflamed the resentment of that, and irritated the passions of all ; then, placing in opposition their interests and prejudices, he sowed divisions and hatreds, promised to the poor the spoils of the rich, to the rich the subjection of the poor ; threatened one man by another, this class by that ; and insulating all by distrust, created his strength out of their weakness, and imposed the yoke of opinion, which they mutually riveted on each other. With the army he levied contributions, and with contributions he disposed of the army: dealing out wealth and office on these principles, he enchained a whole people in indissoluble bonds, and they languished under the slow consumption of despotism.

Thus the same principle, varying its action under every possible form, was forever attenuating the consistence of states, and an eternal circle of vicissitudes flowed from an eternal circle of passions.

And this spirit of egotism and usurpation produced two effects equally operative and fatal : the one a division and subdivision of societies into their smallest fractions, inducing a debility which facilitated their dissolution ; the other, a preserving tendency to concentrate power in a single hand,* which, engulfing successively societies and states, was fatal to their peace and social existence.

Thus, as in a state, a party absorbed the nation, a family the party, and an individual the family; so a movement of absorption took place between state and state, and exhibited on a larger scale in the political order, all the particular evils of the civil order. Thus a state having subdued a state, held it in subjection in the form of a province ; and two provinces being joined together formed a kingdom; two kingdoms being united by conquest, gave birth to empires of gigantic size; and in this conglomeration, the internal strength of states, instead of increasing, diminished; and the condition of the people, instead of ameliorating, became daily more abject and wretched, for causes derived from the nature of things.

Because, in proportion as states increased in extent, their administration becoming more difficult and complicated, greater energies of power were necessary to move such masses ; and there was no longer any proportion between the duties of sovereigns and their ability to perform their duties :

Because despots, feeling their weakness, feared whatever

---

* It is remarkable that this has in all instances been the constant progress of societies ; beginning with a state of anarchy or democracy, that is, with a great division of power they have passed to aristocracy, and from aristocracy to monarchy. Does it not hence follow that those who constitute states under the democratic form, destine them to undergo all the intervening troubles between that and monarchy ; but it should at the same time be proved that social experience is already exhausted for the human race, and that this spontaneous movement is not solely the effect of ignorance.

might develop the strength of nations, and studied only how to enfeeble them :

Because nations, divided by the prejudices of ignorance and hatred, seconded the wickedness of their governments; and availing themselves reciprocally of subordinate agents, aggravated their mutual slavery :

Because, the balance between states being destroyed, the strong more easily oppressed the weak.

Finally, because in proportion as states were concentrated, the people, despoiled of their laws, of their usages, and of the government of their choice, lost that spirit of personal identification with their government, which had caused their energy.

And despots, considering empires as their private domains, and the people as their property, gave themselves up to depredations, and to all the licentiousness of the most arbitrary authority.

And all the strength and wealth of nations were diverted to private expense and personal caprice ; and kings, fatigued with gratification, abandoned themselves to all the extravagancies of factitious and depraved taste.* They must have gardens mounted on arcades, rivers raised over mountains, fertile fields converted into haunts for wild beasts; lakes scooped in dry lands, rocks erected in lakes, palaces built of marble and porphyry, furniture of gold and diamonds. Under the cloak of religion, their pride founded temples, endowed indolent priests, built, for vain skeletons, extravagant tombs, mausoleums and pyramids ; † millions of hands were em-

---

* It is equally worthy of remark, that the conduct and manners of princes and kings of every country and every age, are found to be precisely the same at similar periods, whether of the formation or dissolution of empires. History every where presents the same pictures of luxury and folly ; of parks, gardens, lakes, rocks, palaces, furniture, excess of the table, wine, women, concluding with brutality.

The absurd rock in the garden of Versailles has alone cost three millions. I have sometimes calculated what might have been done with the expense of the three pyramids of Gizah, and I have found that it would easily have constructed, from the Red Sea to Alexandria, a canal one hundred and fifty feet wide and thirty deep, completely covered in with cut stones and a parapet, together with a fortified and commercial town, consisting of four hundred houses, furnished with cisterns. What a difference in point of utility between such a canal and these pyramids !

† The learned Dupuis could not be persuaded that the pyramids were tombs ; but besides the positive testimony of historians, read what Diodorus says of the

ployed in sterile labors ; and the luxury of princes, imitated
by their parasites, and transmitted from grade to grade to the
lowest ranks, became a general source of corruption and im-
poverishment.

And in the insatiable thirst of enjoyment, the ordinary
revenues no longer sufficing, they were augmented ; the cultivator, seeing his labors increase without compensation, lost
all courage ; the merchant, despoiled, was disgusted with
industry ; the multitude, condemned to perpetual poverty,
restrained their labor to simple necessaries ; and all productive industry vanished.

The surcharge of taxes rendering lands a burdensome possession, the poor proprietor abandoned his field, or sold it to
the powerful ; and fortune became concentrated in a few
hands. All the laws and institutions favoring this accumula-
tion, the nation became divided into a group of wealthy
drones, and a multitude of mercenary poor ; the people were
degraded with indigence, the great with satiety, and the
number of those interested in the preservation of the state
decreasing, its strength and existence became proportionally
precarious.

On the other hand, emulation finding no object, science no
encouragement, the mind sunk into profound ignorance.

The administration being secret and mysterious, there
existed no means of reform or amelioration. The chiefs
governing by force or fraud, the people viewed them as a
faction of public enemies ; and all harmony ceased between
the governors and governed.

religious and superstitious importance every Egyptian attached to building his
dwelling eternal, b. 1.

During twenty years, says Herodotus, a hundred thousand men labored every
day to build the pyramid of the Egyptian Cheops. Supposing only three hundred days a year, on account of the sabbath, there will be 30 millions of days' work
in a year, and 600 millions in twenty years ; at 15 sous a day, this makes 450
millions of francs lost, without any further benefit. With this sum, if the king
had shut the isthmus of Suez by a strong wall, like that of China, the destinies
of Egypt might have been entirely changed. Foreign invasions would have been
prevented, and the Arabs of the desert would neither have conquered nor
harassed that country. Sterile labors ! how many millions lost in putting one
stone upon another, under the forms of temples and churches ! Alchymists convert
stones into gold ; but architects change gold into stone. Woe to the kings (as well
as subjects) who trust their purse to these two classes of empirics !

And these vices having enervated the states of the wealthy part of Asia, the vagrant and indigent people of the adjacent deserts and mountains coveted the enjoyments of the fertile plains; and, urged by a cupidity common to all, attacked the polished empires, and overturned the thrones of their despots. These revolutions were rapid and easy; because the policy of tyrants had enfeebled the subjects, razed the fortresses, destroyed the warriors; and because the oppressed subjects remained without personal interest, and the mercenary soldiers without courage.

And hordes of barbarians having reduced entire nations to slavery, the empires, formed of conquerors and conquered, united in their bosom two classes essentially opposite and hostile. All the principles of society were dissolved: there was no longer any common interest, no longer any public spirit; and there arose a distinction of casts and races, which reduced to a regular system the maintenance of disorder; and he who was born of this or that blood, was born a slave or a tyrant — property or proprietor.

The oppressors being less numerous than the oppressed, it was necessary to perfect the science of oppression, in order to support this false equilibrium. The art of governing became the art of subjecting the many to the few. To enforce an obedience so contrary to instinct, the severest punishments were established, and the cruelty of the laws rendered manners atrocious. The distinction of persons establishing in the state two codes, two orders of criminal justice, two sets of laws, the people, placed between the propensities of the heart and the oath uttered from the mouth, had two consciences in contradiction with each other; and the ideas of justice and injustice had no longer any foundation in the understanding.

Under such a system, the people fell into dejection and despair; and the accidents of nature were added to the other evils which assailed them. Prostrated by so many calamities, they attributed their causes to superior and hidden powers; and, because they had tyrants on earth, they fancied others in heaven; and superstition aggravated the misfortunes of nations.

Fatal doctrines and gloomy and misanthropic systems of

religion arose, which painted their gods, like their despots, wicked and envious. To appease them, man offered up the sacrifice of all his enjoyments. He environed himself in privations, and reversed the order of nature. Conceiving his pleasures to be crimes, his sufferings expiations, he endeavored to love pain, and to abjure the love of self. He persecuted his senses, hated his life ; and a self-denying and anti-social morality plunged nations into the apathy of death.

But provident nature having endowed the heart of man with hope inexhaustible, when his desires of happiness were baffled on this earth, he pursued it into another world. By a sweet illusion he created for himself another country — an asylum where, far from tyrants, he should recover the rights of nature, and thence resulted new disorders. Smitten with an imaginary world, man despised that of nature. For chimerical hopes, he neglected realities. His life began to appear a troublesome journey — a painful dream; his body a prison, the obstacle to his felicity ; and the earth, a place of exile and of pilgrimage, not worthy of culture. Then a holy indolence spread over the political world; the fields were deserted, empires depopulated, monuments neglected and deserts multiplied ; ignorance, superstition and fanaticism, combining their operations, overwhelmed the earth with devastation and ruin.

Thus agitated by their own passions, men, whether collectively or individually taken, always greedy and improvident, passing from slavery to tyranny, from pride to baseness, from presumption to despondency, have made themselves the perpetual instruments of their own misfortunes.

These, then, are the principles, simple and natural, which regulated the destiny of ancient states. By this regular and connected series of causes and effects, they rose or fell, in proportion as the physical laws of the human heart were respected or violated ; and in the course of their successive changes, a hundred different nations, a hundred different empires, by turns humbled, elevated, conquered, overthrown, have repeated for the earth their instructive lessons. Yet these lessons were lost for the generations which have followed ! The disorders in times past have reappeared in the present age ! The chiefs of the nations have continued to walk in the paths of falsehood and tyranny!—the people to wander in the darkness of superstition and ignorance!

Since then, continued the Genius, with renewed energy, since the experience of past ages is lost for the living—since the errors of progenitors have not instructed their descendants, the ancient examples are about to reappear; the earth will see renewed the tremendous scenes it has forgotten. New revolutions will agitate nations and empires; powerful thrones will again be overturned, and terrible catastrophes will again teach mankind that the laws of nature and the precepts of wisdom and truth cannot be infringed with impunity.

CHAPTER XII.

LESSONS OF TIMES PAST REPEATED ON THE PRESENT.

THUS spoke the Genius. Struck with the justice and coherence of his discourse, assailed with a crowd of ideas, repugnant to my habits yet convincing to my reason, I remained absorbed in profound silence. At length, while with serious and pensive mien, I kept my eyes fixed on Asia, suddenly in the north, on the shores of the Black sea, and in the fields of the Crimea, clouds of smoke and flame attracted my attention. They appeared to rise at the same time from all parts of the peninsula; and passing by the isthmus into the continent, they ran, as if driven by a westerly wind, along the oozy lake of Azof, and disappeared in the grassy plains of Couban; and following more attentively the course of these clouds, I observed that they were preceded or followed by swarms of moving creatures, which, like ants or grasshoppers disturbed by the foot of a passenger, agitated themselves with vivacity. Sometimes these swarms appeared to advance and rush against each other; and numbers, after the concussion, remained motionless. While disquieted at this spectacle, I strained my sight to distinguish the objects.

Do you see, said the Genius, those flames which spread

over the earth, and do you comprehend their causes and effects?

Oh! Genius, I answered, I see those columns of flame and smoke, and something like insects, accompanying them; but, when I can scarcely discern the great masses of cities and monuments, how should I discover, such little creatures? I can just perceive that these insects mimic battle, for they advance, retreat, attack and pursue.

It is no mimicry, said the Genius, these are real battles.

And what, said I, are those mad animalculæ, which destroy each other? Beings of a day! will they not perish soon enough?

Then the Genius, touching my sight and hearing, again directed my eyes towards the same object. Look, said he, and listen!

Ah! wretches, cried I, oppressed with grief, these columns of flame! these insects! oh! Genius, they are men. These are the ravages of war! These torrents of flame rise from towns and villages! I see the squadrons who kindle them, and who, sword in hand overrun the country: they drive before them crowds of old men, women, and children, fugitive and desolate: I perceive other horsemen, who with shouldered lances, accompany and guide them. I even recognize them to be Tartars by their led horses,* their kalpacks, and tufts of hair: and, doubtless, they who pursue, in triangular hats and green uniforms, are Muscovites. Ah! I now comprehend, a war is kindled between the empire of the Czars and that of the Sultans.

Not yet, replied the Genius; this is only a preliminary. These Tartars have been, and might still be troublesome neighbors. The Muscovites are driving them off, finding their country would be a convenient extension of their own limits; and as a prelude to another revolution, the throne of the Guerais is destroyed.

* A Tartar horseman has always two horses, of which he leads one in hand. The *Kalpeck* is a bonnet made of the skin of a sheep or other animal. The part of the head covered by this bonnet is shaved, with the exception of a tuft, about the size of a crown piece, and which is suffered to grow to the length of seven or eight inches, precisely where our priests place their tonsure. It is by this tuft of hair, worn by the majority of Mussulmen, that the angel of the tomb is to take the elect and carry them into paradise.

And in fact, I saw the Russian standards floating over the Crimea : and soon after their flag waving on the Euxine.

Meanwhile, at the cry of the flying Tartars, the Mussulman empire was in commotion. They are driving off our brethren, cried the children of Mahomet: the people of the prophet are outraged! infidels occupy a consecrated land and profane the temples of Islamism.* Let us arm ; let us rush to combat, to avenge the glory of God and our own cause.

And a general movement of war took place in both empires. In every part armed men assembled. Provisions, stores, and all the murderous apparatus of battle were displayed. The temples of both nations, besieged by an immense multitude, presented a spectacle which fixed all my attention.

On one side, the Mussulmen gathered before their mosques, washed their hands and feet, pared their nails, and combed their beards ; then spreading carpets upon the ground, and turning towards the south, with their arms sometimes crossed and sometimes extended, they made genuflexions and prostrations, and recollecting the disasters of the late war, they exclaimed :

God of mercy and clemency ! hast thou then abandoned thy faithful people? Thou who hast promised to thy Prophet dominion over nations, and stamped his religion by so many triumphs, dost thou deliver thy true believers to the swords of infidels ?

And the Imans and the Santons said to the people :

It is in chastisement of your sins. You eat pork ; you drink wine ; you touch unclean things. God hath punished you. Do penance therefore ; purify ; repeat the profession of faith ;† fast from the rising to the setting sun ; give the tenth of your goods to the mosques ; go to Mecca ; and God will render you victorious.

And the people, recovering courage, uttered loud cries:

There is but one God, said they transported with fury, and Mahomet is his prophet ! Accursed be he who believeth not!

* It is not in the power of the Sultan to cede to a foreign power a province inhabited by true believers. The people, instigated by the lawyers, would not fail to revolt. This is one reason which has led those who know the Turks, to regard as chimerical the ceding of Candia, Cyprus, and Egypt, projected by certain European potentates.

† There is but one God, and Mahomet is his prophet.

God of goodness, grant us to exterminate these Christians; it is for thy glory we fight, and our death is a martyrdom for thy name. And then, offering victims, they prepared for battle.

On the other side, the Russians, kneeling, said:

We render thanks to God, and celebrate his power. He hath strengthened our arm to humble his enemies. Hear our prayers, thou God of mercy! To please thee, we will pass three days without eating either meat or eggs. Grant us to extirpate these impious Mahometans, and to overturn their empire. To thee we will consecrate the tenth of our spoil; to thee we will raise new temples.

And the priests filled the churches with clouds of smoke, and said to the people:

We pray for you, God accepteth our incense, and blesseth your arms. Continue to fast and to fight; confess to us your secret sins; give your wealth to the church; we will absolve you from your crimes, and you shall die in a state of grace.

And they sprinkled water upon the people, dealt out to them, as amulets and charms, small relics of the dead, and the people breathed war and combat.

Struck with this contrast of the same passions, and grieving for their fatal consequences, I was considering the difficulty with which the common judge could yield to prayers so contradictory; when the Genius, glowing with anger, spoke with vehemence:

What accents of madness strike my ear? What blind and perverse delirium disorders the spirits of the nations? Sacrilegious prayers rise not from the earth! and you, oh Heavens, reject their homicidal vows and impious thanksgivings! Deluded mortals! is it thus you revere the Divinity? Say then; how should he, whom you style your common father, receive the homage of his children murdering one another? Ye victors! with what eye should he view your hands reeking in the blood he hath created? And, what do you expect, oh vanquished, from useless groans? Hath God the heart of a mortal, with passions ever changing? Is he, like you, agitated with vengeance or compassion, with wrath or repentance? What base conception of the most sublime of beings! According to them, it would seem, that God whimsical and capricious, is angered or appeased as a man: that he loves and hates alternately; that he punishes or favors; that, weak or wicked, he broods over his hatred; that, contradictory or perfidious, he lays snares to entrap; that he punishes the evils he permits; that he foresees but hinders not crimes; that, like a corrupt judge, he is bribed by offerings; like an ignorant despot, he makes laws and revokes them; that, like a savage tyrant, he grants or resumes favors without reason, and can only be appeased by servility. Ah! now I know the lying spirit of man! Contemplating the picture which he hath drawn of the Divinity: No, said I, it is not God who hath made man after the image of God; but man hath made God after the image of man; he hath given him his own mind, clothed him with his own propensities; ascribed to him his own judgments. And when in this medley he finds the contradiction of his own principles, with hypocritical humility, he imputes weakness to his reason, and names the absurdities of his own mind the mysteries of God.

He hath said, God is immutable, yet he offers prayers to change him; he hath pronounced him incomprehensible, yet he interprets him without ceasing.

Imposters have arisen on the earth who have called themselves the confidants of God; and, erecting themselves into teachers of the people, have opened the ways of falsehood and iniquity; they have ascribed merit to practices indifferent or ridiculous; they have supposed a virtue in certain postures, in pronouncing certain words, articulating certain names; they have transformed into a crime the eating of certain meats, the drinking of certain liquors, on one day rather than another. The Jew would rather die than labor on the sabbath; the Persian would endure suffocation, before he would blow the fire with his breath; the Indian places supreme perfection in besmearing himself with cow-dung, and pronouncing mysteriously the word Aûm;* the Mussulman

* This word is, in the religion of the Hindoos, a sacred emblem of the Divinity. It is only to be pronounced in secret, without being heard by any one. It is formed of three letters, of which the first, a, signifies the principal of all, the creator, Brama; the second, û, the conservator, Vichenou; and the last, m, the destroyer, who puts an end to all, Chiven. It is pronounced like the monosyllable ôm, and expresses the unity of those three Gods. The idea is precisely that of the Alpha and Omega mentioned in the New Testament.

believes he has expiated everything in washing his head and
arms; and disputes, sword in hand, whether the ablution
should commence at the elbow, or finger ends;* the Christian
would think himself damned, if he ate flesh instead of milk or
butter. Oh sublime doctrines! Doctrines truly from heaven!
Oh perfect morals, and worthy of martyrdom or the aposto-
late! I will cross the seas to teach these admirable laws to
the savage people — to distant nations; I will say unto them:

Children of nature, how long will you walk in the paths
of ignorance? how long will you mistake the true principles
of morality and religion?   Come and learn its lessons
from nations truly pious and learned, in civilized countries.
They will inform you how, to gratify God, you must in certain months of the year, languish the whole day with hunger
and thirst; how you may shed your neighbor's blood, and
purify yourself from it by professions of faith and methodical
ablutions; how you may steal his property and be absolved
on sharing it with certain persons, who devote themselves to
its consumption.

Sovereign and invisible power of the universe! mysterious
mover of nature! universal soul of beings! thou who art unknown, yet revered by mortals under so many names! being
incomprehensible and infinite! God, who in the immensity
of the heavens directest the movement of worlds, and peoplest
the abyss of space with millions of suns! say what do these
human insects, which my sight no longer discerns on the
earth, appear in thy eyes?   To thee, who art guiding stars in
their orbits, what are those wormlings writhing themselves in
the dust? Of what import to thy immensity, their distinctions
of parties and sects?   And of what concern the subtleties
with which their folly torments itself?

And you, credulous men, show me the effect of your practices! In so many centuries, during which you have been
following or altering them, what changes have your pre-
scriptions wrought in the laws of nature? Is the sun brighter?

* This is one of the grand points of schism between the partisans of Omar and
those of Ali. Suppose two Mahometans to meet on a journey, and to accost each
other with brotherly affection: the hour of prayer arrives; one begins his ablution
at his fingers, the other at the elbow, and instantly they are mortal enemies. O
sublime importance of religious opinions ! O profound philosophy of the authors
of them !

Is the course of the seasons varied? Is the earth more fruitful, or its inhabitants more happy? If God be good, can your penances please him? If infinite, can your homage add to his glory? If his decrees have been formed on foresight of every circumstance, can your prayers change them? Answer, O inconsistent mortals!

Ye conquerors of the earth, who pretend you serve God! doth he need your aid? If he wishes to punish, hath he not earthquakes, volcanoes, and thunder? And cannot a merciful God correct without extermination?

Ye Mussulmans, if God chastiseth you for violating the five precepts, how hath he raised up the Franks who ridicule them? If he governeth the earth by the Koran, by what did he govern it before the days of the prophet, when it was covered with so many nations who drank wine, ate pork, and went not to Mecca, whom he nevertheless permitted to raise powerful empires? How did he judge the Sabeans of Nineveh and of Babylon; the Persian, worshipper of fire; the Greek and Roman idolators; the ancient kingdoms of the Nile; and your own ancestors, the Arabians and Tartars? How doth he yet judge so many nations who deny, or know not your worship—the numerous castes of Indians, the vast empire of the Chinese, the sable race of Africa, the islanders of the ocean, the tribes of America?

Presumptuous and ignorant men, who arrogate the earth to yourselves! if God were to gather all the generations past and present, what would be, in their ocean, the sects calling themselves universal, of Christians and Mussulmans? What would be the judgments of his equal and common justice over the real universality of mankind? Therein it is that your knowledge loseth itself in incoherent systems; it is there that truth shines with evidence; and there are manifested the powerful and simple laws of nature and reason—laws of a common and general mover—of a God impartial and just, who sheds rain on a country without asking who is its prophet; who causeth his sun to shine alike on all the races of men, on the white as on the black, on the Jew, on the Mussulman, the Christian, and the Idolater; who reareth the harvest wherever cultivated with diligence; who multiplieth every nation where industry and order prevaileth; who prospereth every empire where justice is practised, where the powerful are restrained, and the poor protected by the laws; where the weak live in safety, and all enjoy the rights given by nature and a compact formed in justice.

These are the principles by which people are judged! this the true religion which regulates the destiny of empires, and which, O Ottomans, hath governed yours! Interrogate your ancestors, ask of them by what means they rose to greatness; when few, poor and idolaters, they came from the deserts of Tartary and encamped in these fertile countries; ask if it was by Islamism, till then unknown to them, that they conquered the Greeks and the Arabs, or was it by their courage, their prudence, moderation, spirit of union—the true powers of the social state? Then the Sultan himself dispensed justice, and maintained discipline. The prevaricating judge, the extortionate governor, were punished, and the multitude lived at ease. The cultivator was protected from the rapine of the janissary, and the fields prospered; the highways were safe, and commerce caused abundance. You were a band of plunderers, but just among yourselves. You subdued nations, but did not oppress them. Harrassed by their own princes, they preferred being your tributaries. What matters it, said the Christian, whether my ruler breaks or adores images, if he renders justice to me? God will judge his doctrines in the heavens above.

You were sober and hardy; your enemies timid and enervated; You were expert in battle, your enemies unskillful; your leaders were experienced, your soldiers warlike and disciplined. Booty excited ardor, bravery was rewarded, cowardice and insubordination punished, and all the springs of the human heart were in action. Thus you vanquished a hundred nations, and of a mass of conquered kingdoms compounded an immense empire.

But other customs have succeeded; and in the reverses attending them, the laws of nature have still exerted their force. After devouring your enemies, your cupidity, still insatiable, has reacted on itself, and, concentrated in your own bowels, has consumed you.

Having become rich, you have quarrelled for partition and enjoyment, and disorder hath arisen in every class of society.

The Sultan, intoxicated with grandeur, has mistaken the object of his functions; and all the vices of arbitrary power have been developed. Meeting no obstacle to his appetites, he has become a depraved being; weak and arrogant, he has kept the people at a distance; and their voice has no longer instructed and guided him. Ignorant, yet flattered, neglecting all instruction, all study, he has fallen into imbecility; unfit for business, he has thrown its burdens on hirelings, and they have deceived him. To satisfy their own passions, they have stimulated and nourished his; they have multiplied his wants, and his enormous luxury has consumed everything. The frugal table, plain clothing, simple dwelling of his ancestors no longer sufficed. To supply his pomp, earth and sea have been exhausted. The rarest furs have been brought from the poles; the most costly tissues from the equator. He has devoured at a meal the tribute of a city, and in a day that of a province. He has surrounded himself with an army of women, eunuchs, and satellites. They have instilled into him that the virtue of kings is to be liberal, and the munificence and treasures of the people have been delivered into the hands of flatterers. In imitation of their master, his servants must also have splendid houses, the most exquisite furniture; carpets embroidered at great cost, vases of gold and silver for the lowest uses, and all the riches of the empire have been swallowed up in the Serai.

To supply this inordinate luxury, the slaves and women have sold their influence, and venality has introduced a general depravation. The favor of the sovereign has been sold to his vizier, and the vizier has sold the empire. The law has been sold to the cadi, and the cadi has made sale of justice. The altar has been sold to the priest, and the priest has sold the kingdom of heaven. And gold obtaining everything, they have sacrificed everything to obtain gold. For gold, friend has betrayed friend, the child his parent, the servant his master, the wife her honor, the merchant his conscience; and good faith, morals, concord, and strength were banished from the state.

The pacha, who had purchased the government of his province, farmed it out to others, who exercised every extortion. He sold in turn the collection of the taxes, the command of

the troops, the administration of the villages ; and as every
employ has been transient, rapine, spread from rank to rank,
has been greedy and implacable. The revenue officer has
fleeced the merchant, and commerce was annihilated ; the aga
has plundered the husbandman, and culture has degenerated.
The laborer, deprived of his stock, has been unable to sow ;
the tax was augmented, and he could not pay it; the basti-
nado has been threatened, and he has borrowed. Money,
from want of security, being locked up from circulation,
interest was therefore enormous, and the usury of the rich
has aggravated the misery of the laborer.

When excessive droughts and accidents of seasons have
blasted the harvest, the government has admitted no delay,
no indulgence for the tax ; and distress bearing hard on the
village, a part of its inhabitants have taken refuge in the
cities ; and their burdens falling on those who remained, has
completed their ruin, and depopulated the country.

If driven to extremity by tyranny and outrage, the villages
have revolted, the pacha rejoices. He wages war on them,
assails their homes, pillages their property, carries off their
stock ; and when the fields have become a desert, he exclaims:
"What care I ?   I leave these fields to-morrow."

The earth wanting laborers, the rain of heaven and overflowing of torrents have stagnated in marshes ; and their
putrid exhalations in a warm climate, have caused epidemics,
plagues, and maladies of all sorts, whence have flowed additional suffering, penury, and ruin.

Oh! who can enumerate all the calamities of tyrannical
government ?

Sometimes the pachas declare war against each other,
and for their personal quarrels the provinces of the same
state are laid waste. Sometimes, fearing their masters, they
attempt independence, and draw on their subjects the chastisement of their revolt. Sometimes dreading their subjects,
they invite and subsidize strangers, and to insure their fidelity
set no bounds to their depredations. Here they persecute
the rich and despoil them under false pretences ; there they
suborn false witnesses, and impose penalties for suppositious
offences ; everywhere they excite the hatred of parties, encourage informations to obtain amercements, extort property,

seize persons; and when their short-sighted avarice has accumulated into one mass all the riches of a country, the government, by an execrable perfidy, under pretence of avenging its oppressed people, takes to itself all their spoils, as if they were the culprits, and uselessly sheds the blood of its agents for a crime of which it is the accomplice.

Oh wretches, monarchs or ministers, who sport with the lives and fortunes of the people! Is it you who gave breath to man, that you dare take it from him? Do you give growth to the plants of the earth, that you may waste them? Do you toil to furrow the field? Do you endure the ardor of the sun, and the torment of thirst, to reap the harvest or thrash the grain? Do you, like the the shepherd, watch through the dews of the night? Do you traverse deserts, like the merchant? Ah! on beholding the pride and cruelty of the powerful, I have been transported with indignation, and have said in my wrath, will there never then arise on the earth men who will avenge the people and punish tyrants? A handful of brigands devour the multitude, and the multitude submits to be devoured! Oh! degenerate people! Know you not your rights? All authority is from you, all power is yours. Unlawfully do kings command you on the authority of God and of their lance—Soldiers be still; if God supports the Sultan he needs not your aid; if his sword suffices, he needs not yours; let us see what he can do alone. The soldiers grounded their arms; and behold these masters of the world, feeble as the meanest of their subjects! People! know that those who govern are your chiefs, not your masters; your agents, not your owners; that they have no authority over you, but by you, and for you; that your wealth is yours and they accountable for it; that, kings or subjects, God has made all men equal, and no mortal has the right to oppress his fellow-creatures.

But this nation and its chiefs have mistaken these holy truths. They must abide then the consequences of their blindness. The decree is past; the day approaches when this colossus of power shall be crushed and crumbled under its own mass. Yes, I swear it, by the ruins of so many empires destroyed. The empire of the Crescent shall follow the fate of the despotism it has copied. A nation of strangers

shall drive the Sultan from his metropolis. The throne of
Orkhan shall be overturned. The last shoot of his trunk shall
be broken off; and the horde of Oguzians,* deprived of their
chief, shall disperse like that of the Nagois. In this dissolution, the people of the empire, loosened from the yoke which
united them, shall resume their ancient distinctions, and a
general anarchy shall follow, as happened in the empire of the
Sophis; † until there shall arise among the Arabians, Arme-
nians, or Greeks, legislators who may compose new states.

Oh! if there were on earth men profound and bold! what
elements for grandeur and glory! But the hour of destiny
has already come; the cry of war strikes my ear; and the
catastrophe begins. In vain the Sultan leads forth his armies;
his ignorant warriors are beaten and dispersed. In vain he
calls his subjects; their hearts are ice. Is it not written? say
they, what matters who is our master? We cannot lose by
the change.

In vain the true believers invoke heaven and the prophet.
The prophet is dead; and heaven without pity answers:

Cease to invoke me. You have caused your own misfortunes; cure them yourselves. Nature has established laws;
your part is to obey them. Observe, reason, and profit by
experience. It is the folly of man which ruins him; let his
wisdom save him. The people are ignorant; let them gain
instruction. Their chiefs are wicked; let them correct and
amend; for such is Nature's decree. Since the evils of society
spring from cupidity and ignorance, men will never cease to
be persecuted, till they become enlightened and wise; till
they practise justice, founded on a knowledge of their relations
and of the laws of their organization.‡

* Before the Turks took the name of their chief, Othman I., they bore that of
Oguzians ; and it was under this appellation that they were driven out of Tartary
by Gengis, and came from the borders of Gihoun to settle themselves in Anatolia.

† In Persia, after the death of Thamas-Koulikan, each province had its chief,
and for forty years these chiefs were in a constant state of war. In this view the
Turks do not say without reason : " Ten years of a tyrant are less destructive
than a single night of anarchy."

‡ A singular moral phenomenon made its appearance in Europe in the year
1788. A great nation, jealous of its liberty, contracted a fondness for a nation the
enemy of liberty : a nation friendly to the arts, for a nation that detests them ; a
mild and tolerant nation, for a persecuting and fanatic one ; a social and gay
nation, for a nation whose characteristics are gloom and misanthropy ; in a word,
the French were smitten with a passion for the Turks : they were desirous of

CHAPTER XIII.

WILL THE HUMAN RACE IMPROVE?

AT these words, oppressed with the painful sentiment with which their severity overwhelmed me: Woe to the nations! cried I, melting in tears; woe to myself! Ah! now it is that I despair of the happiness of man! Since his miseries proceed from his heart; since the remedy is in his own power, woe for ever to his existence! Who, indeed will ever be able to restrain the lust of wealth in the strong and powerful? Who can enlighten the ignorance of the weak? Who can teach the multitude to know their rights, and force their chiefs to perform their duties? Thus the race of man is always doomed to suffer! Thus the individual will not cease to oppress the individual, a nation to attack a nation; and days of prosperity, of glory, for these regions, shall never return. Alas! conquerors will come; they will drive out the oppressors, and fix themselves in their place; but, inheriting their power, they will inherit their rapacity; and the earth will have changed tyrants, without changing the tyranny.

Then, turning to the Genius, I exclaimed:

O Genius, despair hath settled on my soul. Knowing the

engaging in a war for them, and that at a time when revolution in their own country was just at its commencement. A man, who perceived the true nature of the situation, wrote a book to dissuade them from the war: it was immediately pretended that he was paid by the government, which in reality wished the war, and which was upon the point of shutting him up in a state prison. Another man wrote to recommend the war: he was applauded, and his word taken for the science, the politeness, and importance of the Turks. It is true that he believed in his own thesis, for he has found among them people who cast a nativity, and alchymists who ruined his fortune; as he found Martinists at Paris, who enabled him to sup with Sesostris, and Magnetizers who concluded with destroying his existence. Notwithstanding this, the Turks were beaten by the Russians, and the man who then predicted the fall of their empire, persists in the prediction. The result of this fall will be a complete change of the political system, as far as it relates to the coast of the Mediterranean. If, however, the French become important in proportion as they become free, and if they make use of the advantage they will obtain, their progress may easily prove of the most honorable sort; inasmuch as, by the wise decrees of fate, the true interest of mankind evermore accords with their true morality.

nature of man, the perversity of those who govern, and the debasement of the governed—this knowledge hath disgusted me with life; and since there is no choice but to be the accomplice or the victim of oppression, what remains to the man of virtue but to mingle his ashes with those of the tomb?

The Genius then gave me a look of severity, mingled with compassion; and after a few moments of silence, he replied:

Virtue, then, consists in dying! The wicked man is indefatigable in consummating his crime, and the just is discouraged from doing good at the first obstacle he encounters! But such is the human heart. A little success intoxicates man with confidence; a reverse overturns and confounds him. Always given up to the sensation of the moment, he seldom judges things from their nature, but from the impulse of his passion.

Mortal, who despairest of the human race, on what profound combination of facts hast thou established thy conclusion? Hast thou scrutinized the organization of sentient beings, to determine with precision whether the instinctive force which moves them on to happiness is essentially weaker than that which repels them from it? or, embracing in one glance the history of the species, and judging the future by the past, hast thou shown that all improvement is impossible? Say! hath human society, since its origin, made no progress toward knowledge and a better state? Are men still in their forests, destitute of everything, ignorant, stupid and ferocious? Are all the nations still in that age when nothing was seen upon the globe but brutal robbers and brutal slaves? If at any time, in any place, individuals have ameliorated, why shall not the whole mass ameliorate? If partial societies have made improvements, what shall hinder the improvement of society in general? And if the first obstacles are overcome, why should the others be insurmountable?

Art thou disposed to think that the human race degenerates? Guard against the illusion and paradoxes of the misanthrope. Man, discontented with the present, imagines for the past a perfection which never existed, and which only serves to cover his chagrin. He praises the dead out of hatred to the living, and beats the children with the bones of their ancestors.

To prove this pretended retrograde progress from perfection

we must contradict the testimony of reason and of fact; and if the facts of history are in any measure uncertain, we must contradict the living fact of the organization of man; we must prove that he is born with the enlightened use of his senses; that, without experience, he can distinguish aliment from poison; that the child is wiser than the old man; that the blind walks with more safety than the clear-sighted; that the civilized man is more miserable than the savage; and, indeed, that there is no ascending scale in experience and instruction.

Believe, young man, the testimony of monuments, and the voice of the tombs. Some countries have doubtless fallen from what they were at certain epochs; but if we weigh the wisdom and happiness of their inhabitants, even in those times, we shall find more of splendor than of reality in their glory; we shall find, in the most celebrated of ancient states, enormous vices and cruel abuses, the true causes of their decay; we shall find in general that the principles of government were atrocious; that insolent robberies, barbarous wars, and implacable hatreds were raging from nation to nation; * that natural right was unknown; that morality was perverted by senseless fanaticism and deplorable superstition; that a dream, a vision, an oracle, were constantly the causes of vast commotions. Perhaps the nations are not yet entirely cured of all these evils; but their intensity at least is diminished, and the experience of the past has not been wholly lost. For the last three centuries, especially, knowledge has increased and been extended; civilization, favored by happy circumstances, has made a sensible progress; inconveniences and abuses have even turned to its advantage; for if states have been too much extended by conquest, the people, by uniting under the same yoke, have lost the spirit of estrangement and division which made them all enemies one to the other. If the powers of government have been more concentrated, there has been more system and harmony in their exercise. If wars have become more extensive in the mass, they are less bloody in detail. If men have gone to battle with less personality, less energy, their struggles have been less sanguinary and

---

* Read the history of the wars of Rome and Carthage, of Sparta and Messina, of Athens and Syracuse, of the Hebrews and the Phœnicians: yet these are the nations of which antiquity boasts as being most polished!

less ferocious; they have been less free, but less turbulent; more effeminate, but more pacific. Despotism itself has rendered them some service; for if governments have been more absolute, they have been more quiet and less tempestuous. If thrones have become a property and hereditary, they have excited less dissensions, and the people have suffered fewer convulsions; finally, if the despots, jealous and mysterious, have interdicted all knowledge of their administration, all concurrence in the management of public affairs, the passions of men, drawn aside from politics, have fixed upon the arts, and the sciences of nature; and the sphere of ideas in every direction has been enlarged; man, devoted to abstract studies, has better understood his place in the system of nature, and his relations in society; principles have been better discussed, final causes better explained, knowledge more extended, individuals better instructed, manners more social, and life more happy. The species at large, especially in certain countries, has gained considerably; and this amelioration cannot but increase in future, because its two principal obstacles, those even which, till then, had rendered it slow and sometimes retrograde,—the difficulty of transmitting ideas and of communicating them rapidly,—have been at last removed.

Indeed, among the ancients, each canton, each city, being isolated from all others by the difference of its language, the consequence was favorable to ignorance and anarchy. There was no communication of ideas, no participation of discoveries, no harmony of interests or of wills, no unity of action or design; besides, the only means of transmitting and of propagating ideas being that of speech, fugitive and limited, and that of writing, tedious of execution, expensive and scarce, the consequence was a hindrance of present instruction, loss of experience from one generation to another, instability, retrogression of knowledge, and a perpetuity of confusion and childhood.

But in the modern world, especially in Europe, great nations having allied themselves in language, and established vast communities of opinions, the minds of men are assimilated, and their affections extended; there is a sympathy of opinion and a unity of action; then that gift of heavenly Genius, the holy art of printing, having furnished the means of communicating in an instant the same idea to millions of men, and of fixing it in a durable manner, beyond the power of tyrants to arrest or annihilate, there arose a mass of progressive instruction, an expanding atmosphere of science, which assures to future ages a solid amelioration. This amelioration is a necessary effect of the laws of nature; for, by the law of sensibility, man as invincibly tends to render himself happy as the flame to mount, the stone to descend, or the water to find its level. His obstacle is his ignorance, which misleads him in the means, and deceives him in causes and effects. He will enlighten himself by experience; he will become right by dint of errors; he will grow wise and good because it is his interest so to be. Ideas being communicated through the nation, whole classes will gain instruction; science will become a vulgar possession, and all men will know what are the principles of individual happiness and of public prosperity. They will know the relations they bear to society, their duties and their rights; they will learn to guard against the illusions of the lust of gain; they will perceive that the science of morals is a physical science, composed, indeed, of elements complicated in their operation, but simple and invariable in their nature, since they are only the elements of the organization of man. They will see the propriety of being moderate and just, because in that is found the advantage and security of each; they will perceive that the wish to enjoy at the expense of another is a false calculation of ignorance, because it gives rise to reprisal, hatred, and vengeance, and that dishonesty is the never-failing offspring of folly.

Individuals will feel that private happiness is allied to public good:

The weak, that instead of dividing their interests, they ought to unite them, because equality constitutes their force:

The rich, that the measure of enjoyment is bounded by the constitution of the organs, and that lassitude follows satiety:

The poor, that the employment of time, and the peace of the heart, compose the highest happiness of man. And public opinion, reaching kings on their thrones, will force them to confine themselves to the limits of regular authority.

Even chance itself, serving the cause of nations, will sometimes give them feeble chiefs, who, through weakness, will suffer them to become free ; and sometimes enlightened chiefs, who, from a principle of virtue, will free them.

And when nations, free and enlightened, shall become like great individuals, the whole species will have the same facilities as particular portions now have; the communication of knowledge will extend from one to another, and thus reach the whole. By the law of imitation, the example of one people will be followed by others, who will adopt its spirit and its laws. Even despots, perceiving that they can no longer maintain their authority without justice and beneficence, will soften their sway from necessity, from rivalship ; and civilization will become universal.

There will be established among the several nations an equilibrium of force, which, restraining them all within the bounds of the respect due to their reciprocal rights, shall put an end to the barbarous practice of war, and submit their disputes to civil arbitration.* The human race will become one great society, one individual family, governed by the same spirit, by common laws, and enjoying all the happiness of which their nature is susceptible.

Doubtless this great work will be long accomplishing ; because the same movement must be given to an immense body ; the same leaven must assimilate an enormous mass of heterogeneous parts. But this movement shall be effected; its presages are already to be seen. Already the great society, assuming in its course the same characters as partial societies have done, is evidently tending to a like result. At first disconnected in all its parts, it saw its members for a long time without cohesion ; and this general solitude of nations formed its first age of anarchy and childhood ; divided afterwards by chance into irregular sections, called states and kingdoms, it has experienced the fatal effects of an extreme inequality of wealth and rank ; and the aristocracy of great empires has formed its second age ; then, these lordly states disputing for preëminence, have exhibited the period of the shock of factions.

* What is a people ? An individual of the society at large. What a war ? A duel between two individual people. In what manner ought a society to act when two of its members fight ? Interfere and reconcile, or repress them. In the days of the Abbé de Saint Pierre this was treated as a dream, but happily for the human race it begins to be realized.

At present the contending parties, wearied with discord, feel the want of laws, and sigh for the age of order and of peace. Let but a virtuous chief arise! a just, a powerful people appear! and the earth will raise them to supreme power. The world is waiting for a legislative people; it wishes and demands it; and my heart attends the cry.

Then turning towards the west: Yes, continued he, a hollow sound already strikes my ear; a cry of liberty, proceeding from far distant shores, resounds on the ancient continent. At this cry, a secret murmur against oppression is raised in a powerful nation; a salutary inquietude alarms her respecting her situation; she enquires what she is, and what she ought to be; while, surprised at her own weakness, she interrogates her rights, her resources, and what has been the conduct of her chiefs.

Yet another day—a little more reflection—and an immense agitation will begin; a new-born age will open! an age of astonishment to vulgar minds, of terror to tyrants, of freedom to a great nation, and of hope to the human race!

CHAPTER XIV.

THE GREAT OBSTACLE TO IMPROVEMENT.

THE Genius ceased. But preoccupied with melancholy thoughts, my mind resisted persuasion; fearing, however, to shock him by my resistance, I remained silent. After a while, turning to me with a look which pierced my soul, he said:

Thou art silent, and thy heart is agitated with thoughts which it dares not utter.

At last, troubled and terrified, I replied:

O Genius, pardon my weakness. Doubtless thy mouth can utter nothing but truth; but thy celestial intelligence can seize its rays, where my gross faculties can discern nothing but clouds. I confess it; conviction has not penetrated my soul, and I feared that my doubts might offend thee.

And what is doubt, replied he, that it should be a crime? Can man feel otherwise than as he is affected? If a truth be palpable, and of importance in practice, let us pity him that misconceives it. His punishment will arise from his blindness. If it be uncertain or equivocal, how is he to find in it what it has not? To believe without evidence or proof, is an act of ignorance and folly. The credulous man loses himself in a labyrinth of contradictions; the man of sense examines and discusses, that he may be consistent in his opinions. The honest man will bear contradiction; because it gives rise to evidence. Violence is the argument of falsehood; and to impose a creed by authority is the act and indication of a tyrant.

O Genius, said I, encouraged by these words, since my reason is free, I strive in vain to entertain the flattering hope with which you endeavor to console me. The sensible and virtuous soul is easily caught with dreams of happiness; but a cruel reality constantly awakens it to suffering and wretchedness. The more I meditate on the nature of man, the more I examine the present state of societies, the less possible it appears to realize a world of wisdom and felicity. I cast my eye over the whole of our hemisphere; I perceive in no place the germ, nor do I foresee the instinctive energy of a happy revolution. All Asia lies buried in profound darkness. The Chinese, governed by an insolent despotism,* by strokes of the bamboo and the cast of lots, restrained by an immutable code of gestures, and by the radical vices of an ill-constructed language,† appear to be in their abortive civilization nothing

---

* The emperor of China calls himself the son of heaven; that is, of God: for in the opinion of the Chinese, the material of heaven, the arbiter of fatality, is the Deity himself. " The emperor only shows himself once in ten months, lest the people, accustomed to see him, might lose their respect ; for he holds it as a maxim that power can only be supported by force, that the people have no idea of justice, and are not to be governed but by coercion." *Narrative of two Mahometan travellers in 851 and 877, translated by the Abbé Renaudot in 1718.*

Notwithstanding what is asserted by the missionaries, this situation has undergone no change. The bamboo still reigns in China, and the son of heaven bastinades, for the most trivial fault, the Mandarin, who in his turn bastinades the people. The Jesuits may tell us that this is the best governed country in the world, and its inhabitants the happiest of men : but a single letter from Amyot has convinced me that China is a truly Turkish government, and the account of Sonnerat confirms it. See Vol. II. of *Voyage aux Indes*, in 4to.

† As long as the Chinese shall in writing make use of their present characters, they can be expected to make no progress in civilization. The necessary intro-

but a race of automatons. The Indian, borne down by prejudices, and enchained in the sacred fetters of his castes, vegetates in an incurable apathy. The Tartar, wandering or fixed, always ignorant and ferocious, lives in the savageness of his ancestors. The Arab, endowed with a happy genius, loses its force and the fruits of his virtue in the anarchy of his tribes and the jealousy of his families. The African, degraded from the rank of man, seems irrevocably doomed to servitude. In the North I see nothing but vilified serfs, herds of men with which landlords stock their estates. Ignorance, tyranny, and wretchedness have everywhere stupified the nations; and vicious habits, depraving the natural senses, have destroyed the very instinct of happiness and of truth.

In some parts of Europe, indeed, reason has begun to dawn, but even there, do nations partake of the knowledge of individuals? Are the talents and genius of governors turned to the benefit of the people? And those nations which call themselves polished, are they not the same that for the last three centuries have filled the earth with their injustice? Are they not those who, under the pretext of commerce, have desolated India, depopulated a new continent, and, at present, subject Africa to the most barbarous slavery? Can liberty be born from the bosom of despots? and shall justice be rendered by the hands of piracy and avarice? O Genius, I have seen the civilized countries; and the mockery of their wisdom has vanished before my sight. I saw wealth accumulated in the hands of a few, and the multitude poor and destitute. I have seen all rights, all powers concentered in certain classes, and the mass of the people passive and dependent. I have seen families of princes, but no families of the nation I have seen government interests, but no public interests or spirit. I have seen that all the science of government was to oppress prudently; and the refined servitude of polished nations appeared to me only the more irremediable.

One obstacle above all has profoundly struck my mind. On looking over the world, I have seen it divided into twenty different systems of religion. Every nation has received, or

ductory step must be the giving them an alphabet like our own, or of substituting in the room of their language that of the Tartars. The improvement made in the latter by M. de Lengles, is calculated to introduce this change. See the Mantchou alphabet, the production of a mind truly learned in the formation of language,

formed, opposite opinions; and every one ascribing to itself the exclusive possession of the truth, must believe the other to be wrong. Now if, as must be the fact in this discordance of opinion, the greater part are in error, and are honest in it, then it follows that our mind embraces falsehood as it does truth; and if so, how is it to be enlightened? When prejudice has once seized the mind, how is it to be dissipated? How shall we remove the bandage from our eyes, when the first article in every creed, the first dogma in all religion, is the absolute proscription of doubt, the interdiction of examination, and the rejection of our own judgment? How is truth to make herself known?—If she resorts to arguments and proofs, the timid man stifles the voice of his own conscience; if she invokes the authority of celestial powers, he opposes it with another authority of the same origin, with which he is preoccupied; and he treats all innovation as blasphemy. Thus man in his blindness, has riveted his own chains, and surrendered himself forever, without defence, to the sport of his ignorance and his passions.

To dissolve such fatal chains, a miracluous concurrence of happy events would be necessary. A whole nation, cured of the delirium of superstition, must be inaccessible to the impulse of fanaticism. Freed from the yoke of false doctrine, a whole people must impose upon itself that of true morality and reason. This people should be courageous and prudent, wise and docile. Each individual, knowing his rights, should not transgress them. The poor should know how to resist seduction, and the rich the allurements of avarice. There should be found leaders disinterested and just, and their tyrants should be seized with a spirit of madness and folly. This people, recovering its rights, should feel its inability to exercise them in person, and should name its representatives. Creator of its magistrates, it should know at once to respect them and to judge them. In the sudden reform of a whole nation, accustomed to live by abuses, each individual displaced should bear with patience his privations, and submit to a change of habits. This nation should have the courage to conquer its liberty, the power to defend it, the wisdom to establish it, and the generosity to extend it to others. And can we ever expect the union of so many circumstances? But

suppose that chance in its infinite combinations should produce them, shall I see those fortunate days. Will not my
ashes long ere then be mouldering in the tomb ?

Here, sunk in sorrow, my oppressed heart no longer found
utterance. The Genius answered not, but I heard him whis-
per to himself:

Let us revive the hope of this man ; for if he who loves his
fellow creatures be suffered to despair, what will become of
nations ? The past is perhaps too discouraging ; I must
anticipate futurity, and disclose to the eye of virtue the astonishing age that is ready to begin ; that, on viewing the object
she desires, she may be animated with new ardor, and
redouble her efforts to attain it.

CHAPTER XV.

THE NEW AGE.

SCARCELY had he finished these words, when a great
tumult arose in the west; and turning to that quarter, I
perceived, at the extremity of the Mediterranean, in one
of the nations of Europe, a prodigious movement—such as
when a violent sedition arises in a vast city—a numberless
people, rushing in all directions, pour through the streets and
fluctuate like waves in the public places. My ear, struck with
the cries which resounded to the heavens, distinguished
these words:

What is this new prodigy? What cruel and mysterious
scourge is this? We are a numerous people and we want
hands! We have an excellent soil, and we are in want of
subsistence? We are active and laborious, and we live in
indigence! We pay enormous tributes, and we are told they
are not sufficient! We are at peace without, and our persons
and property are not safe within. Who, then, is the secret
enemy that devours us?

Some voices from the midst of the multitude replied:

Raise a discriminating standard; and let all those who

maintain and nourish mankind by useful labors gather round it; and you will discover the enemy that preys upon you.

The standard being raised, this nation divided itself at once into two bodies of unequal magnitude and contrasted appearance. The one, innumerable, and almost total, exhibited in the poverty of its clothing, in its emaciated appearance and sun-burnt faces, the marks of misery and labor; the other, a little group, an insignificant faction, presented in its rich attire embroidered with gold and silver, and in its sleek and ruddy faces, the signs of leisure and abundance.

Considering these men more attentively, I found that the great body was composed of farmers, artificers, merchants, all professions useful to society; and that the little group was made up of priests of every order, of financiers, of nobles, of men in livery, of commanders of armies; in a word, of the civil, military, and religious agents of government.

These two bodies being assembled face to face, and regarding each other with astonishment, I saw indignation and rage arising in one side, and a sort of panic in the other. And the large body said to the little one: Why are you separated from us? Are you not of our number?

No, replied the group; you are the people; we are a privileged class, who have our laws, customs, and rights, peculiar to ourselves.

PEOPLE.—And what labor do you perform in our society?

PRIVILEGED CLASS.—None; we are not made to work.

PEOPLE.—How, then, have you acquired these riches?

PRIVILEGED CLASS.—By taking the pains to govern you.

PEOPLE.—What! is this what you call governing? We toil and you enjoy! we produce and you dissipate! Wealth proceeds from us, and you absorb it. Privileged men! class who are not the people; form a nation apart, and govern yourselves.*

---

* This dialogue between the people and the indolent classes, is applicable to every society; it contains the seeds of all the political vices and disorders that prevail, and which may thus be defined: Men who do nothing, and who devour the substance of others; and men who arrogate to themselves particular rights and exclusive privileges of wealth and indolence. Compare the Mamlouks of Egypt, the nobility of Europe, the Nairs of India, the Emirs of Arabia, the patricians of Rome, the Christian clergy, the Imans, the Bramins, the Bonzes, the Lamas, etc., etc., and you will find in all the same characteristic feature :— Men living in idleness at the expense of those who labor.

Then the little group, deliberating on this new state of things, some of the most honorable among them said: We must join the people and partake of their labors and burdens, for they are men like us, and our riches come from them; but others arrogantly exclaimed: It would be a shame, an infamy, for us to mingle with the crowd; they are born to serve us. Are we not men of another race—the noble and pure descendants of the conquerors of this empire? This multitude must be reminded of our rights and its own origin.

THE NOBLES.—People! know you not that our ancestors conquered this land, and that your race was spared only on condition of serving us? This is our social compact! this the government constituted by custom and prescribed by time.

PEOPLE.—O conquerors, pure of blood! show us your genealogies! we shall then see if what in an individual is robbery and plunder, can be virtuous in a nation.

And forthwith, voices were heard in every quarter calling out the nobles by their names; and relating their origin and parentage, they told how the grandfather, great-grandfather, or even father, born traders and mechanics, after acquiring wealth in every way, had purchased their nobility for money: so that but very few families were really of the original stock. See, said these voices, see these purse-proud commoners who deny their parents! see these plebian recruits who look upon themselves as illustrious veterans! and peals of laughter were heard.

And the civil governors said: these people are mild, and naturally servile; speak to them of the king and of the law, and they will return to their duty. People! the king wills, the sovereign ordains!

PEOPLE.—The king can will nothing but the good of the people; the sovereign can only ordain according to law.

CIVIL GOVERNORS.—The law commands you to be submissive.

PEOPLE.—The law is the general will; and we will a new order of things.

CIVIL GOVERNORS.—You are then a rebel people.

PEOPLE.—A nation cannot revolt; tyrants only are rebels.

CIVIL GOVERNORS.—The king is on our side; he commands you to submit.

PEOPLE.—Kings are inseperable from their nations. Our king cannot be with you ; you possess only his phantom.

And the military governors came forward. The people are timorous, said they ; we must threaten them ; they will submit only to force. Soldiers, chastise this insolent multitude.

PEOPLE.—Soldiers, you are of our blood! Will you strike your brothers, your relatives ? If the people perish who will nourish the army ?

And the soldiers, grounding their arms, said to the chiefs : We are likewise the people ; show us the enemy !

Then the ecclesiastical governors said : There is but one resource left. The people are superstitious ; we must frighten them with the names of God and religion.

Our dear brethren! our children! God has ordained us to govern you.

PEOPLE.—Show us your credentials from God!

PRIESTS.—You must have faith ; reason leads astray.

PEOPLE.— Do you govern without reason ?

PRIESTS.— God commands peace! Religion prescribes obedience.

PEOPLE.— Peace supposes justice. Obedience implies conviction of a duty.

PRIESTS.—Suffering is the business of this world.

PEOPLE.—Show us the example.

PRIESTS.—Would you live without gods or kings ?

PEOPLE.—We would live without oppressors.

PRIESTS.—You must have mediators, intercessors.

PEOPLE.—Mediators with God and with the king! courtiers and priests, your services are too expensive : we will henceforth manage our own affairs.

And the little group said : We are lost! the multitude are enlightened.

And the people answered : You are safe ; since we are enlightened we will commit no violence ; we only claim our rights. We feel resentments, but we will forget them. We were slaves, we might command ; but we only wish to be free, and liberty is but justice.

CHAPTER XVI.

A FREE AND LEGISLATIVE PEOPLE.

CONSIDERING that all public power was now suspended, and that the habitual restraint of the people had suddenly ceased, I shuddered with the apprehension that they would fall into the dissolution of anarchy. But, taking their affairs into immediate deliberation, they said:

It is not enough that we have freed ourselves from tyrants and parasites; we must prevent their return. We are men, and experience has abundantly taught us that every man is fond of power, and wishes to enjoy it at the expense of others. It is necessary, then, to guard against a propensity which is the source of discord; we must establish certain rules of duty and of right. But the knowledge of our rights, and the estimation of our duties, are so abstract and difficult as to require all the time and all the faculties of a man. Occupied in our own affairs, we have not leisure for these studies; nor can we exercise these functions in our own persons. Let us choose, then, among ourselves, such persons as are capable of this employment. To them we will delegate our powers to institute our government and laws. They shall be the representatives of our wills and of our interests. And in order to attain the fairest representation possible of our wills and our interests, let it be numerous, and composed of men resembling ourselves.

Having made the election of a numerous body of delegates, the people thus addressed them:

We have hitherto lived in a society formed by chance, without fixed agreements, without free conventions, without a stipulation of rights, without reciprocal engagements,—and a multitude of disorders and evils have arisen from this precarious state. We are now determined on forming a regular compact; and we have chosen you to adjust the articles. Examine, then, with care what ought to be its basis and its conditions; consider what is the end and the principles of every association; recognize the rights which every member brings, the powers which he delegates, and those which he reserves to himself. Point out to us the rules of conduct — the basis of just and equitable laws. Prepare for us a new system of government; for we realize that the one which has hitherto guided us is corrupt. Our fathers have wandered in the paths of ignorance, and habit has taught us to follow in their footsteps. Everything has been done by fraud, violence, and delusion; and the true laws of morality and reason are still obscure. Clear up, then, their chaos; trace out their connection; publish their code, and we will adopt it.

And the people raised a large throne, in the form of a pyramid, and seating on it the men they had chosen, said to them:

We raise you to-day above us, that you may better discover the whole of our relations, and be above the reach of our passions. But remember that you are our fellow-citizens; that the power we confer on you is our own; that we deposit it with you, but not as a property or a heritage; that you must be the first to obey the laws you make; that to-morrow you redescend among us, and that you will have acquired no other right but that of our esteem and gratitude. And consider what a tribute of glory the world, which reveres so many apostles of error, will bestow on the first assembly of rational men, who shall have declared the unchangeable principles of justice, and consecrated, in the face of tyrants, the rights of nations.

CHAPTER XVII.

UNIVERSAL BASIS OF ALL RIGHT AND ALL LAW.

THE men chosen by the people to investigate the true principles of morals and of reason then proceeded in the sacred object of their mission; and, after a long examination, having discovered a fundamental and universal principle, a legislator arose and said to the people:

Here is the primordial basis, the physical origin of all justice and of all right.

Whatever be the active power, the moving cause, that

governs the universe, since it has given to all men the same organs, the same sensations, and the same wants, it has thereby declared that it has given to all the same right to the use of its treasures, and that all men are equal in the order of nature.

And, since this power has given to each man the necessary means of preserving his own existence, it is evident that it has constituted them all independent one of another; that it has created them free; that no one is subject to another; that each one is absolute proprietor of his own person.

Equality and liberty are, therefore, two essential attributes of man, two laws of the Divinity, constitutional and unchangeable, like the physical properties of matter.

Now, every individual being absolute master of his own person, it follows that a full and free consent is a condition indispensable to all contracts and all engagements.

Again, since each individual is equal to another, it follows that the balance of what is received and of what is given, should be strictly in equilibrium; so that the idea of justice, of equity, necessarily imports that of equality.*

Equality and liberty are therefore the physical and unalterable basis of every union of men in society, and of course the necessary and generating principle of every law and of every system of regular government.†

A disregard of this basis has introduced in your nation, and in every other, those disorders which have finally roused you. It is by returning to this rule that you may reform them, and reorganize a happy order of society.

But observe, this reorganization will occasion a violent shock in your habits, your fortunes, and your prejudices. Vicious contracts and abusive claims must be dissolved,

---

* The etymology of the words themselves trace out to us this connection: *equilibrium, equalitas, equitas,* are all of one family, and the physical idea of equality, in the scales of a balance, is the source and type of all the rest.

† In the Declaration of Rights, there is an inversion of ideas in the first article, liberty being placed before equality, from which it in reality springs. This defect is not to be wondered at; the science of the rights of man is a new science: it was invented yesterday by the Americans, to-day the French are perfecting it, but there yet remains a great deal to be done. In the ideas that constitute it there is a genealogical order which, from its basis, physical equality, to the minutest and most remote branches of government, ought to proceed in an uninterrupted series of inferences.

unjust distinctions and ill founded property renounced; you must indeed recur for a moment to a state of nature. Consider whether you can consent to so many sacrifices.

Then, reflecting on the cupidity inherent in the heart of man, I thought that this people would renounce all ideas of amelioration.

But, in a moment, a great number of men, advancing toward the pyramid, made a solemn abjuration of all their distinctions and all their riches.

Establish for us, said they, the laws of equality and liberty; we will possess nothing in future but on the title of justice.

Equality, liberty, justice,—these shall be our code, and shall be written on our standards.

And the people immediately raised a great standard, inscribed with these three words, in three different colors. They displayed it over the pyramid of the legislators, and for the first time the flag of universal justice floated on the face of the earth.

And the people raised before the pyramid a new altar, on which they placed a golden balance, a sword, and a book with this inscription:

TO EQUAL LAW, WHICH JUDGES AND PROTECTS.

And having surrounded the pyramid and the altar with a vast amphitheatre, all the people took their seats to hear the publication of the law. And millions of men, raising at once their hands to heaven, took the solemn oath to live equal, free, and just; to respect their reciprocal properties and rights; to obey the law and its regularly chosen representatives.

A spectacle so impressive and sublime, so replete with generous emotions, moved me to tears; and addressing myself to the Genius, I exclaimed: Let me now live, for in future I have everything to hope.

CHAPTER XVIII.

CONSTERNATION AND CONSPIRACY OF TYRANTS.

BUT scarcely had the solemn voice of liberty and equality resounded through the earth, when a movement of confusion, of astonishment, arose in different nations. On the one hand, the people, warmed with desire, but wavering between hope and fear, between the sentiment of right and the habit of obedience, began to be in motion. The kings, on the other hand, suddenly awakened from the sleep of indolence and despotism, were alarmed for the safety of their thrones; while, on all sides, those clans of civil and religious tyrants, who deceive kings and oppress the people, were seized with rage and consternation; and, concerting their perfidious plans, they said: Woe to us, if this fatal cry of liberty comes to the ears of the multitude! Woe to us, if this pernicious spirit of justice be propagated!

And, pointing to the floating banner, they continued:

Consider what a swarm of evils are included in these three words! If all men are equal, where is our exclusive right to honors and to power? If all men are to be free, what becomes of our slaves, our vassals, our property? If all are equal in the civil state, where is our prerogative of birth, of inheritance? and what becomes of nobility? If they are all equal in the sight of God, what need of mediators?— where is the priesthood? Let us hasten, then, to destroy a germ so prolific, and so contagious. We must employ all our cunning against this innovation. We must frighten the kings, that they may join us in the cause. We must divide the people by national jealousies, and occupy them with commotions, wars, and conquests. They must be alarmed at the power of this free nation. Let us form a league against the common enemy, demolish that sacrilegious standard, overturn that throne of rebellion, and stifle in its birth the flame of revolution.

And, indeed, the civil and religious tyrants of nations formed a general combination; and, multiplying their followers by force and seduction, they marched in hostile array against the free nation; and, surrounding the altar and the pyramid of natural law, they demanded with loud cries:

What is this new and heretical doctrine? what this impious altar, this sacrilegious worship? True believers and loyal subjects! can you suppose that truth has been first discovered to-day, and that hitherto you have been walking in error? that those men, more fortunate than you, have the sole privilege of wisdom? And you, rebel and misguided nation, perceive you not that your new leaders are misleading you? that they destroy the principles of your faith, and overturn the religion of your ancestors? Ah, tremble! lest the wrath of heaven should kindle against you; and hasten by speedy repentance to retrieve your error.

But, inaccessible to seduction as well as to fear, the free nation kept silence, and rising universally in arms, assumed an imposing attitude.

And the legislator said to the chiefs of nations:

If while we walked with a bandage on our eyes the light guided our steps, why, since we are no longer blindfold, should it fly from our search? If guides, who teach mankind to see for themselves, mislead and deceive them, what can be expected from those who profess to keep them in darkness?

But hark, ye leaders of nations! If you possess the truth, show it to us, and we will receive it with gratitude, for we seek it with ardor, and have a great interest in finding it. We are men, and liable to be deceived; but you are also men, and equally fallible. Aid us then in this labyrinth, where the human race has wandered for so many ages; help us to dissipate the illusion of so many prejudices and vicious habits. Amid the shock of so many opinions which dispute for our acceptance, assist us in discovering the proper and distinctive character of truth. Let us this day terminate the long combat with error. Let us establish between it and truth a solemn contest, to which we will invite the opinions of men of all nations. Let us convoke a general assembly of the nations. Let them be judges in their own cause; and in the debate of all systems, let no champion, no argument, be wanting, either on the side of prejudice or of reason; and let the sentiment of a general and common mass of evidence give birth to a universal concord of opinions and of hearts.

CHAPTER XIX.

GENERAL ASSEMBLY OF THE NATIONS.

THUS spoke the legislator; and the multitude, seized with those emotions which a reasonable proposition always inspires, expressed its applause; while the tyrants, left without support, were overwhelmed with confusion.

A scene of a new and astonishing nature then opened to my view. All that the earth contains of people and of nations; men of every race and of every region, converging from their various climates, seemed to assemble in one allotted place; where, forming an immense congress, distinguished in groups by the vast variety of their dresses, features, and complexion, the numberless multitude presented a most unusual and affecting sight.

On one side I saw the European, with his short close coat, pointed triangular hat, smooth chin, and powdered hair; on the other side the Asiatic, with a flowing robe, long beard, shaved head, and round turban. Here stood the nations of Africa, with their ebony skins, their woolly hair, their body girt with white and blue tissues of bark, adorned with bracelets and necklaces of coral, shells, and glass; there the tribes of the north, enveloped in their leathern bags; the Laplander, with his pointed bonnet and his snow-shoes; the Samoyede, with his feverish body and strong odor; the Tongouse, with his horned cap, and carrying his idols pendant from his neck; the Yakoute, with his freckled face; the Kalmuc, with his flat nose and little retorted eyes. Farther distant were the Chinese, attired in silk, with their hair hanging in tresses; the Japanese, of mingled race; the Malays, with wide-spreading ears, rings in their noses, and palm-leaf hats of vast circumference;* and the tattooed races of the isles of the southern ocean and of the continent of the antipodes.† The view of

---

* This species of the palm-tree is called *Latanier*. Its leaf, similar to a fan-mount, grows upon a stalk issuing directly from the earth. A specimen may be seen in the botanic garden.

† The country of the *Papons* of New Guinea.

so many varieties of the same species, of so many extravagant
inventions of the same understanding, and of so many modifi-
cations of the same organization, affected me with a thousand
feelings and a thousand thoughts.* I contemplated with astonishment this gradation of color, which, passing from a
bright carnation to a light brown, a deeper brown, dusky,
bronze, olive, leaden, copper, ends in the black of ebony and
of jet. And finding the Cassimerian, with his rosy cheek,
next to the sun-burnt Hindoo, and the Georgian by the side
of the Tartar, I reflected on the effects of climate hot or cold,
of soil high or low, marshy or dry, open or shaded. I compared the dwarf of the pole with the giant of the temperate
zones, the slender body of the Arab with the ample chest of
the Hollander ; the squat figure of the Samoyede with the
elegant form of the Greek and the Sclavonian ; the greasy
black wool of the Negro with the bright silken locks of the
Dane ; the broad face of the Kalmuc, his little angular eyes
and flattened nose, with the oval prominent visage, large blue
eyes, and aquiline nose of the Circassian and Abazan. I contrasted the brilliant calicoes of the Indian, the well-wrought
stuffs of the European, the rich furs of the Siberian, with the
tissues of bark, of osiers, leaves and feathers of savage nations ;
and the blue figures of serpents, flowers, and stars, with
which they painted their bodies. Sometimes the variegated
appearance of this multitude reminded me of the enamelled
meadows of the Nile and the Euphrates, when, after rains or
inundations, millions of flowers are rising on every side.
Sometimes their murmurs and their motions called to mind
the numberless swarms of locusts which, issuing from the
desert, cover in the spring the plains of Hauran.

* A hall of costumes in one of the galleries of the Louvre would, in every point
of view, be an interesting establishment. It would furnish an admirable treat to
the curiosity of a great number of persons, excellent models to the artist, and
useful subjects of meditation to the physician, the philosopher and the legislator.

Picture to yourself a collection of the various faces and figures of every
country and nation, exhibiting accurately, color, features and form ; what a
field for investigation and enquiry as to the influence of climate, customs, food,
etc. It might truly be called the science of man ! Buffon has attempted a
chapter of this nature, but it only serves to exhibit more strikingly our actual
ignorance. Such a collection is said to have been begun at St. Petersburg, but it
is also said at the same time to be as imperfect as the vocabulary of the three
hundred languages. The enterprise would be worthy of the French nation.

At the sight of so many rational beings, considering on the one hand the immensity of thoughts and sensations assembled in this place, and on the other hand, reflecting on the opposition of so many opinions, and the shock of so many passions of men so capricious, I struggled between astonishment, admiration, and secret dread — when the legislator commanded silence, and attracted all my attention.

Inhabitants of earth! a free and powerful nation addresses you with words of justice and peace, and she offers you the sure pledges of her intentions in her own conviction and experience. Long afflicted with the same evils as yourselves, we sought for their source, and found them all derived from violence and injustice, erected into law by the inexperience of past ages, and maintained by the prejudices of the present. Then abolishing our artificial and arbitrary institutions, and recurring to the origin of all right and reason, we have found that there existed in the very order of nature and in the physical constitution of man, eternal and immutable laws, which only waited his observance to render him happy.

O men! cast your eyes on the heavens that give you light, and on the earth that gives you bread! Since they offer the same bounties to you all — since from the power that gives them motion you have all received the same life, the same organs, have you not likewise all received the same right to enjoy its benefits? Has it not hereby declared you all equal and free? What mortal shall dare refuse to his fellow that which nature gives him?

O nations! let us banish all tyranny and all discord; let us form but one society, one great family; and, since human nature has but one constitution, let there exist in future but one law, that of nature — but one code, that of reason — but one throne, that of justice — but one altar, that of union.

He ceased; and an immense acclamation resounded to the skies. Ten thousand benedictions announced the transports of the multitude; and they made the earth re-echo *justice*, *equality* and *union*.

But different emotions soon succeeded; soon the doctors and the chiefs of nations exciting a spirit of dispute, there was heard a sullen murmur, which growing louder, and spreading from group to group, became a vast disorder; and each nation setting up exclusive pretensions, claimed a preference for its own code and opinion.

You are in error, said the parties, pointing one to the other. We alone are in possession of reason and truth. We alone have the true law, the real rule of right and justice, the only means of happiness and perfection. All other men are either blind or rebellious.

And great agitation prevailed.

Then the legislator, after enforcing silence, loudly exclaimed:

What, O people! is this passionate emotion? Whither will this quarrel conduct you? What can you expect from this dissension? The earth has been for ages a field of disputation, and you have shed torrents of blood in your controversies. What have you gained by so many battles and tears? When the strong has subjected the weak to his opinion, has he thereby aided the cause of truth?

O nations! take counsel of your own wisdom. When among yourselves disputes arise between families and individuals, how do you reconcile them? Do you not give them arbitrators?

Yes, cried the whole multitude.

Do so then to the authors of your present dissensions. Order those who call themselves your instructors, and who force their creeds upon you, to discuss before you their reasons. Since they appeal to your interests, inform yourselves how they support them.

And you, chiefs and governors of the people! before dragging the masses into the quarrels resulting from your diverse opinions, let the reasons for and against your views be given. Let us establish one solemn controversy, one public scrutiny of truth—not before the tribunal of a corruptible individual, or of a prejudiced party, but in the grand forum of mankind—guarded by all their information and all their interests. Let the natural sense of the whole human race be our arbiter and judge.

CHAPTER XX.

THE SEARCH OF TRUTH.

THE people expressed their applause, and the legislator continued: To proceed with order, and avoid all confusion, let a spacious semicircle be left vacant in front of the altar of peace and union ; let each system of religion, and each particular sect, erect its proper distinctive standard on the line of this semicircle ; let its chiefs and doctors place themselves around the standard, and their followers form a column behind them.

The semicircle being traced, and the order published, there instantly rose an innumerable multitude of standards, of all colors and of every form, like what we see in a great commercial port, when, on a day of rejoicing, a thousand different flags and streamers are floating from a forest of masts.

At the sight of this prodigious diversity, I turned towards the Genius and said :

I thought that the earth was divided only into eight or ten systems of faith, and I then despaired of a reconciliation; I now behold thousands of different sects, and how can I hope for concord?

But these, replied the Genius, are not all ; and yet they will be intolerant !

Then, as the groups advanced to take their stations, he pointed out to me their distinctive marks, and thus began to explain their characters :

That first group, said he, with a green banner bearing a crescent, a bandage, and a sabre, are the followers of the Arabian prophet. To say there is a God, *without knowing what he is ;* to believe the words of a man, *without understanding his language ;* to go into the desert to pray to God, *who is everywhere ;* to wash the hands with water, *and not abstain from blood ;* to fast all day, *and eat all night ;* to give alms of their own goods, *and to plunder those of others ;* such are the means of perfection instituted by Mahomet—

such are the symbols of his followers ; and whoever does not
bear them is a reprobate, stricken with anathema, and devoted
to the sword.

A God of clemency, the author of life, has instituted these
laws of oppression and murder : he made them for all the
world, but has revealed them only to one man ; he established
them from all eternity, though he made them known but
yesterday. These laws are abundantly sufficient for all pur-
poses, and yet a volume is added to them. This volume was
to diffuse light, to exhibit evidence, to lead men to perfection
and happiness ; and yet every page was so full of obscurities,
ambiguities, and contradictions, that commentaries and explanations became necessary, even in the life-time of its
apostle. Its interpreters, differing in opinion, divided into
opposite and hostile sects. One maintains that Ali is the
true successor ; the other contends for Omar and Aboubekre.
This denies the eternity of the Koran ; that the necessity of
ablutions and prayers. The Carmite forbids pilgrimages,
and allows the use of wine ; the Hakemite preaches the transmigration of souls. Thus they make up the number of
seventy-two sects, whose banners are before you.* In this
contestation, every one attributing the evidence of truth exclusively to himself, and taxing all others with heresy and
rebellion, turns against them its sanguinary zeal. And their
religion, which celebrates a mild and merciful God, the common father of all men,— changed to a torch of discord, a signal
for war and murder, has not ceased for twelve hundred years
to deluge the earth in blood, and to ravage and desolate the
ancient hemisphere from centre to circumference.†

Those men, distinguished by their enormous white turbans,
their broad sleeves, and their long rosaries, are the Imans, the

---

* The Mussulmen enumerate in common seventy-two sects, but I read, while I
resided among them, a work which gave an account of more than eighty,—all
equally wise and important.

† Read the history of Islamism by its own writers, and you will be convinced
that one of the principal causes of the wars which have desolated Asia and Africa.
since the days of Mahomet, has been the apostolical fanaticism of its doctrine.
Cæsar has been supposed to have destroyed three millions of men : it would be
interesting to make a similar calculation respecting every founder of a religious
system.

Mollas, and the Muftis ; and near them are the Dervishes with
pointed bonnets, and the Santons with dishevelled hair. Behold with what vehemence they recite their professions of
faith! They are now beginning a dispute about the greater
and lesser impurities,— about the matter and the manner of
ablutions,— about the attributes of God and his perfections,—
about the Chaitan, and the good and wicked angels,— about
death, the resurrection, the interrogatory in the tomb, the
judgment, the passage of the narrow bridge not broader than
a hair, the balance of works, the pains of hell, and the joys of
paradise.

Next to these, that second more numerous group, with
white banners intersected with crosses, are the followers of
Jesus. Acknowledging the same God with the Mussulmans,
founding their belief on the same books, admitting, like them,
a first man who lost the human race by eating an apple, they
hold them, however, in a holy abhorrence ; and, out of pure
piety, they call each other impious blasphemers.

The great point of their dissension consists in this, that
after admitting a God *one and indivisible*, the Christian divides
him into three persons, each of which he believes to be a
complete and entire God, without ceasing to constitute an
identical whole, by the indivisibility of the three. And he
adds, that this being, who fills the universe, has reduced
himself to the body of a man ; and has assumed material,
perishable, and limited organs, without ceasing to be immaterial, infinite, and eternal. The Mussulman, who does not
comprehend these mysteries, rejects them as follies, and the
visions of a distempered brain ; though he conceives perfectly
well the eternity of the Koran, and the mission of the prophet :
hence their implacable hatreds.

Again, the Christians, divided among themselves on many
points, have formed parties not less violent than the Mussulmans ; and their quarrels are so much the more obstinate, as
the objects of them are inaccessible to the senses, and incapable of demonstration : their opinions, therefore, have no
other basis but the will and caprice of the parties. Thus,
while they agree that God is a being incomprehensible and
unknown, they dispute, nevertheless, about his essence, his

mode of acting, and his attributes. While they agree that his pretended transformation into man is an enigma above the human understanding, they dispute on the junction or distinction of his two wills and his two natures, on his change of substance, on the real or fictitious presence, on the mode of incarnation, etc.

Hence those innumerable sects, of which two or three hundred have already perished, and three or four hundred others, which still subsist, display those numberless banners which here distract your sight.

The first in order, surrounded by a group in varied and fantastic dress, that confused mixture of violet, red, white, black and speckled garments — with heads shaved, or with tonsures, or with short hair — with red hats, square bonnets, pointed mitres, or long beards, is the standard of the Roman pontiff, who, uniting the civil government to the priesthood, has erected the supremacy of his city into a point of religion, and made of his pride an article of faith.

On his right you see the Greek pontiff, who, proud of the rivalship of his metropolis, sets up equal pretensions, and supports them against the Western church by the priority of that of the East. On the left are the standards of two recent chiefs,* who, shaking off a yoke that had become tyrannical, have raised altar against altar in their reform, and wrested half of Europe from the pope. Behind these are the subaltern sects, subdivided from the principal divisions, the Nestorians, the Eutycheans, the Jacobites, the Iconoclasts, the Anabaptists, the Presbyterians, the Wicliffites, the Osiandrians, the Manicheans, the Pietists, the Adamites, the Contemplatives, the Quakers, the Weepers, and a hundred others,† all of distinct parties, persecuting when strong, tolerant when weak, hating each other in the name of a God of peace, forming each an exclusive heaven in a religion of universal charity, dooming each other to pains without end in a future state, and realizing in this world the imaginary hell of the other.

* Luther and Calvin.

† Consult upon this subject *Dictionnaire des Hérséies par l' Abbé Pluquet*, in two volumes 8vo. ; a work admirably calculated to inspire the mind with philosophy, in the sense that the Lacedemonians taught the children temperance by showing to them the drunken Helots.

After this group, observing a lonely standard of the color of hyacinth, round which were assembled men clad in all the different dresses of Europe and Asia :

At least, said I, to the Genius, we shall find unanimity here.

Yes, said he, at first sight and by a momentary accident. Dost thou not know that system of worship ?

Then, perceiving in Hebrew letters the monogram of the name of God, and the palms which the Rabbins held in their hands :

True, said I, these are the children of Moses, dispersed even to this day, abhorring every nation, and abhorred and persecuted by all.

Yes, he replied, and for this reason, that, having neither the time nor liberty to dispute, they have the appearance of unanimity. But no sooner will they come together, compare their principles, and reason on their opinions, than they will separate as formerly, at least into two principal sects ;* one of which, taking advantage of the silence of their legislator, and adhering to the literal sense of his books, will deny everything that is not clearly expressed therein; and on this principle will reject as profane inventions, the immortality of the soul, its transmigration to places of pain or pleasure, its resurrection, the final judgment, the good and bad angels, the revolt of the evil Genius, and all the poetical belief of a world to come. And this highly-favored people, whose perfection consists in a slight mutilation of their persons,—this atom of a people, which forms but a small wave in the ocean of mankind, and which insists that God has made nothing but for them, will by its schism reduce to one-half, its present trifling weight in the scale of the universe.

He then showed me a neighboring group, composed of men dressed in white robes, wearing a veil over their mouths, and ranged around a banner of the color of the morning sky, on which was painted a globe cleft in two hemispheres, black and white : The same thing will happen, said he, to these children of Zoroaster,† the obscure remnant of a people once

* The Sadducees and Pharisees.

† They are the Parses, better known by the opprobrious name of Gaures or Guebres, another word for infidels. They are in Asia what the Jews are in Europe. The name of their pope or high priest is Mobed.

so powerful. At present, persecuted like the Jews, and dispersed among all nations, they receive without discussion the
precepts of the representative of their prophet. But as soon
as the Mobed and the Destours * shall assemble, they will
renew the controversy about the good and the bad principle ;
on the combats of Ormuzd, God of light, and Ahrimanes, God
of darkness ; on the direct and allegorical sense ; on the good
and evil Genii ; on the worship of fire and the elements ; on
impurities and ablutions ; on the resurrection of the soul and
body, or only of the soul ; † on the renovation of the present
world, and on that which is to take its place. And the
Parses will divide into sects, so much the more numerous,
as their families will have contracted, during their dispersion,
the manners and opinions of different nations.

Next to these, remark those banners of an azure ground,
painted with monstrous figures of human bodies, double,
triple, and quadruple, with heads of lions, boars, and elephants,
and tails of fishes and tortoises ; these are the ensigns of the
sects of India, who find their gods in various animals, and
the souls of their fathers in reptiles and insects. These men
support hospitals for hawks, serpents, and rats, and they abhor
their fellow creatures ! They purify themselves with the
dung and urine of cows, and think themselves defiled by the
touch of a man ! They wear a net over the mouth, lest, in a
fly, they should swallow a soul in a state of penance,‡ and
they can see a Pariah § perish with hunger ! They acknowledge the same gods, but they separate into hostile bands.

The first standard, retired from the rest, bearing a figure
with four heads, is that of Brama, who, though the creator of
the universe, is without temples or followers ; but, reduced to

* That is to say, their priests. See, respecting the rites of this religion, *Henry
Lord Hyde*, and the *Zendavesta*. Their costume is a robe with a belt of four
knots, and a veil over their mouth for fear of polluting the fire with their breath.

† The Zoroastrians are divided between two opinions ; one party believing that
both soul and body will rise, the other that it will be the soul only. The Christians
and Mahometans have embraced the most solid of the two.

‡ According to the system of the Metempsychosis, a soul, to undergo purification, passes into the body of some insect or animal. It is of importance not to
disturb this penance, as the work must in that case begin afresh.

§ This is the name of a cast or tribe reputed unclean, because they eat of what
has enjoyed life.

serve as a pedestal to the Lingam,* he contents himself with
a little water which the Bramin throws every morning on his
shoulder, reciting meanwhile an idle canticle in his praise.

The second, bearing a kite with a scarlet body and a white
head, is that of Vichenou, who, though preserver of the world,
has passed part of his life in wicked actions. You sometimes
see him under the hideous form of a boar or a lion, tearing
human entrails, or under that of a horse,† shortly to come
armed with a sword to destroy the human race, blot out the
stars, annihilate the planets, shake the earth, and force the
great serpent to vomit a fire which shall consume the
spheres.

The third is that of Chiven, God of destruction and desolation, who has, however, for his emblem the symbol of generation. He is the most wicked of the three, and he has the
most followers. These men, proud of his character, express
in their devotions to him their contempt for the other gods, ‡
his equals and brothers ; and, in imitation of his inconsisten-
cies, while they profess great modesty and chastity, they
publicly crown with flowers, and sprinkle with milk and
honey, the obscene image of the *Lingam.*

In the rear of these, approach the smaller standards of a
multitude of gods — male, female, and hermaphrodite. These
are friends and relations of the principal gods, who have
passed their lives in wars among themselves, and their
followers imitate them. These gods have need of nothing,
and they are constantly receiving presents ; they are omnipotent and omnipresent, and a priest, by muttering a few words,
shuts them up in an idol or a pitcher, to sell their favors
for his own benefit.

Beyond these, that cloud of standards, which, on a yellow
ground, common to them all, bear various emblems, are those
of the same god, who reins under different names in the na-

---

* See *Sonnerat, Voyage aux Indes,* vol. i.

† These are the incarnations of Vichenou, or metamorphoses of the sun. He is
to come at the end of the world, that is, at the expiration of the great period, in
the form of a horse, like the four horses of the Apocalypse.

‡ When a sectary of Chiven hears the name of Vichenou pronounced, he stops
his ears, runs, and purifies himself.

tions of the East. The Chinese adores him in Fot,* the
Japanese in Budso, the Ceylonese in Bedhou, the people of
Laos in Chekia, of Pegu in Phta, of Siam in Sommona-Kodom,
of Thibet in Budd and in La. Agreeing in some points of
his history, they all celebrate his life of penitence, his mortifications, his fastings, his functions of mediator and expiator,
the enmity between him and another god, his adversary, their
battles, and his ascendency. But as they disagree on the
means of pleasing him, they dispute about rites and ceremonies, and about the dogmas of interior doctrine and of public
doctrine. That Japanese Bonze, with a yellow robe and
naked head, preaches the eternity of souls, and their successive transmigrations into various bodies; near him, the
Sintoist denies that souls can exist separate from the senses,†
and maintains that they are only the effect of the organs to
which they belong, and with which they must perish, as the
sound of the flute perishes with the flute. Near him, the
Siamese, with his eyebrows shaved, and a talipat screen‡ in his
hand, recommends alms, offerings, and expiations, at the same
time that he preaches blind necessity and inexorable fate. The
Chinese vo-chung sacrifices to the souls of his ancestors ; and
next him, the follower of Confucius interrogates his destiny in
the cast of dice and the movement of the stars.§ That child,
surrounded by a swarm of priests in yellow robes and hats, is

* The original name of this god is *Baits*, which in Hebrew signifies an egg.
The Arabs pronounce it *Baidh*, giving to the *dh* an emphatic sound which makes
it approach to *dz*. Kempfer, an acurate traveler, writes it *Budso*, which must be
pronounced *Boudso*, whence is derived the name of Budsoist and of Bonze,
applied to the priests. Clement of Alexandria, in his *Stromata*, writes it *Bedou*,
as it is pronounced also by the Chingulais; and Saint Jerome, *Boudda* and
Boutta. At Thibet they call it Budd ; and hence the name of the country called
Boud-tan and *Ti-budd :* it was in this province that this system of religion was
first inculcated in Upper Asia ; *La* is a corruption of *Allah*, the name of God in
the Syriac language, from which many of the eastern dialects appear to be derived. The Chinese having neither *b* nor *d*, have supplied their place by *f* and *t*,
and have therefore said *Fout*.

† See in Kempfer the doctrine of the Sintoists, which is a mixture of that of
Epicurus and of the Stoics.

‡ It is a leaf of the *Latanier* species of the palm-tree. Hence the bonzes of
Siam take the appellation of *Talapoin*. The use of this screen is an exclusive
privilege.

§ The sectaries of Confucius are no less addicted to astrology than the bonzes.
It is indeed the malady of every eastern nation.

the Grand Lama, in whom the god of Thibet has just become incarnate.* But a rival has arisen who partakes this benefit with him ; and the Kalmouc on the banks of the Baikal, has a God similar to the inhabitant of Lasa. And they agree, also, in one important point — that god can inhabit only a human body. They both laugh at the stupidity of the Indian who pays homage to cow-dung, though they themselves consecrate the excrements of their high-priest.†

After these, a crowd of other banners, which no man could number, came forward into sight ; and the genius exclaimed :

I should never finish the detail of all the systems of faith which divide these nations. Here the hordes of Tartars adore, in the forms of beasts, birds, and insects, the good and evil Genii ; who, under a principal, but indolent god, govern the universe. In their idolatry they call to mind the ancient paganism of the West. You observe the fantastical dress of the Chamans ; who, under a robe of leather, hung round with bells and rattles, idols of iron, claws of birds, skins of snakes and heads of owls, invoke, with frantic cries and factitious convulsions, the dead to deceive the living. There, the black tribes of Africa exhibit the same opinions in the worship of their fetiches. See the inhabitant of Juida worship god in a great snake, which, unluckily, the swine delight to eat.‡ The Teleutean attires his god in a coat of several colors, like a

---

* *The Delai-La-Ma*, or immense high priest of *La*, is the same person whom we find mentioned in our old books of travels, by the name of Prester John, from a corruption of the Persian word *Djehan*, which signifies the world, to which has been prefixed the French word *prestre or prêtre*, priest. Thus the *priest world*, and the *god world* are in the Persian idiom the same.

† In a recent expedition the English have found certain idols of the Lamas filled in the inside with sacred pastils from the close stool of the high priest. Mr. Hastings, and Colonel Pollier, who is now at Lausanne, are living witnesses of this fact, and undoubtedly worthy of credit. It will be very extraordinary to observe, that this disgusting ceremony is connected with a profound philosophical system, to wit, that of the metempsychosis, admitted by the Lamas. When the Tartars swallow, the sacred relics, which they are accustomed to do, they imitate the laws of the universe, the parts of which are incessantly absorbed and pass into the substance of each other. It is upon the model of the serpent who devours his tail, and this serpent is Budd and the world.

‡ It frequently happens that the swine devour the very species of serpents the negroes adore, which is a source of great desolation in the country. President de Brosses has given us, in his *History of the Fetiche*, a curious collection of absurdities of this nature.

Russian soldier.* The Kamchadale, observing that everything goes wrong in his frozen country, considers god as an old ill-natured man, smoking his pipe and hunting foxes and martins in his sledge.†

But you may still behold a hundred savage nations who have none of the ideas of civilized people respecting God, the soul, another world, and a future life; who have formed no system of worship; and who nevertheless enjoy the rich gifts of nature in the irreligion in which she has created them.

CHAPTER XXI.

PROBLEM OF RELIGIOUS CONTRADICTIONS.

THE various groups having taken their places, an unbounded silence succeeded to the murmurs of the multitude; and the legislator said:

Chiefs and doctors of mankind! You remark how the nations, living apart, have hitherto followed different paths, each believing its own to be that of truth. If, however, truth is one, and opinions are various, it is evident that some are in error. If, then, such vast numbers of us are in the wrong, who shall dare to say, " I am in the right? " Begin, therefore, by being indulgent in your dissensions. Let us all seek truth as if no one possessed it. The opinions which to this day have governed the world, originating from chance, propagated in obscurity, admitted without discussion, accredited by a love of novelty and imitation, have usurped their empire

---

*The Teleuteans, a Tartar nation, paint God as wearing a vesture of all colors, particularly red and green; and as these constitute the uniform of the Russian dragoons, they compare him to this description of soldiers. The Egyptians also dress the God World in a garment of every color. *Eusebius Præp. Evang.* p 115. The Teleuteans call God *Bou*, which is only an alteration of Boudd, the God Egg and World.

† Consult upon this subject a work entitled, *Description des Peuples, soumis à la Russie*, and it will be found that the picture is not overcharged.

in a clandestine manner. It is time, if they are well founded, to give a solemn stamp to their certainty, and legitimize their existence. Let us summon them this day to a general scrutiny, let each propound his creed, let the whole assembly be the judge, and let that alone be acknowledged as true which is so for the whole human race.

Then, by order of position, the representative of the first standard on the left was allowed to speak:

"You are not permitted to doubt," said their chief, "that our doctrine is the only true and infallible one. *First*, it is revealed by God himself—"

" So is ours," cried all the other standards, " and you are not permitted to doubt it."

"But at least," said the legislator, "you must prove it, for we cannot believe what we do not know."

"Our doctrine is proved," replied the first standard, "by numerous facts, by a multitude of miracles, by resurrections of the dead, by rivers dried up, by mountains removed—"

"And we also have numberless miracles," cried all the others, and each began to recount the most incredible things.

" *Their* miracles," said the first standard, " are imaginary, or the fictions of the evil spirit, who has deluded them."

" They are yours," said the others, " that are imaginary ; " and each group, speaking of itself, cried out:

" None but ours are true, all the others are false."

The legislator then asked: " Have you living witnesses of the facts ? "

" No," replied they all; " the facts are ancient, the witnesses are dead, but their writings remain."

" Be it so," replied the legislator; "but if they contradict each other, who shall reconcile them ? "

" Just judge ! " cried one of the standards, "the proof that our witnesses have seen the truth is, that they died to confirm it ; and our faith is sealed by the blood of martyrs."

" And ours too," said the other standards ; " we have thousands of martyrs who have died in the most excruciating torments, without ever denying the truth."

Then the Christians of every sect, the Mussulmans, the Indians, the Japanese, recited endless legends of confessors, martyrs, penitents, etc.

And one of these parties, having denied the martyrology of the others : "Well," said they, "we will then die ourselves to prove the truth of our belief."

And instantly a crowd of men, of every religion and of every sect, presented themselves to suffer the torments of death. Many even began to tear their arms, and to beat their heads and breasts, without discovering any symptom of pain.

But the legislator, preventing them — "O men!" said he, "hear my words with patience. If you die to prove that two and two make four, will your death add any thing to this truth?"

"No!" answered all.

"And if you die to prove that they make five, will that make them five?"

Again they all answered, "No."

"What, then, is your persuasion to prove, if it changes not the existence of things? Truth is one — your persuasions are various; many of you, therefore, are in error. Now, if man, as is evident, can persuade himself of error, what is the persuasion of man to prove?

"If error has its martyrs, what is the sure criterion of truth?

"If the evil spirit works miracles, what is the distinctive character of God?

"Besides, why resort forever to incomplete and insufficient miracles? Instead of changing the course of nature, why not rather change opinions? Why murder and terrify men, instead of instructing and correcting them?

"O credulous, but opinionated mortals! none of us know what was done yesterday, what is doing to-day even under our eyes; and we swear to what was done two thousand years ago!

"Oh, the weakness and yet the pride of men! The laws of nature are unchangeable and profound — our minds are full of illusion and frivolity — and yet we would comprehend every thing — determine every thing! Forgetting that it is easier for the whole human race to be in error, than to change the nature of the smallest atom."

"Well, then," said one of the doctors, "let us lay aside the evidence of fact, since it is uncertain ; let us come to argument — to the proofs inherent in the doctrine."

Then came forward, with a look of confidence, an Iman of the law of Mahomet; and, having advanced into the circle, turned towards Mecca, and recited with great fervor his confession of faith. "Praise be to God," said he, with a solemn and imposing voice, "the light shines with full evidence, and the truth has no need of examination." Then, showing the Koran, he exclaimed: "Here is the light of truth in its proper essence. There is no doubt in this book. It conducts with safety him who walks in darkness, and who receives without discussion the divine word which descended on the prophet, to save the simple and confound the wise. God has established Mahomet his minister on earth; he has given him the world, that he may subdue with the sword whoever shall refuse to receive his law. Infidels dispute, and will not believe; their obduracy comes from God, who has hardened their hearts to deliver them to dreadful punishments." *

At these words a violent murmur arose on all sides, and silenced the speaker. "Who is this man," cried all the groups, "who thus insults us without a cause? What right has he to impose his creed on us as conqueror and tyrant? Has not God endowed us, as well as him, with eyes, understanding, and reason? And have we not an equal right to use them, in choosing what to believe and what to reject? If he attacks us, shall we not defend ourselves? If he likes to believe without examination, must we therefore not examine before we believe?

"And what is this luminous doctrine that fears the light? What is this apostle of a God of clemency, who preaches nothing but murder and carnage? What is this God of justice, who punishes blindness which he himself has made? If violence and persecution are the arguments of truth, are gentleness and charity the signs of falsehood?"

A man then advancing from a neighboring group, said to the Iman:

"Admitting that Mahomet is the apostle of the best doctrine,—the prophet of the true religion,—have the goodness

---

* This passage contains the sense and nearly the very words of the first chapter of the Koran; and the reader will observe in general, that, in the pictures that follow, the writer has endeavored to give as accurately as possible the letter and spirit of the opinions of each party.

at least to tell us whether, in the practice of his doctrine,
we are to follow his son-in-law Ali, or his vicars Omar
and Aboubekre ? " *

At the sound of these names a terrible schism arose among
the Mussulmans themselves. The partisans of Ali and those
of Omar, calling out heretics and blasphemers, loaded each
other with execrations. The quarrel became so violent that
neighboring groups were obliged to interfere, to prevent their
coming to blows. At length, tranquillity being somewhat
restored, the legislator said to the Imans:

" See the consequences of your principles ! If you yourselves were to carry them into practice, you would destroy
each other to the last man. Is it not the first law of God that
man should live ? "

Then, addressing himself to the other groups, he continued:

" Doubtless this intolerant and exclusive spirit shocks every
idea of justice, and overturns the whole foundation of morals
and society ; but before we totally reject this code of doctrine,
is it not proper to hear some of its dogmas?   Let us not pronounce on the forms, without having some knowledge of the
substance."

The groups having consented, the Iman began to expound
how God, having sent to the nations lost in idolatry twenty-
four thousand prophets, had finally sent the last, the seal and
perfection of all, Mahomet ; on whom be the salvation of
peace : how, to prevent the divine word from being any
longer perverted by infidels, the supreme goodness had itself
written the pages of the Koran. Then, explaining the particular dogmas of Islamism, the Iman unfolded how the Koran,
partaking of the divine nature, was uncreated and eternal,
like its author : how it had been sent leaf by leaf, in twenty-
four thousand nocturnal apparitions of the angel Gabriel :
how the angel announced himself by a gentle knocking, which
threw the prophet into a cold sweat : how in the vision of one
night he had travelled over ninety heavens, riding on the
beast Borack, half horse and half woman : how, endowed with
the gift of miracles, he walked in the sunshine without a
shadow, turned dry trees to green, filled wells and cisterns

* These are the two grand parties into which the Mussulmans are divided. The
Turks have embraced the second, the Persians the first.

with water, and split in two the body of the moon: how, by divine command, Mahomet had propagated, sword in hand, the religion the most worthy of God by its sublimity, and the most proper for men by the simplicity of its practice; since it consisted in only eight or ten points: — To profess the unity of God; to acknowledge Mahomet as his only prophet; to pray five times a day; to fast one month in the year; to go to Mecca once in our life; to pay the tenth of all we possess; to drink no wine; to eat no pork; and to make war upon the infidels.* He taught that by these means every Mussulman, becoming himself an apostle and martyr, should enjoy in this world many blessings; and at his death, his soul, weighed in the balance of works, and absolved by the two black angels, should pass the infernal pit on the bridge as narrow as a hair and as sharp as the edge of a sword, and should finally be received to a region of delight, which is watered with rivers of milk and honey, and embalmed in all the perfumes of India and Arabia; and where the celestial Houris,— virgins always chaste,— are eternally crowning with repeated favors the elect of God, who preserve an eternal youth.

At these words an involuntary smile was seen on all their lips; and the various groups, reasoning on these articles of faith, exclaimed with one voice:

" Is it possible that reasonable beings can admit such reveries? Would you not think it a chapter from *The Thousand and One Nights?* "

A Samoyede advanced into the circle: " The paradise of Mahomet," said he, " appears to me very good; but one of the means of gaining it is embarrassing: for if we must neither eat nor drink between the rising and setting sun, as he has ordered, how are we to practise that fast in my country, where the sun continues above the horizon six months without setting? "

" That is impossible," cried all the Mussulman doctors, to support the teaching of the prophet; but a hundred nations having attested the fact, the infallibility of Mahomet could not but receive a severe shock.

" It is singular," said an European, " that God should be

---

* Whatever the advocates for the philosophy and civilization of the Turks may assert, to make war upon infidels is considered by them as an obligatory precept and an act of religion. See *Reland de Relig. Mahom.*

constantly revealing what takes place in heaven, without ever
instructing us what is doing on the earth."

" For my part," said an American, " I find a great difficulty
in the pilgrimage. For suppose twenty-five years to a generation, and only a hundred millions of males on the globe,—
each being obliged to go to Mecca once in his life,—there
must be four millions a year on the journey ; and as it would
be impracticable for them to return the same year, the numbers would be doubled — that is, eight millions : where would
you find provisions, lodgings, water, vessels, for this universal procession ? Here must be miracles indeed ! "

" The proof," said a catholic doctor, "that the religion of
Mahomet is not revealed, is that the greater part of the ideas
which serve for its basis existed a long time before, and that
it is only a confused mixture of truths disfigured and taken
from our holy religion and from that of the Jews ; which an
ambitious man has made to serve his projects of domination,
and his worldly views. Look through his book ; you will see
nothing there but the histories of the Bible and the Gospel
travestied into absurd fables — into a tissue of vague and
contradictory declamations, and ridiculous or dangerous
precepts.

" Analyze the spirit of these precepts, and the conduct of
their apostle ; you will find there an artful and audacious
character, which, to obtain its end, works ably it is true, on
the passions of the people it had to govern. It is speaking
to simple men, and it entertains them with miracles ; they are
ignorant and jealous, and it flatters their vanity by despising
science ; they are poor and rapacious, and it excites their
cupidity by the hope of pillage ; having nothing at first to
give them on earth, it tells them of treasures in heaven ; it
teaches them to desire death as a supreme good ; it threatens
cowards with hell ; it rewards the brave with paradise ; it
sustains the weak with the opinion of fatality ; in short, it produces the attachment it wants by all the allurements of sense,
and all the power of the passions.

" How different is the character of our religion ! and how
completely does its empire, founded on the counteraction of
the natural temper, and the mortification of all our passions,
prove its divine origin ! How forcibly does its mild and

compassionate morality, its affections altogether spiritual, attest its emanation from God! Many of its doctrines, it is true, soar above the reach of the understanding, and impose on reason a respectful silence; but this more fully demonstrates its revelation, since the human mind could never have imagined such mysteries."

Then, holding the Bible in one hand and the four Gospels in the other, the doctor began to relate that, in the beginning, God, after passing an eternity in idleness, took the resolution, without any known cause, of making the world out of nothing; that having created the whole universe in six days, he found himself fatigued on the seventh; that having placed the first human pair in a garden of delights, to make them completely happy, he forbade their tasting a particular fruit which he placed within their reach; that these first parents, having yielded to the temptation, all their race (which were not yet born) had been condemned to bear the penalty of a fault which they had not committed; that, after having left the human race to damn themselves for four or five thousand years, this God of mercy ordered a well beloved son, whom he had engendered without a mother, and who was as old as himself, to go and be put to death on the earth; and this for the salvation of mankind; of whom much the greater portion, nevertheless, have ever since continued in the way of perdition; that to remedy this new difficulty, this same God, born of a virgin, having died and risen from the dead, assumes a new existence every day, and in the form of a piece of bread, multiplies himself by millions at the voice of one of the basest of men. Then, passing on to the doctrine of the sacraments, he was going to treat at large on the power of absolution and reprobation, of the means of purging all sins by a little water and a few words, when, uttering the words *indulgence, power of the pope, sufficient grace*, and *efficacious grace*, he was interrupted by a thousand cries.

"It is a horrible abuse," cried the Lutherans, "to pretend to remit sins for money."

"The notion of the *real presence*," cried the Calvinists, "is contrary to the text of the Gospel."

"The pope has no right to decide anything of himself," cried the Jansenists; and thirty other sects rising up, and accusing each other of heresies and errors, it was no longer possible to hear anything distinctly.

Silence being at last restored, the Mussulmans observed to the legislator :

" Since you have rejected our doctrine as containing things incredible, can you admit that of the Christians ? Is not theirs still more contrary to common sense and justice ? A God, immaterial and infinite, to become a man! to have a son as old as himself! This god-man to become bread, to be eaten and digested! Have we any thing equal to that ? Have the Christians an exclusive right of setting up a blind faith ? And will you grant them privileges of belief to our detriment ? "

Some savage tribes then advanced: "What!" said they, " because a man and woman ate an apple six thousand years ago, all the human race are damned? And you call God just ? What tyrant ever rendered children responsible for the faults of their fathers ? What man can answer for the actions of another ? Does not this overturn every idea of justice and of reason ? "

Others exclaimed: " Where are the proofs, the witnesses of these pretended facts ? Can we receive them without examining the evidence ? The least action in a court of justice requires two witnesses ; and we are ordered to believe all this on mere tradition and hearsay ! "

A Jewish Rabbin then addressing the assembly, said : " As to the fundamental facts, we are sureties ; but with regard to their form and their application, the case is different, and the Christians are here condemned by their own arguments. For they cannot deny that we are the original source from which they are derived—the primitive stock on which they are grafted; and hence the reasoning is very short : Either our law is from God, and then theirs is a heresy, since it differs from ours, or our law is not from God, and then theirs falls at the same time."

" But you must make this distinction," replied the Christian: " Your law is from God as *typical* and *preparative*, but not as *final* and *absolute :* you are the image of which we are the substance."

" We know," replied the Rabbin, " that such are your pretensions ; but they are absolutely gratuitous and false. Your system turns altogether on mystical meanings, visionary and allegorical interpretations.* With violent distortions on the letter of our books, you substitute the most chimerical ideas for the true ones, and find in them whatever pleases you; as a roving imagination will find figures in the clouds. Thus you have made a spiritual Messiah of that which, in the spirit of our prophets, is only a temporal king. You have made a redemption of the human race out of the simple re-establishment of our nation. Your conception of the Virgin is founded on a single phrase, of which you have changed the meaning. Thus you make from our Scriptures whatever your fancy dictates; you even find there your *trinity;* though there is not a word that has the most distant allusion to such a thing; and it is an invention of profane writers, admitted into your system with a host of other opinions, of every religion and of every sect, during the anarchy of the first three centuries of your era."

At these words, the Christian doctors, crying sacrilege and blasphemy, sprang forward in a transport of fury to fall upon the Jew; and a troop of monks, in motley dresses of black and white, advanced with a standard on which were painted pincers, gridirons, lighted fagots, and the words *Justice, Charity, Mercy.*† "It is necessary," said they, "to make an example of these impious wretches, and burn them for the glory of God." They began even to prepare the pile, when a Mussulman answered in a strain of irony:

"This, then, is that religion of peace, that meek and beneficent system which you so much extol! This is that evangelical charity which combats infidelity with persuasive mildness, and repays injuries with patience! Ye hypocrites! It is thus that you deceive mankind — thus that you propagate your accursed errors! When you were weak, you preached liberty, toleration, peace; when you are strong, you practise persecution and violence — "

---

* When we read the Fathers of the church, and see upon what arguments they have built the edifice of religion, we are inexpressibly astonished with their credulity or their knavery: but allegory was the rage of that period; the Pagans employed it to explain the actions of their gods, and the Christians acted in the same spirit when they employed it after their fashion.

† This description answers exactly to the banner of the Inquisition of Spanish Jacobins.

And he was going to begin the history of the wars and slaughters of Christianity, when the legislator, demanding silence, suspended this scene of discord.

The monks, affecting a tone of meekness and humility, exclaimed: " It is not ourselves that we would avenge ; it is the cause of God ; it is the glory of God that we defend."

" And what right have you, more than we," said the Imans, "to constitute yourselves the representatives of God ? Have you privileges that we have not ? Are you not men like us ? "

" To defend God," said another group, " to pretend to avenge him, is to insult his wisdom and his power. Does he not know, better than men, what befits his dignity ? "

" Yes," replied the monks, " but his ways are secret."

" And it remains for you to prove," said the Rabbins, " that you have the exclusive privilege of understanding them."

Then, proud of finding supporters to their cause, the Jews thought that the books of Moses were going to be triumphant, when the Mobed (high priest) of the Parses obtained leave to speak.

" We have heard," said he, " the account of the Jews and Christians of the origin of the world ; and, though greatly mutilated, we find in it some facts which we admit. But we deny that they are to be attributed to the legislator of the Hebrews. It was not he who made known to men these sublime truths, these celestial events. It was not to him that God revealed them, but to our holy prophet Zoroaster : and the proof of this is in the very books that they refer to. Examine with attention the laws, the ceremonies, the precepts established by Moses in those books ; you will not find the slightest indication, either expressed or understood, of what constitutes the basis of the Jewish and Christian theology. You nowhere find the least trace of the immortality of the soul, or of a future life, or of heaven, or of hell, or of the revolt of the principal angel, author of the evils of the human race. These ideas were not known to Moses, and the reason is very obvious : it was not till four centuries afterwards that Zoroaster first evangelized them in Asia.*

*See the Chronology of the Twelve Ages, in which I conceive myself to have clearly proved that Moses lived about 1,400 years before Jesus Christ, and Zoroaster about a thousand.

"Thus," continued the Mobed, turning to the Rabbins, "it was not till after that epoch, that is to say, in the time of your first kings, that these ideas began to appear in your writers; and then their appearance was obscure and gradual, according to the progress of the political relations between your ancestors and ours. It was especially when, having been conquered by the kings of Nineveh and Babylon and transported to the banks of the Tygris and the Euphrates, where they resided for three successive generations, that they imbibed manners and opinions which had been rejected as contrary to their law. When our king Cyrus had delivered them from slavery, their heart was won to us by gratitude; they became our disciples and imitators; and they admitted our dogmas in the revision of their books;* for your Genesis, in particular, was never the work of Moses, but a compilation drawn up after the return from the Babylonian captivity, in which are inserted the Chaldean opinions of the origin of the world.

"At first the pure followers of the law, opposing to the emigrants the letter of the text and the absolute silence of the prophet, endeavored to repel these innovations; but they ultimately prevailed, and our doctrine, modified by your ideas, gave rise to a new sect.

* In the first periods of the Christian church, not only the most learned of those who have since been denominated heretics, but many of the orthodox conceived Moses to have written neither the law nor the Pentateuch, but that the work was a compilation made by the elders of the people and the Seventy, who, after the death of Moses, collected his scattered ordinances, and mixed with them things that were extraneous; similar to what happened as to the Koran of Mahomet. See *Les Clementines*, Homel. 2. sect. 51. and Homel. 3. sect. 42.

Modern critics, more enlightened or more attentive than the ancients, have found in Genesis in particular, marks of its having been composed on the return from the captivity; but the principal proofs have escaped them. These I mean to exhibit in an analysis of the book of Genesis, in which I shall demonstrate that the tenth chapter, among others, which treats of the pretended generations of the man called Noah, is a real geographical picture of the world, as it was known to the Hebrews at the epoch of the captivity, which was bounded by Greece or Hellas at the West, mount Caucasus at the North, Persia at the East, and Arabia and Upper Egypt at the South. All the pretended personages from Adam to Abraham, or his father Terah, are mythological beings, stars, constellations, countries. Adam is Bootes: Noah is Osiris: Xisuthrus Janus, Saturn; that is to say Capricorn, or the celestial Genius that opened the year. The *Alexandrian Chronicle* says expressly, page 85, that Nimrod was supposed by the Persians to be their first king, as having invented the art of hunting, and that he was translated into heaven, where he appears under the name of Orion.

"You expected a king to restore your political independence; we announced a God to regenerate and save mankind. From this combination of ideas, your Essenians laid the foundation of Christianity : and whatever your pretensions may be, Jews, Christians, Mussulmans, you are, in your system of spiritual beings, only the blundering followers of Zoroaster. "

The Mobed, then passing on to the details of his religion, quoting from the Zadder and the Zendavesta, recounted, in the same order as they are found in the book of Genesis, the creation of the world in six *gahans*,* the formation of a first man and a first woman, in a divine place, under the reign of perfect good ; the introduction of evil into the world by the great snake, emblem of *Ahrimanes ;* the revolt and battles of the Genius of evil and darkness against *Ormuzd*, God of good and of light ; the division of the angels into white and black, or good and bad ; their hierarchal orders, *cherubim, seraphim, thrones, dominions*, etc. ; the end of the world at the close of six thousand years ; the coming of the lamb, the regenerator of nature ; the new world ; the future life, and the regions of happiness and misery ; the passage of souls over the bridge of the bottomless pit ; the celebration of the mysteries of Mithras ; the unleavened bread which the initiated eat ; the baptism of new-born children ; the unction of the dead ; the confession of sins ; and, in a word, he recited so many things analagous to those of the three preceding religions, that his

---

* Or periods, or in six gahan-bars, that is six periods of time. These periods are what Zoroaster calls the thousands of God or of light, meaning the six summer months. In the first, say the Persians, God created (arranged in order) the heavens ; in the second the waters ; in the third the earth ; in the fourth trees ; in the fifth animals ; and in the sixth man ; corresponding with the account in Genesis. For particulars see Hyde, ch. 9, and Henry Lord, ch. 2, on the religion of the ancient Persians. It is remarkable that the same tradition is found in the sacred books of the Etrurians, which relate that the fabricator of all things had comprised the duration of his work in a period of twelve thousand years, which period was distributed to the twelve houses of the sun. In the first thousand, God made heaven and earth ; in the second the firmament ; in the third the sea and the waters ; in the fourth the sun, moon and stars ; in the fifth the souls of animals, birds, and reptiles ; in the sixth man. See Suidas, at the word Tyrrhena ; which shows first the identity of their theological and astrological opinions ; and, secondly, the identity, or rather confusion of ideas, between absolute and system-atical creation ; that is, the periods assigned for renewing the face of nature, which were at first the period of the year, and afterwards periods of 60, of 600, of 25,000, of 36,000 and of 432,000 years.

discourse seemed like a commentary or a continuation of the Koran or the Apocalypse.*

But the Jewish, Christian, and Mahometan doctors, crying out against this recital, and treating the Parses as idolaters and worshippers of fire, charged them with falsehood, interpolations, falsification of facts; and there arose a violent dispute as to the dates of the events, their order and succession, the origin of the doctrines, their transmission from nation to nation, the authenticity of the books on which they are founded, the epoch of their composition, the character of their compilers, and the validity of their testimony. And the various parties, pointing out reciprocally to each other, the contradictions, improbabilities, and forgeries, accused one another of having established their belief on popular rumors, vague traditions, and absurd fables, invented without discernment, and admitted without examination by unknown, partial, or ignorant writers, at uncertain or unknown epochs.

A great murmur now arose from under the standards of the various Indian sects; and the Bramins, protesting against the pretensions of the Jews and the Parses, said:

" What are these new and almost unheard of nations, who arrogantly set themselves up as the sources of the human race, and the depositaries of its archives? To hear their calculations of five or six thousand years, it would seem that the world was of yesterday; whereas our monuments prove a duration of many thousands of centuries. And for what reason are their books to be preferred to ours? Are then the *Vedes*, the *Chastres*, and the *Pourans* inferior to the *Bibles*,

---

* The modern Parses and the ancient Mithriacs, who are the same sect, observe all the Christian sacraments, even the laying on of hands in confirmation. The priest of Mithra, says Tertullian, (*de Præscriptione*, ch. 40) promises absolution from sin on confession and baptism; and, if I rightly remember, Mithra marks his soldiers in the forehead, with the chrism called in the Egyptian Kouphi; he celebrates the sacrifice of bread, which is the resurrection, and presents the crown to his followers, menacing them at the same time with the sword, etc.

In these mysteries they tried the courage of the initiated with a thousand terrors, presenting fire to his face, a sword to his breast, etc. ; they also offered him a crown, which he refused, saying, God is my crown: and this crown is to be seen in the celestial sphere by the side of Bootes. The personages in these mysteries were distinguished by the names of the animal constellations. The ceremony of mass is nothing more than an imitation of these mysteries and those of Eleusis. The benediction, *the Lord be with you*, is a literal translation of the formula of admission *chou-k, am, p-ka*. See *Beausob. Hist. Du Manicheisme*, vol. ii.

the *Zendavestas*, and the *Zadders* ? * And is not the testimony
of our fathers and our gods as valid as that of the fathers and
the gods of the West? Ah! if it were permitted to reveal our
mysteries to profane men! if a sacred veil did not justly con-
ceal them from every eye!"

The Bramins stopping short at these words: "How can we
admit your doctrine," said the legislator, "if you will not
make it known? And how did its first authors propagate it,
when, being alone possessed of it, their own people were to
them profane? Did heaven reveal it to be kept a secret?"†

But the Bramins persisting in their silence: "Let them

---

* These are the sacred volumes of the Hindoos; they are sometimes written
Vedams, Pouranams, Chastrans, because the Hindoos, like the Persians, are
accustomed to give a nasal sound to the terminations of their words, which we
represent by the affixes *on* and *an*, and the Portuguese by the affixes *om* and *am*.
Many of these books have been translated, thanks to the liberal spirit of Mr.
Hastings, who has founded at Calcutta a literary society, and a printing press.
At the same time, however, that we express our gratitude to this society, we
must be permitted to complain of its exclusive spirit; the number of copies
printed of each book being such as it is impossible to purchase them even in
England; they are wholly in the hands of the East India proprietors. Scarcely
even is the *Asiatic Miscellany* known in Europe; and a man must be very learned
in oriental antiquity before he so much as hears of the Jones's, the Wilkins's, and
the Halhed's, etc. As to the sacred books of the Hindoos, all that are yet in our
hands are the *Bhagvat Geeta*, the *Ezour-Vedam*, the *Bagavadam*, and certain
fragments of the *Chastres* printed at the end of the *Bhagvat Geeta*. These books
are in Indostan what the *Old and New Testament* are in Christendom, the *Koran*
in Turkey, the *Zadder* and the *Zendavesta* among the Parses, etc. When I have
taken an extensive survey of their contents, I have sometimes asked myself, what
would be the loss to the human race if a new Omar condemned them to the
flames; and, unable to discover any mischief that would ensue, I call the imaginary chest that contains them, the box of Pandora.

† The Vedas or Vedams are the sacred volumes of the Hindoos, as the Bibles
with us. They are three in number; the Rick Veda, the Yadjour Veda, and the
Sama Veda; they are so scarce in India, that the English could with great difficulty find an original one, of which a copy is deposited in the British Museum;
they who reckon four Vedas, include among them the Attar Veda, concerning
ceremonies, but which is lost. There are besides commentaries named Upanish-
ada, one of which was published by Anquetil du Peron, and entitled Oupnekhat,
a curious work. The date of these books is more than twenty-five centuries prior
to our era; their contents prove that all the reveries of the Greek metaphysicians
come from India and Egypt. Since the year 1788, the learned men of England
are working in India a mine of literature totally unknown in Europe, and which
proves that the civilization of India ascends to a very remote antiquity. After
the Vedas come the Chastras amounting to six. They treat of theology and the
Sciences. Afterwards eighteen Pouranas, treating of Mythology and History.
See the Bahgouet-guita, the Baga Vadam, and the Ezour-Vedam, etc.

have the honor of the secret," said a European : "Their doctrine is now divulged ; we have their books, and I can give
you the substance of them."

Then beginning with an abstract of the four *Vedes*, the
eighteen *Pourans*, and the five or six *Chastres*, he recounted
how a being, infinite, eternal, immaterial and round, after
having passed an eternity in self-contemplation, and deter-
mining at last to manifest himself, separated the male and
female faculties which were in him, and performed an act of
generation, of which the Lingam remains an emblem ; how
that first act gave birth to three divine powers, *Brama, Bichen*
or *Vichenou*, and *Chib* or *Chiven ;* * whose functions were — the
first to create, the second to preserve, and the third to destroy,
or change the form of the universe.   Then, detailing the history of their operations and adventures, he explained how
Brama, proud of having created the world and the eight
bobouns, or spheres of probation, thought himself superior to
Chib, his equal; how his pride brought on a battle between
them, in which these celestial globes were crushed like a
basket of eggs; how Brama, vanquished in this conflict, was
reduced to serve as a pedestal to Chib, metamorphosed into
a Lingam ; how Vichenou, the god mediator, has taken at
different times to preserve the world, nine mortal forms of
animals ; how first, in shape of a fish, he saved from the
universal deluge a family who repeopled the earth ; how afterwards, in the form of a tortoise,† he drew from the sea of milk
the mountain Mandreguiri (the pole) ; then, becoming a boar,
he tore the belly of the giant Ereuniachessen, who was
drowning the earth in the abyss of Djole, from whence he
drew it out with his tusks ; how, becoming incarnate in a
black shepherd, and under the name of *Christ-en*, he delivered

---

* These names are differently pronounced according to the different dialeĉts ;
thus they say *Birmah, Bremma, Brouma*. *Bichen* has been turned into *Vichen*
by the easy exchange of a *B* for a *V*, and into *Vichenou* by means of a grammatical
affix. In the same manner *Chib*, which is synonymous with Satan, and signifies
adversary, is frequently written *Chiba* and *Chiv-en ;* he is called also *Rouder* and
Routr-en, that is, the destroyer.

† This is the constellation testudo, or the lrye, which was at first a tortoise, on
account of its slow motion round the Pole ; then a lyre, because it is the shell of
this reptile on which the strings of the lyre are mounted. See an excellent
memoir of *M. Dupuis sur l' Origine des Constellations.*

the world of the enormous serpent Calengem, and then crushed his head, after having been wounded by him in the heel.

Then, passing on to the history of the secondary Genii, he
related how the Eternal, to display his own glory, created
various orders of angels, whose business it was to sing his
praises and to direct the universe ; how a part of these angels
revolted under the guidance of an ambitious chief, who strove
to usurp the power of God, and to govern all ; how God
plunged them into a world of darkness, there to undergo the
punishment for their crimes ; how at last, touched with compassion, he consented to release them, to receive them into
favor, after they should undergo a long series of probations ;
how, after creating for this purpose fifteen orbits or regions
of planets, and peopling them with bodies, he ordered these
rebel angels to undergo in them eighty-seven transmigrations ;
he then explained how souls, thus purified, returned to the first
source, to the ocean of life and animation from which they had
proceeded ; and since all living creatures contain portions of
this universal soul, he taught how criminal it was to deprive
them of it.   He was finally proceeding to explain the rites and
ceremonies, when, speaking of offerings and libations of milk
and butter made to gods of copper and wood, and then of
purifications by the dung and urine of cows, there arose a
universal murmur, mixed with peals of laughter, which interrupted the orator.

Each of the different groups began to reason on that
religion : " They are idolators," said the Mussulmans ; " and
should be exterminated."   " They are deranged in their
intellect," said the followers of Confucius ; " we must try to
cure them."   " What ridiculous gods," said others, " are these
puppets, besmeared with grease and smoke ! Are gods to be
washed like dirty children, from whom you must brush away
the flies, which, attracted by honey, are fouling them with
their excrements ! "

But a Bramin exclaimed with indignation : " These are
profound mysteries,— emblems of truth, which you are not
worthy to hear."

" And in what respect are you more worthy than we ? " exclaimed a *Lama* of Tibet.   " Is it because you pretend to
have issued from the head of Brama, and the rest of the

human race from the less noble parts of his body? But to support the pride of your distinctions of origin and castes, prove to us in the first place that you are different from other men; establish, in the next place, as historical facts, the allegories which you relate; show us, indeed, that you are the authors of all this doctrine; for we will demonstrate, if necessary, that you have only stolen and disfigured it; that you are only the imitators of the ancient paganism of the West; to which, by an ill assorted mixture, you have allied the pure and spiritual doctrine of our gods—a doctrine totally detached from the senses, and entirely unknown on earth till Beddou taught it to the nations."*

A number of groups having asked what was this doctrine, and who was this god, of whom the greater part had never heard the name, the Lama resumed and said:

"In the beginning, a sole-existent and self-existent God, having passed an eternity in the contemplation of his own being, resolved to manifest his perfections out of himself, and created the matter of the world. The four elements being produced, but still in a state of confusion, he breathed on the face of the waters, which swelled like an immense bubble in form of an egg, which unfolding, became the vault or orb of heaven, enclosing the world.† Having made the earth, and the bodies of animals, this God, essence of motion, imparted to them a part of his own being to animate them; for this reason, the soul of everything that breathes being a portion

---

* All the ancient opinions of the Egyptian and Grecian theologians are to be found in India, and they appear to have been introduced, by means of the commerce of Arabia and the vicinity of Persia, time immemorial.

† This cosmogony of the Lamas, the Bonzes, and even the Bramins, as Henry Lord asserts, is literally that of the ancient Egyptians. The Egyptians, says Porphyry, call Kneph, intelligence, or efficient cause of the universe. They relate that this God vomited an egg, from which was produced another God named Phtha or Vulcan, (igneous principle or the sun) and they add, that this egg is the world. Euseb. *Præp. Evang.* p. 115.

They represent, says the same author in another place, the God Kneph, or efficient cause, under the form of a man in deep blue (the color of the sky) having in his hand a sceptre, a belt round his body, and a small bonnet royal of light feathers on his head, to denote how very subtile and fugacious the idea of that being is. Upon which I shall observe that Kneph in Hebrew signifies a wing, a feather, and that this color of sky-blue is to be found in the majority of the Indian Gods, and is, under the name of Narayan, one of their most distinguishing epithets.

of the universal soul, no one of them can perish; they only change their form and mould in passing successively into different bodies. Of all these forms, the one most pleasing to God is that of man, as most resembling his own perfections. When a man, by an absolute disengagement from his senses, is wholly absorbed in self-contemplation, he then discovers the divinity, and becomes himself God. Of all the incarnations of this kind that God has hitherto taken, the greatest and most solemn was that in which he appeared thirty centuries ago in Kachemire, under the name of *Fôt* or *Beddou*, to preach the doctrines of self-denial and self-annihilation."

Then, pursuing the history of *Fôt*, the Lama continued :

" He was born from the right flank of a virgin of royal blood, who did not cease to be a virgin for having become a mother; that the king of the country, uneasy at his birth, wished to destroy him, and for this purpose ordered a massacre of all the males born at that period, that being saved by shepherds, Beddou lived in the desert till the age of thirty years, at which time he began his mission to enlighten men and cast out devils ; that he performed a multitude of the most astonishing miracles ; that he spent his life in fasting and severe penitence, and at his death, bequeathed to his disciples a book containing his doctrines."

And the Lama began to read :

" He that leaveth his father and mother to follow me," says *Fôt*, " becomes a perfect Samanean (a heavenly man).

" He that practices my precepts to the fourth degree of perfection, acquires the faculty of flying in the air, of moving heaven and earth, of prolonging or shortening his life (rising from the dead).

" The Samanean despises riches, and uses only what is strictly necessary ; he mortifies his body, silences his passions, desires nothing, forms no attachments, meditates my doctrines without ceasing, endures injuries with patience, and bears no malice to his neighbor.

" Heaven and earth shall perish," says *Fôt :* " despise therefore your bodies, which are composed of the four perishable elements, and think only of your immortal soul.

" Listen not to the flesh : fear and sorrow spring from the passions : stifle the passions and you destroy fear and sorrow,

" Whoever dies without having embraced my religion,"
says *Fôt*, " returns among men, until he embraces it."

The Lama was going on with his reading, when the Christians interrupted him, crying out that this was their own
religion adulterated — that Fôt was no other than Jesus himself disfigured, and that the Lamas were the Nestorians and
the Manicheans disguised and bastardized.*

But the Lama, supported by the Chamans, Bonzes, Gonnis,
Talapoins of Siam, of Ceylon, of Japan, and of China, proved
to the Christians, even from their own authors, that the doctrine of the Samaneans was known through the East more
than a thousand years before the Christian era ; that their
name was cited before the time of Alexander, and that Boutta,
or Beddou, was known before Jesus.†

---

* This is asserted by our missionaries, and among others by Georgi in his un-
finished work of the Thibetan alphabet : but if it can be proved that the Manicheans were but plagiarists, and the ignorant echo of a doctrine that existed fifteen
hundred years before them, what becomes of the declarations of Georgi? See
upon this subject, Beausob. *Hist. du Manicheisme.*

† The eastern writers in general agree in placing the birth of *Beddou* 1027 years
before Jesus Christ, which makes him the contemporary of Zoroaster, with
whom, in my opinion, they confound him. It is certain that his doctrine notori-
ously existed at that epoch ; it is found entire in that of Orpheus, Pythagoras, and
the Indian gymnosophists. But the gymnosophists are cited at the time of Alexander as an ancient sect already divided into Brachmans and Samaneans. See
Bardesanes en Saint Jerome, Epitre à Jovien. Pythagoras lived in the ninth
century before Jesus Christ ; See Chronology of the twelve ages ; and Orpheus is
of still greater antiquity. If, as is the case, the doctrine of Pythagoras and that
of Orpheus are of Egyptian origin, that of Beddou goes back to the common
source ; and in reality the Egyptian priests recite, that Hermes as he was dying
said : " I have hitherto lived an exile from my country, to which I now return.
Weep not for me, I ascend to the celestial abode where each of you will follow in
his turn : there God is : this life is only death." — Chalcidius in Thinæum.

Such was the profession of faith of the Samaneans, the sectaries of Orpheus, and
the Pythagoreans. Farther, Hermes is no other than Beddou himself; for among
the Indians, Chinese, Lamas, etc., the planet Mercury and the corresponding day
of the week (Wednesday) bear the name of Beddou, and this accounts for his
being placed in the rank of mythological beings, and discovers the illusion of his
pretended existence as a man ; since it is evident that Mercury was not a human
being, but the Genius or Decan, who, placed at the summer solstice, opened the
Egyptian year ; hence his attributes taken from the constellation Syrius, and his
name of Anubis, as well as that of Esculapius, having the figure of a man and the
head of a dog : hence his serpent, which is the Hydra, emblem of the Nile (Hydor,
humidity) ; and from this serpent he seems to have derived his name of Hermes,
as Remes (with a schin) in the oriental languages, signifies serpent. Now Beddou
and Hermes being the same names, it is manifest of what antiquity is the system
ascribed to the former. As to the name of Samanean, it is precisely that of

Then, retorting the pretensions of the Christians against themselves : " Prove to us," said the Lama, " that you are not Samaneans degenerated, and that the man you make the author of your sect is not Fôt himself disguised. Prove to us by historical facts that he even existed at the epoch you pretend ; for, it being destitute of authentic testimony,* we absolutely deny it ; and we maintain that your very gospels are only the books of some Mithriacs of Persia, and the Essenians of Syria, who were a branch of reformed Samaneans." †

Chaman, still preserved in Tartary, China, and India. The interpretation given to it is, man of the woods, a hermit mortifying the flesh, such being the characteristic of this sect ; but its literal meaning is, celestial (Samâoui) and explains the system of those who are called by it. — The system is the same as that of the sectaries of Orpheus, of the Essenians, of the ancient Anchorets of Persia, and the whole eastern country. See Porphyry, *de Abstin. Animal.*

These celestial and penitent men carried in India their insanity to such an extreme as to wish not to touch the earth, and they accordingly lived in cages suspended from the trees, where the people, whose admiration was not less absurd, brought them provisions. During the night there were frequent robberies, rapes and murders, and it was at length discovered that they were committed by those men, who, descending from their cages, thus indemnified themselves for their restraint during the day. The Bramins, their rivals, embraced the opportunity of exterminating them ; and from that time their name in India has been synonymous with hypocrite. See *Hist. de la Chine*, in 5 vols. quarto, at the note page 30; *Hist. de Huns*, 2 vols. and preface to the *Ezour-Vedam.*

* There are absolutely no other monuments of the existence of Jesus Christ as a human being, than a passage in Josephus (*Antiq. Jud. lib. 18, c. 3,*) a single phrase in Tacitus (*Annal. lib. 15, c. 44,*) and the Gospels. But the passage in Josephus is unanimously acknowledged to be apocryphal, and to have been interpolated towards the close of the third century, (See *Trad. de Joseph, par M. Gillet*) ; and that of Tacitus in so vague and so evidently taken from the deposition of the Christians before the tribunals, that it may be ranked in the class of evangelical records. It remains to enquire of what authority are these records. " All the world knows," says Faustus, who, though a Manichean, was one of the most learned men of the third century, " All the world knows that the gospels were neither written by Jesus Christ, nor his apostles, but by certain unknown persons, who rightly judging that they should not obtain belief respecting things which they had not seen, placed at the head of their recitals the names of contemporary apostles." See *Beausob.* vol. i. and *Hist. des Apologistes de la Relig. Chret. par Burigni*, a sagacious writer, who has demonstrated the absolute uncertainty of those foundations of the Christian religion ; so that the existence of Jesus is no better proved than that of Osiris and Hercules, or that of Fôt or Beddou, with whom, says M. de Guignes, the Chinese continually confound him, for they never call Jesus by any other name than Fôt. *Hist. de Huns.*

† That is to say, from the pious romances formed out of the sacred legends of the mysteries of Mithra, Ceres, Isis, etc., from whence are equally derived the books of the Hindoos and the Bonzes. Our missionaries have long remarked a striking resemblance between those books and the gospels. M. Wilkins expressly

At these words, the Christians set up a general cry, and a new dispute was about to begin ; when a number of Chinese Chamans, and Talapoins of Siam, came forward and said that they would settle the whole controversy. And one of them speaking for the whole exclaimed : " It is time to put an end to these frivolous contests by drawing aside the veil from the interior doctrine that Fôt himself revealed to his disciples on his death bed.*

" All these theological opinions," continued he, " are but chimeras. All the stories of the nature of the gods, of their actions and their lives, are but allegories and mythological emblems, under which are enveloped ingenious ideas of morals, and the knowledge of the operations of nature in the action of the elements and the movement of the planets.

" The truth is, that all is reduced to nothing — that all is illusion, appearance, dream ; that the moral metempsychosis is only the figurative sense of the physical metempsychosis, or the successive movement of the elements of bodies which perish not, but which, having composed one body, pass when that is dissolved, into other mediums and form other combinations. The soul is but the vital principle which results from the properties of matter, and from the action of the elements in those bodies where they create a spontaneous movement. To suppose that this product of the play of the organs, born with them, matured with them, and which sleeps with them, can subsist when they cease, is the romance of a wandering imagination, perhaps agreeable enough, but really chimerical.

God itself is nothing more than the moving principle, the occult force inherent in all beings — the sum of their laws and

mentions it in a note in the *Bhagvat Geeta*. All agree that Krisna, Fôt, and Jesus have the same characteristic features : but religious prejudice has stood in the way of drawing from this circumstance the proper and natural inference. To time and reason must it be left to display the truth.

* The Budsoists have two doctrines, the one public and ostensible, the other interior and secret, precisely like the Egyptian priests. It may be asked, why this distinction ? It is, that as the public doctrine recommends offerings, expiations, endowments, etc., the priests find their profit in preaching it to the people ; whereas the other, teaching the vanity of worldly things, and attended with no lucre, it is thought proper to make it known only to adepts. Can the teachers and followers of this religion be better classed than under the heads of knavery and credulity ?

properties — the animating principle; in a word, the soul of the universe; which on account of the infinite variety of its connections and its operations, sometimes simple, sometimes multiple, sometimes active, sometimes passive, has always presented to the human mind an unsolvable enigma. All that man can comprehend with certainty is, that matter does not perish; that it possesses essentially those properties by which the world is held together like a living and organized being; that the knowledge of these laws with respect to man is what constitutes wisdom; that virtue and merit consist in their observance; and evil, sin, and vice, in the ignorance and violation of them; that happiness and misery result from these by the same necessity which makes heavy bodies descend and light ones rise, and by a fatality of causes and effects, whose chain extends from the smallest atom to the greatest of the heavenly bodies." *

At these words, a crowd of theologians of every sect cried out that this doctrine was materialism, and that those who profess it were impious atheists, enemies to God and man, who must be exterminated. " Very well," replied the *Chamans*, " suppose we are in error, which is not impossible, since the first attribute of the human mind is to be subject to illusion; but what right have you to take away from men like yourselves, the life which Heaven has given them? If Heaven holds us guilty and in abhorrence, why does it impart to us the same blessings as to you? And if it treats us with forbearance, what authority have you to be less indulgent? Pious men! who speak of God with so much certainty and confidence, be so good as to tell us what it is; give us to comprehend what those abstract and metaphysical beings are, which you call *God* and *soul*, substance without matter, existence without body, life without organs or sensation. If you know those beings by your senses or their reflections, render them in like manner perceptible to us; or if you speak of them on testimony and tradition, show us a uniform account, and give a determinate basis to our creed."

* These are the very expressions of La Loubre, in his description of the kingdom of Siam and the theology of the Bronzes. Their dogmas, compared with those of the ancient philosophers of Greece and Italy, give a complete representation of the whole system of the Stoics and Epicureans, mixed with astrological superstitions, and some traits of Pythagorism.

There now arose among the theologians a great controversy respecting God and his nature, his manner of acting, and of manifesting himself; on the nature of the soul and its union with the body; whether it exists before the organs, or only after they are formed; on the future life, and the other world. And every sect, every school, every individual, differing on all these points, and each assigning plausible reasons, and respectable though opposite authorities for his opinion, they fell into an inextricable labyrinth of contradictions.

Then the legislator, having commanded silence and recalled the dispute to its true object, said: "Chiefs and instructors of nations; you came together in search of truth. At first, every one of you, thinking he possessed it, demanded of the others an implicit faith; but perceiving the contrariety of your opinions, you found it necessary to submit them to a common rule of evidence, and to bring them to one general term of comparison; and you agreed that each should exhibit the proofs of his doctrine. You began by alleging facts; but each religion and every sect, being equally furnished with miracles and martyrs, each producing an equal number of witnesses, and offering to support them by a voluntary death, the balance on this first point, by right of parity, remained equal.

"You then passed to the trial of reasoning; but the same arguments applying equally to contrary positions — the same assertions, equally gratuitous, being advanced and repelled with equal force, and all having an equal right to refuse his assent, nothing was demonstrated. What is more, the confrontation of your systems has brought up more and extraordinary difficulties; for amid the apparent or adventitious diversities, you have discovered a fundamental resemblance, a common groundwork; and each of you pretending to be the inventor, and first depositary, have taxed each other with adulterations and plagiarisms; and thence arises a difficult question concerning the transmission of religious ideas from people to people.

"Finally, to complete your embarrassment: when you endeavored to explain your doctrines to each other, they appeared confused and foreign, even to their adherents; they were founded on ideas inaccessible to your senses; you

consequently had no means of judging of them, and you confessed yourselves in this respect to be only the echoes of
your fathers. Hence follows this other question : how came
they to the knowledge of your fathers, who themselves had
no other means than you to conceive them ? So that, on the
one hand, the succession of these ideas being unknown, and
on the other, their origin and existence being a mystery, all
the edifice of your religious opinions becomes a complicated
problem of metaphysics and history.

"Since, however, these opinions, extraordinary as they
may be, must have had some origin ; since even the most
abstract and fantastical ideas have some physical model, it
may be useful to recur to this origin, and discover this model
—in a word, to find out from what source the human understanding has drawn these ideas, at present so obscure, of God,
of the soul, of all immaterial beings, which make the basis of
so many systems ; to unfold the filiation which they have followed, and the alterations which they have undergone in their
transmissions and ramifications. If, then, there are any persons present who have made a study of these objects, let them
come forward, and endeavor, in the face of nations, to dissipate the obscurity in which their opinions have so long
remained."

CHAPTER XXII.

ORIGIN AND FILIATION OF RELIGIOUS IDEAS.

AT these words, a new group, formed in an instant by men
from various standards, but not distinguished by any,
came forward into the circle ; and one of them spoke
in the name of the whole :

"Delegates, friends of evidence and virtue ! It is not surprising that the subject in question should be enveloped in so
many clouds, since, besides its inherent difficulties, thought
itself has always been encumbered with superadded obstacles
peculiar to this study, where all free enquiry and discussion

have been interdicted by the intolerance of every system. But now that our views are permitted to expand, we will expose to open day, and submit to the judgment of nations, that which unprejudiced minds, after long researches, have found to be the most reasonable; and we do this, not with the pretension of imposing a new creed, but with the hope of provoking new lights, and obtaining better information.

" Doctors and instructors of nations! You know what thick darkness covers the nature, the origin, the history of the dogmas which you teach. Imposed by authority, inculcated by education, and maintained by example, they pass from age to age, and strengthen their empire from habit and inattention. But if man, enlightened by reflection and experience, brings to mature examination the prejudices of his childhood, he soon discovers a multitude of incongruities and contradictions which awaken his sagacity and excite his reasoning powers.

" At first, remarking the diversity and opposition of the creeds which divide the nations, he takes courage to question the infallibility which each of them claims, and arming himself with their reciprocal pretensions, he conceives that his senses and his reason, derived immediately from God, are a law not less holy, a guide not less sure, than the mediate and contradictory codes of the prophets.

" If he then examines the texture of these codes themselves, he observes that their laws, pretended to be divine, that is, immutable and eternal, have arisen from circumstances of times, places, and persons; that they have issued one from the other, in a kind of genealogical order, borrowing from each other reciprocally a common and similar fund of ideas, which every lawgiver modifies according to his fancy.

" If he ascends to the source of these ideas, he finds it involved in the night of time, in the infancy of nations, even to the origin of the world, to which they claim alliance; and there, placed in the darkness of chaos, in the empire of fables and traditions, they present themselves, accompanied with a state of things so full of prodigies, that it seems to forbid all access to the judgment: but this state itself excites a first effort of reason, which resolves the difficulty; for if the prodigies, found in the theological systems, have really existed — if, for instance, the metamorphoses, the apparitions, the conversations with one or many gods, recorded in the books of the Indians, the Hebrews, the Parses, are historical events, he must agree that nature in those times was totally different from what it is at present; that the present race of men are quite another species from those who then existed; and, therefore, he ought not to trouble his head about them.

"If, on the contrary, these miraculous events have really not existed in the physical order of things, then he readily conceives that they are creatures of the human intellect; and this faculty being still capable of the most fantastical combinations, explains at once the phenomenon of these monsters in history. It only remains, then, to find how and wherefore they have been formed in the imagination. Now, if we examine with care the subjects of these intellectual creations, analyze the ideas which they combine and associate, and carefully weigh all the circumstances which they allege, we shall find that this first obscure and incredible state of things is explained by the laws of nature. We find that these stories of a fabulous kind have a figurative sense different from the apparent one; that these events, pretended to be marvellous, are simple and physical facts, which, being misconceived or misrepresented, have been disfigured by accidental causes dependent on the human mind, by the confusion of signs employed to represent the ideas, the want of precision in words, permanence in language, and perfection in writing; we find that these gods, for instance, who display such singular characters in every system, are only the physical agents of nature, the elements, the winds, the stars, and the meteors, which have been personified by the necessary mechanism of language and of the human understanding; that their lives, their manners, their actions, are only their mechanical operations and connections; and that all their pretended history is only the description of these phenomena, formed by the first naturalists who observed them, and misconceived by the vulgar who did not understand them, or by succeeding generations who forgot them. In a word, all the theological dogmas on the origin of the world, the nature of God, the revelation of his laws, the manifestation of his person, are known to be only the recital of astronomical facts, only figurative and emblematical accounts of the motion of the heavenly bodies. We are con-

vinced that the very idea of a God, that idea at present so
obscure, is, in its first origin, nothing but that of the physical
powers of the universe, considered sometimes as a plurality
by reason of their agencies and phenomena, sometimes as
one simple and only being by reason of the universality of the
machine and the connection of its parts ; so that the being
called God has been sometimes the wind, the fire, the water,
all the elements ; sometimes the sun, the stars, the planets,
and their influence ; sometimes the matter of the visible
world, the totality of the universe ; sometimes abstract and
metaphysical qualities, such as space, duration, motion, intelligence ; and we everywhere see this conclusion, that the idea
of God has not been a miraculous revelation of invisible
beings, but a natural offspring of the human intellect — an
operation of the mind, whose progress it has followed and
whose revolutions it has undergone, in all the progress that
has been made in the knowledge of the physical world and
its agents.

"It is then in vain that nations attribute their religion to
heavenly inspirations ; it is in vain that their dogmas pretend
to a primeval state of supernatural events : the original barbarity of the human race, attested by their own monuments,[*]
belies these assertions at once. But there is one constant and
indubitable fact which refutes beyond contradiction all these
doubtful accounts of past ages. From this position, that man
acquires and receives no ideas but through the medium of his
senses,[†] it follows with certainty that every notion which
claims to itself any other origin than that of sensation and
experience, is the erroneous supposition of a posterior reasoning : now, it is sufficient to cast an eye upon the sacred
systems of the origin of the world, and of the actions of the
gods, to discover in every idea, in every word, the anticipation
of an order of things which could not exist till a long time
after. Reason, strengthened by these contradictions, rejecting

---

[*] It is the unanimous testimony of history, and even of legends, that the first
human beings were every where savages, and that it was to civilize them, and
teach them to *make bread*, that the Gods manifested themselves.

[†] The rock on which all the ancients have split, and which has occasioned all
their errors, has been their supposing the idea of God to be innate and co-eternal
with the soul ; and hence all the reveries developed in Plato and Jamblicus. See
the *Timæus*, the *Phedon*, and *De Mysteriis Egyptiorum*, sect. 1, c. 3.

everything that is not in the order of nature, and admitting
no historical facts but those founded on probabilities, lays
open its own system, and pronounces itself with assurance.

" Before one nation had received from another nation dogmas already invented; before one generation had inherited
ideas acquired by a preceding generation, none of these complicated systems could have existed in the world. The first
men, being children of nature, anterior to all events, ignorant
of all science, were born without any idea of the dogmas
arising from scholastic disputes; of rites founded on the
practice of arts not then known; of precepts framed after the
development of passions; or of laws which suppose a language, a state of society not then in being; or of God, whose
attributes all refer to physical objects, and his actions to a
despotic state of government; or of the soul, or of any of
those metaphysical beings, which we are told are not the
objects of sense, and for which, however, there can be no other
means of access to the understanding. To arrive at so many
results, the necessary circle of preceding facts must have been
observed; slow experience and repeated trials must have
taught the rude man the use of his organs; the accumulated
knowledge of successive generations must have invented and
improved the means of living; and the mind, freed from the
cares of the first wants of nature, must have raised itself to the
complicated art of comparing ideas, of digesting arguments,
and seizing abstract similitudes.

I. *Origin of the idea of God: Worship of the elements and of
the physical powers of nature.*

" It was not till after having overcome these obstacles, and
gone through a long career in the night of history, that man,
reflecting on his condition, began to perceive that he was
subjected to forces superior to his own, and independent of
his will. The sun enlightened and warmed him, the fire
burned him, the thunder terrified him, the wind beat upon
him, the water overwhelmed him. All beings acted upon
him powerfully and irresistibly. He sustained this action for
a long time, like a machine, without enquiring the cause; but
the moment he began his enquiries, he fell into astonishment;

and, passing from the surprise of his first reflections to the reverie of curiosity, he began a chain of reasoning.

" *First*, considering the action of the elements on him, he conceived an idea of weakness and subjection on his part, and of power and domination on theirs; and this idea of power was the primitive and fundamental type of every idea of God.

" *Secondly*, the action of these natural existences excited in him sensations of pleasure or pain, of good or evil; and by a natural effect of his organization, he conceived for them love or aversion; he desired or dreaded their presence; and fear or hope gave rise to the first idea of religion.

" Then, judging everything by comparison, and remarking in these beings a spontaneous movement like his own, he supposed this movement directed by a will,—an intelligence of the nature of his own; and hence, by induction, he formed a new reasoning. Having experienced that certain practices towards his fellow creatures had the effect to modify their affections and direct their conduct to his advantage, he resorted to the same practices towards these powerful beings of the universe. He reasoned thus with himself: When my fellow creature, stronger than I, is disposed to do me injury, I abase myself before him, and my prayer has the art to calm him. I will pray to these powerful beings who strike me. I will supplicate the intelligences of the winds, of the stars, of the waters, and they will hear me. I will conjure them to avert the evil and give me the good that is at their disposal; I will move them by my tears, I will soften them by offerings, and I shall be happy.

" Thus simple man, in the infancy of his reason, spoke to the sun and to the moon; he animated with his own understanding and passions the great agents of nature; he thought by vain sounds, and vain actions, to change their inflexible laws. Fatal error! He prayed the stone to ascend, the water to mount above its level, the mountains to remove, and substituting a fantastical world for the real one, he peopled it with imaginary beings, to the terror of his mind and the torment of his race.

" In this manner the ideas of God and religion have sprung, like all others, from physical objects; they were produced in the mind of man from his sensations, from his wants, from the circumstances of his life, and the progressive state of his knowledge.

" Now, as the ideas of God had their first models in physical agents, it followed that God was at first varied and manifold, like the form under which he appeared to act. Every being was a Power, a Genius; and the first men conceived the universe filled with innumerable gods.

" Again the ideas of God have been created by the affections of the human heart ; they became necessarily divided into two classes, according to the sensations of pleasure or pain, love or hatred, which they inspired.

" The forces of nature, the gods and genii, were divided into beneficent and malignant, good and evil powers ; and hence the universality of these two characters in all the systems of religion.

" These ideas, analogous to the condition of their inventors, were for a long time confused and ill-digested. Savage men, wandering in the woods, beset with wants and destitute of resources, had not the leisure to combine principles and draw conclusions ; affected with more evils than they found pleasures, their most habitual sentiment was that of fear, their theology terror ; their worship was confined to a few salutations and offerings to beings whom they conceived as greedy and ferocious as themselves. In their state of equality and independence, no man offered himself as mediator between men and gods as insubordinate and poor as himself. No one having superfluities to give, there existed no parasite by the name of priest, no tribute by the name of victim, no empire by the name of altar. Their dogmas and their morals were the same thing, it was only self-preservation ; and *religion*, that arbitrary idea, without influence on the mutual relations of men, was a vain homage rendered to the visible powers of nature.

" Such was the necessary and original idea of God."

And the orator, addressing himself to the savage nations, continued :

" We appeal to you, men who have received no foreign and factitious ideas ; tell us, have you ever gone beyond what I have described? And you, learned doctors, we call you to witness; is not this the unanimous testimony of all ancient monuments? *

II. *Second system : Worship of the Stars, or Sabeism.*

" But those same monuments present us likewise a system more methodical and more complicated — that of the worship of all the stars ; adored sometimes in their proper forms, sometimes under figurative emblems and symbols ; and this worship was the effect of the knowledge men had acquired in physics, and was derived immediately from the first causes of the social state; that is, from the necessities and arts of the first degree, which are among the elements of society.

* It clearly results, says Plutarch, from the verses of Orpheus and the sacred books of the Egyptians and Phrygians, that the ancient theology, not only of the Greeks, but of all nations, was nothing more than a system of physics, a picture of the operations of nature, wrapped up in mysterious allegories and enigmatical symbols, in a manner that the ignorant multitude attended rather to their apparent than to their hidden meaning, and even in what they understood of the latter, supposed there to be something more deep than what they perceived. Fragment of a work of Plutarch now lost, quoted by Eusebius, *Præpar. Evang.* lib. 3, ch. 1, p. 83.

The majority of philosophers, says Porphyry, and among others Hæremon (who lived in Egypt in the first age of Christianity), imagine there never to have been any other world than the one we see, and acknowledged no other Gods of all those recognized by the Egyptians, than such as are commonly called planets, signs of the Zodiac, and constellations; whose aspects, that is, rising and setting, are supposed to influence the fortunes of men ; to which they add their divisions of the signs into decans and dispensers of time, whom they style lords of the ascendant, whose names, virtues in relieving distempers, rising, setting, and presages of future events, are the subjects of almanacs (for be it observed, that the Egyptian priests had almanacs the exact counterpart of Matthew Lansberg's); for when the priests affirmed that the sun was the architect of the universe, Chæremon presently concludes that all their narratives respecting Isis and Osiris, together with their other sacred fables, referred in part to the planets, the phases of the moon, and the revolution of the sun, and in part to the stars of the daily and nightly hemispheres and the river Nile; in a word, in all cases to physical and natural existences and never to such as might be immaterial and incorporeal. . . .

All these philosophers believe that the acts of our will and the motion of our bodies depend on those of the stars to which they are subjected, and they refer every thing to the laws of physical necessity, which they call destiny or *Fatum*, supposing a chain of causes and effects which binds, by I know not what connection, all beings together, from the meanest atom to the supremest power and primary influence of the Gods ; so that, whether in their temples or in their idols, the only subject of worship is the power of destiny. *Porphyr. Epist. ad Janebonem.*

" Indeed, as soon as men began to unite in society, it became necessary for them to multiply the means of subsistence,
and consequently to attend to agriculture : agriculture, to be
carried on with success, requires the observation and knowledge of the heavens. It was necessary to know the periodical
return of the same operations of nature, and the same phenomena in the skies ; indeed to go so far as to ascertain the
duration and succession of the seasons and the months of the
year. It was indispensable to know, in the first place, the
course of the sun, who, in his zodiacal revolution, shows himself the supreme agent of the whole creation ; then, of the
moon, who, by her phases and periods, regulates and dis-
tributes time ; then, of the stars, and even of the planets,
which by their appearance and disappearance on the horizon
and nocturnal hemisphere, marked the minutest divisions.
Finally, it was necessary to form a whole system of astronomy,* or a calendar ; and from these works there naturally
followed a new manner of considering these predominant and
governing powers.   Having observed that the productions
of the earth had a regular and constant relation with the
heavenly bodies ; that the rise, growth, and decline of each
plant kept pace with the appearance, elevation, and declination of the same star, or the same group of stars ; in short,
that the languor or activity of vegetation seemed to depend
on celestial influences, men drew from thence an idea of
action, of power, in those beings, superior to earthly bodies ;
and the stars, dispensing plenty or scarcity, became powers,
genii,† gods, authors of good and evil.

" As the state of society had already introduced a regular
hierarchy of ranks, employments and conditions, men, con-

* It continues to be repeated every day, on the indirect authority of the book of
Genesis, that astronomy was the invention of the children of Noah. It has been
gravely said, that while wandering shepherds in the plains of Shinar, they employed their leisure in composing a planetary system : as if shepherds had
occasion to know more than the polar star ; and if necessity was not the sole
motive of every invention ! If the ancient shepherds were so studious and
sagacious, how does it happen that the modern ones are so stupid, ignorant, and
inattentive ? And it is a fact that the Arabs of the desert know not so many as
six constellations, and understand not a word of astronomy.

† It appears that by the word genius, the ancients denoted a quality, a generative power ; for the following words, which are all of one family, convey this
meaning : generare, genos, genesis, genus, gens.

tinuing to reason by comparison, carried their new notions into their theology, and formed a complicated system of divinities by gradation of rank, in which the sun, as first god,* was a military chief or a political king: the moon was his wife and queen ; the planets were servants, bearers of commands, messengers ; and the multitude of stars were a nation, an army of heroes, genii, whose office was to govern the world under the orders of their chiefs. All the individuals had names, functions, attributes, drawn from their relations and influences ; and even sexes, from the gender of their appellations.†

" And as the social state had introduced certain usages and ceremonies, religion, keeping pace with the social state, adopted similar ones ; these ceremonies, at first simple and private, became public and solemn ; the offerings became rich and more numerous, and the rites more methodical ; they assigned certain places for the assemblies, and began to have chapels and temples ; they instituted officers to administer them, and these became priests and pontiffs ; they established liturgies, and sanctified certain days, and religion became a civil act, a political tie.

" But in this arrangement, religion did not change its first principles ; the idea of God was always that of physical beings, operating good or evil, that is, impressing sensations of pleasure or pain : the dogma was the knowledge of their laws, or their manner of acting ; virtue and sin, the observance or infraction of these laws ; and morality, in its native simplicity, was the judicious practice of whatever contributes to the preservation of existence, the well-being of one's self and his fellow creatures.‡

*The Sabeans, ancient and modern, says Maimonides, acknowledge a principal God, the maker and inhabitant of heaven ; but on account of his great distance they conceive him to be inaccessible ; and in imitation of the conduct of people towards their kings, they employ as mediators with him, the planets and their angels, whom they call princes and potentates, and whom they suppose to reside in those luminous bodies as in palaces or tabernacles, etc. *More-Nebuchim.*

† According as the gender of the object was in the language of the nation masculine or feminine, the Divinity who bore its name was male or female. Thus the Cappadocians called the moon God, and the sun Goddess ; a circumstance which gives to the same beings a perpetual variety in ancient mythology.

‡ We may add, says Plutarch, that these Egyptian priests always regarded the preservation of health as a point of the first importance, and as indispensably necessary to the practice of piety and the service of the gods. See his account of *Isis and Osiris*, towards the end.

" Should it be asked at what epoch this system took its
birth, we shall answer on the testimony of the monuments of
astronomy itself, that its principles appear with certainty to
have been established about seventeen thousand years ago.*
and if it be asked to what people it is to be attributed, we
shall answer that the same monuments, supported by unanimous traditions, attribute it to the first tribes of Egypt ; and
when reason finds in that country all the circumstances which
could lead to such a system ; when it finds there a zone of
sky, bordering on the tropic, equally free from the rains of the
equator and the fogs of the North ; † when it finds there a
central point of the sphere of the ancients, a salubrious climate,
a great, but manageable river, a soil fertile without art or
labor, inundated without morbid exhalations, and placed between two seas which communicate with the richest countries, it conceives that the inhabitant of the Nile, addicted to
agriculture from the nature of his soil, to geometry from the
annual necessity of measuring his lands, to commerce from

---

* The historical orator follows here the opinion of M. Dupuis, who, in his learned
memoirs concerning the *Origin of the Constellations* and *Origin of all Worship*,
has assigned many plausible reasons to prove that *Libra* was formerly the sign of
the vernal, and *Aries* of the autumnal equinox ; that is, that since the origin of
the actual astronomical system, the precession of the equinoxes has carried forward by seven signs the primitive order of the Zodiac. Now estimating the precession at about seventy years and a half to a degree, that is, 2,115 years to each
sign ; and observing that *Aries* was in its fifteenth degree, 1,447 years before
Christ, it follows that the first degree of *Libra* could not have coincided with the
vernal equinox more lately than 15,194 years before Christ ; now, if you add 1790
years since Christ, it appears that 16,984 years have elapsed since the origin of the
Zodiac. The vernal equinox coincided with the first degree of *Aries*, 2,504 years
before Christ, and with the first degree of *Taurus* 4,619 years before Christ. Now
it is to be observed, that the worship of the Bull is the principal article in the
theological creed of the Egyptians, Persians, Japanese, etc. ; from whence it
clearly follows, that some general revolution took place among these nations at
that time. The chronology of five or six thousand years in Genesis is little agreeable to this hypothesis ; but as the book of Genesis cannot claim to be considered
as a history farther back than Abraham, we are at liberty to make what arrange-
ments we please in the eternity that preceded. See on this subject the analysis
of Genesis, in the first volume of *New Researches on Ancient History;* see also
Origin of Constellations, by Dupuis, 1781 ; the *Origin of Worship*, in 3 vols. 1794,
and the *Chronological Zodiac*, 1806.

† M. Balli, in placing the first astronomers at Selingenskoy, near the Baikal
paid no attention to this twofold circumstance : it equally argues against their
being placed at Axoum on account of the rains, and the *Zimb fly* of which Mr.
Bruce speaks.

the facility of communications, to astronomy from the state of his sky, always open to observation, must have been the first to pass from the savage to the social state ; and consequently to attain the physical and moral sciences necessary to civilized life.

" It was, then, on the borders of the upper Nile, among a black race of men, that was organized the complicated system of the worship of the stars, considered in relation to the productions of the earth and the labors of agriculture ; and this first worship, characterized by their adoration under their own forms and natural attributes, was a simple proceeding of the human mind. But in a short time, the multiplicity of the objects of their relations, and their reciprocal influence, having complicated the ideas, and the signs that represented them, there followed a confusion as singular in its cause as pernicious in its effects.

III. *Third system. Worship of Symbols, or Idolatry.*

" As soon as this agricultural people began to observe the stars with attention, they found it necessary to individualize or group them ; and to assign to each a proper name, in order to understand each other in their designation. A great difficulty must have presented itself in this business : First, the heavenly bodies, similar in form, offered no distinguishing characteristics by which to denominate them ; and, secondly, the language in its infancy and poverty, had no expressions for so many new and metaphysical ideas. Necessity, the usual stimulus of genius, surmounted everything. Having remarked that in the annual revolution, the renewal and periodical appearance of terrestrial productions were constantly associated with the rising and setting of certain stars, and to their position as relative to the sun, the fundamental term of all comparison, the mind by a natural operation connected in thought these terrestrial and celestial objects, which were connected in fact ; and applying to them a common sign, it gave to the stars, and their groups, the names of the terrestrial objects to which they answered.*

* " The ancients," says Maimonides, " directing all their attention to agriculture, gave names to the stars derived from their occupation during the year." *More Neb. pars 3.*

" Thus the Ethopian of Thebes named stars of inundation, or Aquarius, those stars under which the Nile began to overflow ; * stars of the ox or the bull, those under which they began to plow ; stars of the lion, those under which that animal, driven from the desert by thirst, appeared on the banks of the Nile ; stars of the sheaf, or of the harvest virgin, those of the reaping season ; stars of the lamb, stars of the two kids, those under which these precious animals were brought forth : and thus was resolved the first part of the difficulty.

" Moreover, man having remarked in the beings which surrounded him certain qualities distinctive and proper to each species, and having thence derived a name by which to designate them, he found in the same source an ingenious mode of generalizing his ideas ; and transferring the name already invented to every thing which bore any resemblance or analogy, he enriched his language with a perpetual round of metaphors.

" Thus the same Ethiopian having observed that the return of the inundation always corresponded with the rising of a beautiful star which appeared towards the source of the Nile, and seemed to warn the husbandman against the coming waters, he compared this action to that of the animal who, by his barking, gives notice of danger, and he called this star the dog, the barker (Sirius). In the same manner he named the stars of the crab, those where the sun, having arrived at the tropic, retreated by a slow retrograde motion like the crab or cancer. He named stars of the wild goat, or Capricorn, those where the sun, having reached the highest point in his annuary tract, rests at the summit of the horary gnomon, and imitates the goat, who delights to climb the summit of the rocks. He named stars of the balance, or libra, those where the days and nights, being equal, seemed in equilibrium, like that instrument ; and stars of the scorpion, those where certain periodical winds bring vapors, burning like the venom of the scorpion. In the same manner he called by the name of rings and serpents the figured traces of the orbits of the stars and the planets, and such was the general mode of naming all the stars and even the planets, taken by groups or as

* This must have been June.

individuals, according to their relations with husbandry and terrestrial objects, and according to the analogies which each nation found between them and the objects of its particular soil and climate.*

" From this it appeared that abject and terrestrial beings became associated with the superior and powerful inhabitants of heaven ; and this association became stronger every day by the mechanism of language and the constitution of the human mind. Men would say by a natural metaphor : The bull spreads over the earth the germs of fecundity (in spring) ; he restores vegetation and plenty : the lamb (or ram) delivers the skies from the malificent powers of winter ; he saves the world from the serpent (emblem of the humid season) and restores the empire of goodness (summer, joyful season) : the scorpion pours out his poison on the earth, and scatters diseases and death. The same of all similar effects.

" This language, understood by every one, was attended at first with no inconvenience ; but in the course of time, when the calendar had been regulated, the people, who had no longer any need of observing the heavens, lost sight of the original meaning of these expressions ; and the allegories remaining in common use became a fatal stumbling block to the understanding and to reason. Habituated to associate to the symbols the ideas of their archetypes, the mind at last confounded them : then the same animals, whom fancy had transported to the skies, returned again to the earth ; but being thus returned, clothed in the livery of the stars, they claimed the stellary attributes, and imposed on their own authors. Then it was that the people, believing that they saw their gods among them, could pray to them with more convenience : they demanded from the ram of their flock the influences which might be expected from the heavenly ram ; they prayed the scorpion not to pour out his venom upon nature ; they revered the crab of the sea, the scarabeus of the mud, the fish of the river ; and by a series of corrupt but inseparable analogies, they lost themselves in a labyrinth of well connected absurdities.

* The ancients had verbs from the substantives *crab, goat, tortoise,* as the French have at present the verbs *serpenter, coquetter.* The history of all languages is nearly the same.

" Such was the origin of that ancient whimsical worship of
the animals ; such is the train of ideas by which the character
of the divinity became common to the vilest of brutes, and by
which was formed that theological system, extremely comprehensive, complicated, and learned, which, rising on the
borders of the Nile, propagated from country to country by
commerce, war, and conquest, overspread the whole of the
ancient world ; and which, modified by time, circumstances
and prejudices, is still seen entire among a hundred nations,
and remains as the essential and secret basis of the theology
of those even who despise and reject it."

Some murmurs at these words being heard from various
groups : "Yes ! " continued the orator, " hence arose, for instance, among you, nations of Africa, the adoration of your
fetiches, plants, animals, pebbles, pieces of wood, before which
your ancestors would not have had the folly to bow, if they
had not seen in them talismans endowed with the virtue of
the stars.*

" Here, ye nations of Tartary, is the origin of your marmo-
sets, and of all that train of animals with which your chamans
ornament their magical robes. This is the origin of those
figures of birds and of snakes which savage nations imprint
upon their skins with sacred and mysterious ceremonies.

" Ye inhabitants of India ! in vain you cover yourselves

---

* The ancient astrologers, says the most learned of the Jews (Maimonides),
having sacredly assigned to each planet a color, an animal, a tree, a metal, a
fruit, a plant, formed from them all a figure or representation of the star, taking
care to select for the purpose a proper moment, a fortunate day, such as the conjunction of the star, or some other favorable aspect. They conceived that by
their magic ceremonies they could introduce into those figures or idols the influences of the superior beings after which they were modeled. These were the
idols that the Chaldean-Sabeans adored ; and in the performance of their worship
they were obliged to be dressed in the proper color. The astrologers, by their
practices, thus introduced idolatry, desirous of being regarded as the dispensers
of the favors of heaven ; and as agriculture was the sole employment of the
ancients, they succeeded in persuading them that the rain and other blessings of
the seasons were at their disposal. Thus the whole art of agriculture was exercised by rules of astrology, and the priests made talismans or charms which were
to drive away locusts, flies, etc. See *Maimonides, More Nebuchim. pars 3, c. 29.*

The priests of Egypt, Persia, India, etc., pretended to bind the Gods to their
idols, and to make them come from heaven at their pleasure. They threatened
the sun and moon, if they were disobedient, to reveal the secret mysteries, to
shake the skies, etc., etc. *Euseb. Pracep. Evang. p. 198, and Jamblicus de
Mysteriis Ægypt.*

with the veil of mystery: the hawk of your god Vichenou is but one of the thousand emblems of the sun in Egypt; and your incarnations of a god in the fish, the boar, the lion, the tortoise, and all his monstrous adventures, are only the metamorphoses of the sun, who, passing through the signs of the twelve animals (or the zodiac), was supposed to assume their figures, and perform their astronomical functions.*

"People of Japan, your bull, which breaks the mundane egg, is only the bull of the zodiac, which in former times opened the seasons, the age of creation, the vernal equinox. It is the same bull Apis which Egypt adored, and which your ancestors, Jewish Rabbins, worshipped in the golden calf. This is still your bull, followers of Zoroaster, which, sacrificed in the symbolic mysteries of Mithra, poured out his blood which fertilized the earth. And ye Christians, your bull of the Apocalypse, with his wings, symbol of the air, has no other origin; and your lamb of God, sacrificed, like the bull of Mithra, for the salvation of the world, is only the same sun, in the sign of the celestial ram, which, in a later age, opening the equinox in his turn, was supposed to deliver the world from evil, that is to say, from the constellation of the serpent, from that great snake, the parent of winter, the emblem of the Ahrimanes, or Satan of the Persians, your school masters. Yes, in vain does your imprudent zeal consign idolaters to the torments of the Tartarus which they invented; the whole basis of your system is only the worship of the sun, with whose attributes you have decorated your principal personage. It is the sun which, under the name of Horus, was born, like your God, at the winter solstice, in the arms of the celestial virgin, and who passed a childhood of obscurity, indigence, and want, answering to the season of cold and frost. It is he that, under the name of Osiris, persecuted by Typhon and by the tyrants of the air, was put to death, shut up in a dark tomb, emblem of the hemisphere of winter, and afterwards, ascending from the inferior zone towards the zenith of heaven, arose again from the dead triumphant over the giants and the angels of destruction.

"Ye priests! who murmur at this relation, you wear his

* These are the very words of Jamblicus de Symbolis Ægyptiorum, c. 2, sect. 7. The sun was the grand Proteus, the universal metamorphist.

emblems all over your bodies; your tonsure is the disk of the sun; your stole is his zodiac;* your rosaries are symbols of the stars and planets. Ye pontiffs and prelates! your mitre, your crozier, your mantle are those of Osiris; and that cross, whose mystery you extol without comprehending it, is the cross of Serapis, traced by the hands of Egyptian priests on the plan of the figurative world; which, passing through the equinoxes and the tropics, became the emblem of the future life and of the resurrection, because it touched the gates of ivory and of horn, through which the soul passed to heaven."

At these words, the doctors of all the groups began to look at each other with astonishment; but no one breaking silence, the orator proceeded:

"Three principal causes concur to produce this confusion of ideas: First, the figurative expressions under which an infant language was obliged to describe the relations of objects; expressions which, passing afterwards from a limited to a general sense, and from a physical to a moral one, caused, by their ambiguities and synonymes, a great number of mistakes.

"Thus, it being first said that the sun had surmounted, or finished, twelve animals, it was thought afterwards that he had killed them, fought them, conquered them; and of this was composed the historical life of Hercules.†

"It being said that he regulated the periods of rural labor, the seed time and the harvest, that he distributed the seasons and occupations, ran through the climates and ruled the earth, etc., he was taken for a legislative king, a conquering

---

* "The Arabs," says Herodotus, "shave their heads in a circle and about the temples, in imitation of Bacchus (that is the sun), who shaves himself in this manner." Jeremiah speaks also of this custom. The tuft of hair which the Mahometans preserve, is taken also from the sun, who was painted by the Egyptians at the winter solstice, as having but a single hair upon his head. . . .

The robes of the goddess of Syria and of Diana of Ephesus, from whence are borrowed the dress of the priests, have the twelve animals of the zodiac painted on them. . . . .

Rosaries are found upon all the Indian idols, constructed more than four thousand years ago, and their use in the East has been universal from time immemorial. . . . .

The *crosier* is precisely the staff of Bootes or Osiris. (See plate.)

All theLamas wear the *mitre* or cap in the shape of a cone, which was an emblem of the sun.

† See the memoir of Dupuis *on the Origin of the Constellations*, before cited.

warrior ; and they framed from this the history of Osiris, of Bacchus, and others of that description.

" Having said that a planet entered into a sign, they made of this conjunction a marriage, an adultery, an incest.* Having said that the planet was hid or buried, when it came back to light, and ascended to its exaltation, they said that it had died, risen again, was carried into heaven, etc.

" A second cause of confusion was the material figures themselves, by which men first painted thoughts ; and which, under the name of hieroglyphics, or sacred characters, were the first invention of the mind. Thus, to give warning of the inundation, and of the necessity of guarding against it, they painted a boat, the ship Argo ; to express the wind, they painted the wing of a bird ; to designate the season, or the month, they painted the bird of passage, the insect, or the animal which made its appearance at that period ; to describe the winter, they painted a hog or a serpent, which delight in humid places, and the combination of these figures carried the known sense of words and phrases.† But as this sense

* These are the very words of Plutarch in his account of Isis and Osiris. The Hebrews say, in speaking of the generations of the Patriarchs, *et ingressus est in eam*. From this continual equivoke of ancient language, proceeds every mistake.

† The reader will doubtless see with pleasure some examples of ancient hiero-glyphics.

" The Egyptians (says Hor-appolo) represent eternity by the figures of the sun and moon. They designate the world by the blue serpent with yellow scales (stars, it is the Chinese Dragon). If they were desirous of expressing the year, they drew a picture of Isis, who is also in their language called *Sothis*, or dog-star, one of the first constellations, by the rising of which the year commences ; its inscription at Sais was, *It is I that rise in the constellation of the Dog*.

" They also represent the year by a palm tree, and the month by one of its branches, because it is the nature of this tree to produce a branch every month. They farther represent it by the fourth part of an acre of land." The whole acre divided into four denotes the bissextile period of four years. The abbreviation of this figure of a field in four divisions, is manifestly the letter *hä* or *hèt*, the seventh in the Samaritan alphabet ; and in general all the letters of the alphabet are merely astronomical hieroglyphics ; and it is for this reason that the mode of writing is from right to left, like the march of the stars. — " They denote a prophet by the image of a dog, because the dog star (*Anoubis*) by its rising gives notice of the inundation. *Noubi* in Hebrew signifies prophet. — They represent inunda-tion by a lion, because it takes place under that sign : and hence, says Plutarch, the custom of placing at the gates of temples figures of lions with water issuing from their mouths. — They express the idea of God and destiny by a star. They also represent God, says Porphyry, by a black stone, because his nature is dark and obscure. All white things express the celestial and luminous Gods : all cir-cular ones the world, the moon, the sun the orbits ; all semicircular ones, as bows

could not be fixed with precision, as the number of these

and crescents are descriptive of the moon. Fire and the Gods of Olympus they
represent by pyramids and obelisks (the name of the sun, *Baal*, is found in this
latter word) : the sun by a cone (the mitre of Osiris) : the earth, by a cylinder
(which revolves) : the generative power of the air by the *phalus*, and that of the
earth by a triangle, emblem of the female organ. *Euseb. Præcep. Evang. p. 98.*
"Clay, says Jamblicus *de Symbolis*, sect. 7, c. 2. denotes matter, the generative
and nutrimental power, every thing which receives the warmth and fermentation
of life."

"A man sitting upon the *Lotos* or *Nenuphar*, represents the moving spirit (the
sun) which, in like manner as that plant lives in the water without any communication with clay, exists equally distinct from matter, swimming in empty space,
resting on itself: it is round also in all its parts, like the leaves, the flowers, and
the fruit of the Lotos. (Brama has the eyes of the Lotos, says Chasler Nesdirsen,
to denote his intelligence : his eye swims over every thing, like the flower of the
Lotos on the waters.) A man at the helm of a ship, adds Jamblicus, is descriptive
of the sun which governs all. And Porphyry tells us that the sun is also represented by a man in a ship resting upon an amphibious crocodile (emblem of air
and water).

"At Elephantine they worshipped the figure of a man in a sitting posture,
painted blue, having the head of a ram, and the horns of a goat which encom-
passed a disk ; all which represented the sun and moon's conjunction at the sign
of the ram ; the blue color denoting the power of the moon, at the period of junction, to raise water into the clouds. *Euseb. Præcep. Evang. p. 116.*

" The hawk is an emblem of the sun and of light, on account of his rapid flight
and his soaring into the highest regions of the air where light abounds.

A fish is the emblem of aversion, and the *Hippopotamus* of violence, because it
is said to kill its father and to ravish its mother. Hence, says Plutarch, the emblematical inscription of the temple of Sais, where we see painted on the vestibule,
1. A child, 2. An old man, 3. A hawk, 4. A fish, 5. A hippopotamus; which
signify, 1. Entrance, into life, 2. Departure, 3. God, 4. Hates, 5. Injustice. See
Isis and Osiris.

" The Egyptians, adds he, represent the world by a Scarabeus, because this
insect pushes, in a direction contrary to that in which it proceeds, a ball containing its eggs, just as the heaven of the fixed stars causes the revolution of the sun,
(the yolk of an egg) in an opposite direction to its own.

" They represent the world also by the number *five*, being that of the elements,
which, says Diodorus, are earth, water, air, fire, and ether, or *spiritus*. The
Indians have the same number of elements, and according to Macrobius's mys-
tics, they are the supreme God, or *primum mobile*, the intelligence, or *mens*, born
of him, the soul of the world which proceeds from him, the celestial spheres, and
all things terrestrial. Hence, adds Plutarch, the analogy between the Greek
pente, five, and *pan* all.

" The ass," says he again, " is the emblem of Typhon, because like that animal
he is of a reddish color. Now Typhon signifies whatever is of a mirey or clayey
nature ; (and in Hebrew I find the three words *clay*, *red*, and *ass* to be formed
from the same root *hamr*. Jamblicus has farther told us that clay was the emblem
of matter ; and he elsewhere adds, that all evil and corruption proceeded from
matter ; which compared with the phrase of Macrobius, *all is perishable*, liable to
change in the celestial sphere, gives us the theory, first physical, then moral, of
the system of good and evil of the ancients."

figures and their combinations became excessive, and over-burdened the memory, the immediate consequence was confusion and false interpretations. Genius afterwards having invented the more simple art of applying signs to sounds, of which the number is limited, and painting words, instead of thoughts, alphabetical writing thus threw into disuetude hieroglyphical painting; and its signification, falling daily into oblivion, gave rise to a multitude of illusions, ambiguities, and errors.

"Finally, a third cause of confusion was the civil organization of ancient states. When the people began to apply themselves to agriculture, the formation of a rural calendar, requiring a continued series of astronomical observations, it became necessary to appoint certain individuals charged with the functions of watching the appearance and disappearance of certain stars, to foretell the return of the inundation, of certain winds, of the rainy season, the proper time to sow every kind of grain. These men, on account of their service, were exempt from common labor, and the society provided for their maintenance. With this provision, and wholly employed in their observations, they soon became acquainted with the great phenomena of nature, and even learned to penetrate the secret of many of her operations. They discovered the movement of the stars and planets, the coincidence of their phases and returns with the productions of the earth and the action of vegetation; the medicinal and nutritive properties of plants and fruits; the action of the elements, and their reciprocal affinities. Now, as there was no other method of communicating the knowledge of these discoveries but the laborious one of oral instruction, they transmitted it only to their relations and friends, it followed therefore that all science and instruction were confined to a few families, who, arrogating it to themselves as an exclusive privilege, assumed a professional distinction, a corporation spirit, fatal to the public welfare. This continued succession of the same researches and the same labors, hastened, it is true, the progress of knowledge; but by the mystery which accompanied it, the people were daily plunged in deeper shades, and became more superstitious and more enslaved. Seeing their fellow mortals produce certain phenomena, announce, as at pleasure,

eclipses and comets, heal diseases, and handle venomous
serpents, they thought them in alliance with celestial powers;
and, to obtain the blessings and avert the evils which they
expected from above, they took them for mediators and interpreters; and thus became established in the bosom of every
state sacrilegious corporations of hypocritical and deceitful
men, who centered all powers in themselves; and the priests,
being at once astronomers, theologians, naturalists, physicians,
magicians, interpreters of the gods, oracles of men, and rivals
of kings, or their accomplices, established, under the name
of religion, an empire of mystery and a monopoly of instruction, which to this day have ruined every nation. . . ."

Here the priests of all the groups interrupted the orator,
and with loud cries accused him of impiety, irreligion, blasphemy; and endeavored to cut short his discourse; but the
legislator observing that this was only an exposition of historical facts, which, if false or forged, would be easily refuted;
that hitherto the declaration of every opinion had been free,
and without this it would be impossible to discover the truth,
the orator proceeded:

"Now, from all these causes, and from the continual associations of ill-assorted ideas, arose a mass of disorders in
theology, in morals, and in traditions; first, because the animals represented the stars, the characters of the animals, their
appetites, their sympathies, their aversions, passed over to
the gods, and were supposed to be their actions; thus, the
god Ichneumon made war against the god Crocodile; the
god Wolf liked to eat the god Sheep; the god Ibis devoured
the god Serpent; and the deity became a strange, capricious,
and ferocious being, whose idea deranged the judgment of
man, and corrupted his morals and his reason.

"Again, because in the spirit of their worship every family,
every nation, took for its special patron a star or a constellation, the affections or antipathies of the symbolic animal were
transferred to its sectaries; and the partisans of the god Dog
were enemies to those of the god Wolf;* those who adored

* These are properly the words of Plutarch, who relates that those various wor-
ships were given by a king of Egypt to the different towns to disunite and enslave
them, and these kings had been taken from the cast of priests. See *Isis and
Osiris.*

the god Ox had an abhorrence to those who ate him ; and religion became the source of hatred and hostility,— the senseless cause of frenzy and superstition.

" Besides, the names of those animal-stars having, for this same reason of patronage, been conferred on countries, nations, mountains, and rivers, these objects were taken for gods, and hence followed a mixture of geographical, historical, and mythological beings, which confounded all traditions.

" Finally, by the analogy of actions which were ascribed to them, the god-stars, having been taken for men, for heroes, for kings, kings and heroes took in their turn the actions of gods for models, and by imitation became warriors, conquerors, proud, lascivious, indolent, sanguinary ; and religion consecrated the crimes of despots, and perverted the principles of government.

IV. *Fourth system. Worship of two Principles, or Dualism.*

" In the mean time, the astronomical priests, enjoying peace and abundance in their temples, made every day new progress in the sciences, and the system of the world unfolding gradually to their view, they raised successively various hypotheses as to its agents and effects, which became so many theological systems.

" The voyages of the maritime nations and the caravans of the nomads of Asia and Africa, having given them a knowledge of the earth from the Fortunate Islands to Serica, and from the Baltic to the sources of the Nile, the comparison of the phenomena of the various zones taught them the rotundity of the earth, and gave birth to a new theory. Having remarked that all the operations of nature during the annual period were reducible to two principal ones, that of producing and that of destroying ; that on the greater part of the globe these two operations were performed in the intervals of the two equinoxes ; that is to say, during the six months of summer every thing was procreating and multiplying, and that during winter everything languished and almost died ; they supposed in Nature two contrary powers, which were in a continual state of contention and exertion ; and considering the celestial sphere in this view, they divided the images

which they figured upon it into two halves or hemispheres;
so that the constellations which were on the summer heaven
formed a direct and superior empire; and those which were
on the winter heaven composed an antipode and inferior empire. Therefore, as the constellations of summer accompanied
the season of long, warm, and unclouded days, and that of
fruits and harvests, they were considered as the powers of
light, fecundity, and creation; and, by a transition from a
physical to a moral sense, they became genii, angels of science,
of beneficence, of purity and virtue. And as the constellations
of winter were connected with long nights and polar fogs,
they were the genii of darkness, of destruction, of death; and
by transition, angels of ignorance, of wickedness, of sin and
vice. By this arrangement the heaven was divided into two
domains, two factions; and the analogy of human ideas
already opened a vast field to the errors of imagination; but
the mistake and the illusion were determined, if not occasioned
by a particular circumstance. (Observe plate *Astrological
Heaven of the Ancients*.)

" In the projection of the celestial sphere, as traced by the
astronomical priests,* the zodiac and the constellations, dis-

---

* The ancient priests had three kinds of spheres, which it may be useful to make
known to the reader.

"We read in Eusebius," says Porphyry, "that Zoroaster was the first who,
having fixed upon a cavern pleasantly situated in the mountains adjacent to
Persia, formed the idea of consecrating it to Mithra (the sun) creator and father
of all things: that is to say, having made in this cavern several geometrical divisions, representing the seasons and the elements, he imitated on a small scale the
order and disposition of the universe by Mithra. After Zoroaster, it became a
custom to consecrate caverns for the celebration of mysteries: so that in like
manner as temples were dedicated to the Gods, rural altars to heroes and terrestrial deities, etc., subterranean abodes to infernal deities, so caverns and grottoes
were consecrated to the world, to the universe, and to the nymphs: and from
hence Pythagoras and Plato borrowed the idea of calling the earth a cavern, a
cave, *de Antro Nympharum.*

Such was the first projection of the sphere in relief; though the Persians give
the honor of the invention to Zoroaster, it is doubtless due to the Egyptians; for
we may suppose from this projection being the most simple that it was the most
ancient; the caverns of Thebes, full of similar pictures, tend to strengthen this
opinion.

The following was the second projection: "The prophets or hierophants," says
Bishop Synnesius, "who had been initiated in the mysteries, do not permit the
common workmen to form idols or images of the Gods; but they descend themselves into the sacred caves, where they have concealed coffers containing certain
spheres upon which they construct those images secretly and without the

posed in circular order, presented their halves in diametrical opposition ; the hemisphere of winter, antipode of that of summer, was adverse, contrary, opposed to it. By a continual metaphor, these words acquired a moral sense ; and the adverse genii, or angels, became revolted enemies.* From that moment all the astronomical history of the constellations was changed into a political history ; the heavens became a human state, where things happened as on the earth. Now, as the earthly states, the greater part despotic, had already their monarchs, and as the sun was apparently the monarch of the skies, the summer hemisphere (empire of light) and its constellations (a nation of white angels) had for king an enlightened God, a creator intelligent and good. And as every rebel faction must have its chief, the heaven of winter, the subterranean empire of darkness and woe, and its stars, a nation of black angels, giants and demons, had for their chief a malignant genius, whose character was applied by different people to the constellation which to them was the most remarkable. In Egypt it was at first the Scorpion, first zodiacal sign after Libra, and for a long time chief of the winter signs ; then it was the Bear, or the polar Ass, called Typhon, that is to say,

knowledge of the people, who despise simple and natural things and wish for prodigies and fables." (Syn. in Calvit.) That is, the ancient priests had armillary spheres like ours ; and this passage, which so well agrees with that of Chæremon, gives us the key to all their theological astrology.

Lastly, they had flat models of the nature of Plate V, with the difference that they were of a very complicated nature, having every fictitious division of decan and subdecan, with the hieroglyphic signs of their influence. Kircher has given us a copy of one of them in his *Egyptian Œdipus*, and Gybelin a figured fragment in his book of the calendar (under the name of the *Egyptian Zodiac*). The ancient Egyptians, says the astrologer Julius Firmicus, (*Astron. lib. ii.* and *lib. iv., c. 16*), divide each sign of the Zodiac into three sections ; and each section was under the direction of an imaginary being whom they called decan or chief of ten ; so that there were three decans a month, and thirty-six a year. Now these decans, who were also called Gods (*Theoi*), regulated the destinies of mankind — and they were placed particularly in certain stars. They afterwards imagined in every ten three other Gods, whom they called arbiters ; so that there were nine for every month, and these were farther divided into an infinite number of powers. The Persians and Indians made their spheres on similar plans ; and if a picture thereof were to be drawn from the description given by Scaliger at the end of Manilius, we should find in it a complete explanation of their hieroglyphics, for every article forms one.

* If it was for this reason the Persians always wrote the name of Ahrimanes inverted thus : ˙sǝuɐɯıɹɥɐ

deluge,* on account of the rains which deluge the earth
during the dominion of that star. At a later period,† in Persia,
it was the Serpent, who, under the name of Ahrimanes, formed
the basis of the system of Zoroaster ; and it is the same, O
Christians and Jews! that has become your serpent of Eve
(the celestial virgin,) and that of the cross ; in both cases it is
the emblem of Satan, the enemy and great adversary of the
Ancient of Days, sung by Daniel.

" In Syria, it was the hog or wild boar, enemy of Adonis ;
because in that country the functions of the Northen Bear
were performed by the animal whose inclination for mire and
dirt was emblematic of winter. And this is the reason, followers of Moses and Mahomet! that you hold him in horror, in
imitation of the priests of Memphis and Balbec, who detested
him as the murderer of their God, the sun. This likewise, O
Indians! is the type of your Chib-en ; and it has been likewise
the Pluto of your brethren, the Romans and Greeks ; in like
manner, your Brama, God the creator, is only the Persian
Ormuzd, and the Egyptian Osiris, whose very name expresses
creative power, producer of forms. And these gods received
a worship analogous to their attributes, real or imaginary ;
which worship was divided into two branches, according to
their characters. The good god receives a worship of love
and joy, from which are derived all religious acts of gaiety,
such as festivals, dances, banquets, offerings of flowers, milk,
honey, perfumes ; in a word, everything grateful to the senses

* Typhon, pronounced Touphon by the Greeks, is precisely the *touphan* of the
Arabs, which signifies deluge ; and these deluges in mythology are nothing more
than winter and the rains, or the overflowing of the Nile: as their pretended fires
which are to destroy the world, are simply the summer season. And it is for this
reason that Aristotle (*De Meteor, lib.* I. *c. xiv*), says, that the winter of the great
cyclic year is a deluge; and its summer a conflagration. " The Egyptians," says
Porphyry, " employ every year a talisman in remembrance of the world: at the
summer solstice they mark their houses, flocks and trees with red, supposing that
on that day the whole world had been set on fire. It was also at the same period
that they celebrated the pyrric or fire dance." And this illustrates the origin of
purification by fire and by water ; for having denominated the tropic of Cancer
the gate of heaven, and the genial heat of celestial fire, and that of Capricorn the
gate of deluge or of water, it was imagined that the spirit or souls who passed
through these gates in their way to and from heaven, were *roasted* or *bathed:*
hence the baptism of Mithra ; and the passage through flames, observed throughout the East long before Moses.

† That is when the ram became the equinoctial sign, or rather when the alteration of the skies showed that it was no longer the bull.

and to the soul.* The evil god, on the contrary, received a worship of fear and pain ; whence originated all religious acts of the gloomy sort,† tears, desolations, mournings, self-denials, bloody offerings, and cruel sacrifices.

"Hence arose that distinction of terrestrial beings into pure and impure, sacred and abominable, according as their species were of the number of the constellations of one of these two gods, and made part of his domain ; and this produced, on the one hand, the superstitions concerning pollutions and purifications ; and, on the other, the pretended efficacious virtues of amulets and talismans.

"You conceive now," continued the orator, addressing himself to the Persians, the Indians, the Jews, the Christians, the Mussulmans, "you conceive the origin of those ideas of battles and rebellions, which equally abound in all your mythologies. You see what is meant by white and black angels, your cherubim and seraphim, with heads of eagles, of lions, or of bulls ; your deus, devils, demons, with horns of goats and tails of serpents ; your thrones and dominions, ranged in seven orders or gradations, like the seven spheres of the planets ; all beings acting the same parts, and endowed with the same attributes in your *Vedas*, *Bibles*, and *Zend-avestas*, whether they have for chiefs Ormuzd or Brama, Typhon or Chiven, Michael or Satan ;—whether they appear under the form of giants with a hundred arms and feet of serpents, or that of gods metamorphosed into lions, storks, bulls or cats, as they are in the sacred fables of the Greeks and Egyptians.

* All the ancient festivals respecting the return and exaltation of the sun were of this description : hence the *hilaria* of the Roman calendar at the period of the passage, Pascha, of the vernal equinox. The dances were imitations of the march of the planets. Those of the Dervises still represent it to this day.

† "Sacrifices of blood," says Porphyry, "were only offered to Demons and evil Genii to avert their wrath. Demons are fond of blood, humidity, stench." *Apud. Euseb. Præp. Ev., p. 173.*

"The Egyptians," says Plutarch, "only offer bloody victims to Typhon. They sacrifice to him a red ox, and the animal immolated is held in execration and loaded with all the sins of the people." The goat of Moses. See *Isis and Osiris.*

Strabo says, speaking of Moses, and the Jews, "Circumcision and the prohibition of certain kinds of meat sprung from superstition." And I observe, respecting the ceremony of circumcision, that its object was to take from the symbol of Osiris, (*Phallus*) the pretended obstacle to fecundity : an obstacle which bore the seal of Typhon, "whose nature," says Plutarch, "is made up of all that *hinders, opposes, causes obstruction.*"

You perceive the successive filiation of these ideas, and how, in proportion to their remoteness from their source, and as the minds of men became refined, their gross forms have been polished, and rendered less disgusting.

" But in the same manner as you have seen the system of two opposite principles or gods arise from that of symbols, interwoven into its texture, your attention shall now be called to a new system which has grown out of, this, and to which this has served in its turn as the basis and support.

V. *Moral and Mystical Worship, or System of a Future State.*

" Indeed, when the vulgar heard speak of a new heaven and another world, they soon gave a body to these fictions ; they erected therein a real theatre of action, and their notions of astronomy and geography served to strengthen, if not to originate, this illusion.

" On the one hand, the Phœnician navigators who passed the pillars of Hercules, to fetch the tin of Thule and the amber of the Baltic, related that at the extremity of the world, the end of the ocean (the Mediterranean), where the sun sets for the countries of Asia, were the Fortunate Islands, the abode of eternal spring ; and beyond were the hyperborean regions, placed under the earth (relatively to the tropics) where reigned an eternal night.*   From these stories, misunderstood, and no doubt confusedly related, the imagination of the people composed the Elysian fields,† regions of delight, placed in a world below, having their heaven, their sun, and their stars ; and Tartarus, a place of darkness, humidity, mire, and frost.   Now, as man, inquisitive of that which he knows not, and desirous of protracting his existence, had already interrogated himself concerning what was to become of him after his death, as he had early reasoned on the principle of life which animates his body, and which leaves it without deforming it, and as he had imagined airy substances, phantoms, and shades, he fondly believed that he should continue, in the subterranean world, that life which it was too painful for him to lose ; and these lower regions seemed commodious for the

---

* Nights of six months duration.

† *Alis*, in the Phœnician or Hebrew language signifies dancing and joyous.

reception of the beloved objects which he could not willingly resign.

" On the other hand, the astrological and geological priests told such stories and made such descriptions of their heavens, as accorded perfectly well with these fictions. Having, in their metaphorical language, called the equinoxes and solstices the gates of heaven, the entrance of the seasons, they explained these terrestrial phenomena by saying, that through the gate of horn (first the bull, afterwards the ram) and through the gate of Cancer, descended the vivifying fires which give life to vegetation in the spring, and the aqueous spirits which bring, at the solstice, the inundation of the Nile ; that through the gate of ivory (Libra, formerly Sagittarius, or the bowman) and that of Capricorn, or the urn, the emanations or influences of the heavens returned to their source, and reascended to their origin ; and the Milky Way, which passed through the gates of the solstices, seemed to be placed there to serve them as a road or vehicle.* Besides, in their atlas, the celestial scene presented a river (the Nile, designated by the windings of the hydra), a boat, (the ship Argo) and the dog Sirius, both relative to this river, whose inundation they foretold. These circumstances, added to the preceding, and still further explaining them, increased their probability, and to arrive at Tartarus or Elysium, souls were obliged to cross the rivers Styx and Acheron in the boat of the ferryman Charon, and to pass through the gates of horn or ivory, guarded by the dog Cerberus. Finally, these inventions were applied to a civil use, and thence received a further consistency.

" Having remarked that in their burning climate the putrefaction of dead bodies was a cause of pestilential diseases, the Egyptians, in many of their towns, had adopted the practice of burying their dead beyond the limits of the inhabited country, in the desert of the West. To go there, it was necessary to pass the channels of the river, and consequently to be received into a boat, and pay something to the ferryman, without which the body, deprived of sepulture, must have been the prey of wild beasts. This custom suggested to the civil and religious legislators the means of a powerful influence on manners ; and, addressing uncultivated and ferocious men

* See *Macrob. Som. Scrip.* c. 12.

with the motives of filial piety and a reverence for the dead, they established, as a necessary condition, their undergoing a previous trial, which should decide whether the deceased merited to be admitted to the rank of the family in the black city. Such an idea accorded too well with all the others, not to be incorporated with them: the people soon adopted it; and hell had its Minos and its Rhadamanthus, with the wand, the bench, the ushers, and the urn, as in the earthly and civil state. It was then that God became a moral and political being, a lawgiver to men, and so much the more to be dreaded, as this supreme legislator, this final judge, was inaccessible and invisible. Then it was that this fabulous and mythological world, composed of such odd materials and disjointed parts, became a place of punishments and of rewards, where divine justice was supposed to correct what was vicious and erroneous in the judgment of men. This spiritual and mystical system acquired the more credit, as it took possession of man by all his natural inclinations. The oppressed found in it the hope of indemnity, and the consolation of future vengeance; the oppressor, expecting by rich offerings to purchase his impunity, formed out of the errors of the vulgar an additional weapon of oppression; the chiefs of nations, the kings and priests, found in this a new instrument of domination by the privilege which they reserved to themselves of distributing the favors and punishments of the great judge, according to the merit or demerit of actions, which they took care to characterize as best suited their system.

"This, then, is the manner in which an invisible and imaginary world has been introduced into the real and visible one; this is the origin of those regions of pleasure and pain, of which you Persians have made your regenerated earth, your city of resurrection, placed under the equator, with this singular attribute, that in it the blessed cast no shade.* Of these

---

* There is on this subject a passage in Plutarch, so interesting and explanatory of the whole of this system, that we shall cite it entire. Having observed that the theory of good and evil had at all times occupied the attention of philosophers and theologians, he adds: "Many suppose there to be two gods of opposite inclinations,—one delighting in good, the other in evil; the first of these is called particularly by the name of God, the second by that of Genius or Demon. Zoroaster has denominated them Oromaze and Ahrimanes, and has said that of whatever falls under the cognizance of our senses, light is the best representation of

materials, Jews and Christians, disciples of the Persians, have you formed your New Jerusalem of the Apocalypse, your paradise, your heaven, copied in all its parts from the astrological heaven of Hermes : and your hell, ye Mussulmans, your bottomless pit, surmounted by a bridge, your balance for weighing souls and good works, your last judgment by the angels Monkir and Nekir, are likewise modeled from the mysterious ceremonies of the cave of Mithras ; * and your heaven differs not in the least from that of Osiris, of Ormuzd, and of Brama.

the one, and darkness and ignorance of the other. He adds, that Mithra is an intermediate being, and it is for this reason the Persians call Mithra the *mediator* or *intermediator*. Each of these Gods has distinct plants and animals consecrated to him : for example, dogs, birds and hedge-hogs belong to the good Genius, and all aquatic animals to the evil one.

" The Persians also say, that Oromaze was born or formed out of the purest light ; Ahrimanes, on the contrary, out of the thickest darkness : that Oromaze made six gods as good as himself, and Ahrimanes opposed to them six wicked ones : that Oromaze afterwards multiplied himself threefold (Hermes trismegistus) and removed to a distance as remote from the sun as the sun is remote from the earth ; that he there formed stars, and, among others, Sirius, which he placed in the heavens as a guard and sentinel. He made also twenty-four other Gods, which he inclosed in an egg ; but Ahrimanes created an equal number on his part, who broke the egg, and from that moment good and evil were mixed (in the universe). But Ahrimanes is one day to be conquered, and the earth to be made equal and smooth, that all men may live happy.

" Theopompus adds, from the books of the Magi, that one of these Gods reigns in turn every three thousand years, during which the other is kept in subjection ; that they afterwards contend with equal weapons during a similar portion of time, but that in the end the evil Genius will fall (never to rise again). Then men will become happy, and their bodies cast no shade. The God who mediates all these things reclines at present in repose, waiting till he shall be pleased to execute them." See *Isis and Osiris*.

There is an apparent allegory through the whole of this passage. The egg is the fixed sphere, the world : the six Gods of Oromaze are the six signs of summer, those of Ahrimanes the six signs of winter. The forty-eight other Gods are the forty-eight constellations of the ancient sphere, divided equally between Ahrimanes and Oromaze. The office of Sirius, as guard and sentinel, tells us that the origin of these ideas was Egyptian : finally, the expression that the earth is to become equal and smooth, and that the bodies of happy beings are to cast no shade, proves that the equator was considered as their true paradise.

* In the caves which priests every where constructed, they celebrated mysteries which consisted (says Origen against Celsus) in imitating the motion of the stars, the planets and the heavens. The initiated took the name of constellations, and assumed the figures of animals. One was a lion, another a raven, and a third a ram. Hence the use of masks in the first representation of the drama. See *Ant. Dev.ilé*, vol. iii., p. 244. " In the mysteries of Ceres the chief in the procession called himself the creator ; the bearer of the torch was denominated the sun ; the person nearest to the altar, the moon ; the herald or deacon, Mercury. In Egypt

VI. *Sixth System.   The Animated World, or Worship of the Universe under diverse Emblems.*

" While the nations were wandering in the dark labyrinth of mythology and fables, the physical priests, pursuing their studies and enquiries into the order and disposition of the universe, came to new conclusions, and formed new systems concerning powers and first causes.

" Long confined to simple appearances, they saw nothing in the movement of the stars but an unknown play of luminous bodies rolling round the earth, which they believed the central point of all the spheres ; but as soon as they discovered the rotundity of our planet, the consequences of this first fact led them to new considerations ; and from induction to induction they rose to the highest conceptions in astronomy and physics.

" Indeed, after having conceived this luminous idea, that the terrestrial globe is a little circle inscribed in the greater circle of the heavens, the theory of concentric circles came naturally into their hypothesis, to determine the unknown circle of the terrestrial globe by certain known portions of the celestial circle ; and the measurement of one or more degrees of the meridian gave with precision the whole circumference. Then, taking for a compass the known diameter of the earth, some fortunate genius applied it with a bold hand to the boundless orbits of the heavens ; and man, the inhabitant of a grain of sand, embracing the infinite distances of the stars, launches into the immensity of space and the eternity of time : there he is presented with a new order of the universe of which the atom-globe which he inhabited appeared no longer to be the centre; this important post was reserved to the enormous mass of the sun ; and that body became the flaming pivot of eight surrounding spheres, whose movements were henceforth subjected to precise calculations.

there was a festival in which the men and women represented the year, the age, the seasons, the different parts of the day, and they walked in precession after Bacchus. Athen. lib. v., ch. 7. In the cave of Mithra was a ladder with seven steps, representing the seven spheres of the planets, by means of which souls ascended and descended. This is precisely the ladder in Jacob's vision, which shows that at that epocha the whole system was formed. There is in the French king's library a superb volume of pictures of the Indian Gods, in which the ladder is represented with the souls of men mounting it."

" It was indeed a great effort for the human mind to have undertaken to determine the disposition and order of the great engines of nature; but not content with this first effort, it still endeavored to develop the mechanism, and discover the origin and the instinctive principle. Hence, engaged in the abstract and metaphysical nature of motion and its first cause, of the inherent or incidental properties of matter, its successive forms and its extension, that is to say, of time and space unbounded, the physical theologians lost themselves in a chaos of subtile reasoning and scholastic controversy.*

" In the first place, the action of the sun on terrestrial bodies, teaching them to regard his substance as a pure and elementary fire, they made it the focus and reservoir of an ocean of igneous and luminous fluid, which, under the name of ether, filled the universe and nourished all beings. Afterwards, having discovered, by a physical and attentive analysis, this same fire, or another perfectly resembling it, in the composition of all bodies, and having perceived it to be the essential agent of that spontaneous movement which is called life in animals and vegetation in plants, they conceived the mechanism and harmony of the universe, as of a homogeneous whole, of one identical body, whose parts, though distant, had nevertheless an intimate relation; † and the world was a living being, animated by the organic circulation of an igneous and even electrical fluid,‡ which, by a term of comparison borrowed first from men and animals, had the sun for a heart and a focus.§

" From this time the physical theologians seem to have

* Consult the *Ancient Astronomy* of M. Bailly, and you will find our assertions respecting the knowledge of the priests amply proved.

† These are the very words of Jamblicus. *De Myst. Egypt.*

‡ The more I consider what the ancients understood by ether and spirit, and what the Indians call *akache*, the stronger do I find the analogy between it and the electrial fluid. A luminous fluid, principle of warmth and motion, pervading the universe, forming the matter of the stars, having small round particles, which insinuate themselves into bodies, and fill them by dilating itself, be their extent what it will. What can more strongly resemble electricity?

§ Natural philosophers, says Macrobius, call the sun the heart of the world. *Som. Scrip.* c. 20. The Egyptians, says Plutarch, call the East the face, the North the right side, and the South the left side of the world, because there the heart is placed. They continually compare the universe to a man; and hence the celebrated microcosm of the Alchymists. We observe, by the bye, that the

divided into several classes ; one class, grounding itself on
these principles resulting from observation ; that nothing can
be annihilated in the world ; that the elements are indestructi-
ble ; that they change their combinations but not their nature ;
that the life and death of beings are but the different modifica-
tions of the same atoms ; that matter itself possesses properties which give rise to all its modes of existence ; that the
world is eternal,* or unlimited in space and duration ; said
that the whole universe was God ; and, according to them,
God was a being, effect and cause, agent and patient, moving
principle and thing moved, having for laws the invariable
properties that constitute fatality; and this class conveyed
their idea by the emblem of Pan (the great whole) ; or of Jupiter,
with a forehead of stars, body of planets, and feet of animals ;
or of the Orphic Egg,† whose yolk, suspended in the center
of a liquid, surrounded by a vault, represented the globe of
the sun, swimming in ether in the midst of the vault of
heaven ; ‡ sometimes by a great round serpent, representing
the heavens where they placed the moving principle, and for
that reason of an azure color, studded with spots of gold, (the
stars) devouring his tail—that is, folding and unfolding himself eternally, like the revolutions of the spheres ; sometimes
by that of a man, having his feet joined together and tied,
to signify immutable existence, wrapped in a cloak of all
colors, like the face of nature, and bearing on his head a

Alchymists, Cabalists, Free-masons, Magnetisers, Martinists, and every other
such sort of visionaries, are but the mistaken disciples of this ancient school: we
say mistaken, because, in spite of their pretensions, the thread of the occult
science is broken.

* See the *Pythagorean, Ocellus Lacunus.*

† *Vide Œdip. Ægypt.* Tome II., page 205.

‡ This comparison of the sun with the yolk of an egg refers: 1. To its round
and yellow figure; 2. To its central situation; 3. To the germ or principle of life
contained in the yolk. May not the oval form of the egg allude to the elipsis of
the orbs? I am inclined to this opinion. The word Orphic offers a farther observation. Macrobius says (*Som. Scrip.* c. 14. and c. 20), that the sun is the brain of
the universe, and that it is from analogy that the skull of a human being is round,
like the planet, the seat of intelligence. Now the word Œrph signifies in Hebrew
the brain and its seat (cervix): Orpheus, then, is the same as Bedou or Baits;
and the Bonzes are those very Orphics which Plutarch represents as quacks, who
ate no meat, vended talismans and little stones, and deceived individuals, and
even governments themselves. See a learned memoir of *Freret sur les Orphiques,
Acad. des Inscrp. vol. 25, in quarto.*

sphere of gold,* emblem of the sphere of the stars; or by that of another man, sometimes seated on the flower of the lotos borne on the abyss of waters, sometimes lying on a pile of twelve cushions, denoting the twelve celestial signs. And here, Indians, Japanese, Siamese, Tibetans, and Chinese, is the theology, which, founded by the Egyptians and transmitted to you, is preserved in the pictures which you compose of Brama, of Beddou, of Somona-Kodom, of Omito. This, ye Jews and Christians, is likewise the opinion of which you have preserved a part in your God moving on the face of the waters, by an allusion to the wind † which, at the beginning of the world, that is, the departure of the sun from the sign of Cancer, announced the inundation of the Nile, and seemed to prepare the creation.

VII. *Seventh System. Worship of the* SOUL *of the* WORLD, *that is to say, the Element of Fire, vital Principle of the Universe.*

" But others, disgusted at the idea of a being at once effect and cause, agent and patient, and uniting contrary natures in the same nature, distinguished the moving principle from the thing moved; and premising that matter in itself was inert, they pretended that its properties were communicated to it by a distinct agent, of which itself was only the cover or the case. This agent was called by some the igneous principle, known to be the author of all motion; by others it was supposed to be the fluid called ether, which was thought more active and subtile; and, as in animals the vital and moving principle was called a soul, a spirit, and as they reasoned constantly by comparisons, especially those drawn from human beings, they gave to the moving principle of the universe the name of soul, intelligence, spirit; and God was the vital spirit, which extended through all beings and animated the vast body of the world. And this class conveyed their idea sometimes by Youpiter,‡ essence of motion and animation, principle of existence, or rather existence itself; sometimes by

---

*See Porphyry in *Eusebus, Præp. Evang.*, lib, 3, p. 115.

† The Northern or Etesian wind, which commences regularly at the solstice, with the inundation.

‡ This is the true pronunciation of the Jupiter of the Latins. . . . *Existence itself.* This is the signification of the word *You.*

Vulcan or Phtha, elementary principle of fire ; or by the altar
of Vesta, placed in the center of her temple like the sun in the
heavens ; sometimes by Kneph, a human figure, dressed in
dark blue, having in one hand a sceptre and a girdle (the
zodiac), with a cap of feathers to express the fugacity of
thought, and producing from his mouth the great egg.

"Now, as a consequence of this system, every being containing in itself a portion of the igneous and etherial fluid,
common and universal mover, and this fluid soul of the world
being God, it followed that the souls of all beings were portions of God himself, partaking of all his attributes, that is,
being a substance indivisible, simple, and immortal ; and
hence the whole system of the immortality of the soul, which
at first was eternity.*

* In the system of the first spiritualists, the soul was not created with, or at the
same time as the body, in order to be inserted in it : its existence was supposed
to be anterior and from all eternity. Such, in a few words, is the doctrine of
Macrobius on this head. *Som. Seip. passim.*

"There exists a luminous, igneous, subtile fluid, which under the name of
ether and spiritus, fills the universe. It is the essential principle and agent of
motion and life, it is the Deity. When an earthly body is to be animated, a small
round particle of this fluid gravitates through the milky way towards the lunar
sphere ; where, when it arrives, it unites with a grosser air, and becomes fit to
associate with matter : it then enters and entirely fills the body, animates it,
suffers, grows, increases, and diminishes with it ; lastly, when the body dies, and
its gross elements dissolve, this incorruptible particle takes its leave of it, and
returns to the grand ocean of ether, if not retained by its union with the lunar
air : it is this air or gas, which, retaining the shape of the body, becomes a phantom or ghost, the perfect representation of the deceased. The Greeks called this
phantom the image or idol of the soul; the Pythagoreans, its chariot, its frame ;
and the Rabbinical school, its vessel, or boat. When a man had conducted himself well in this world, his whole soul, that is its chariot and ether, ascended to
the moon, where a separation took place : the chariot lived in the lunar Elysium,
and the ether returned to the fixed sphere, that is, to God : for the fixed heaven,
says Macrobius, was by many called by the name of God (c. 14). If a man had
not lived virtuously, the soul remained on earth to undergo purification, and was
to wander to and fro, like the ghosts of Homer, to whom this doctrine must have
been known, since he wrote after the time of Pherecydes and Pythagoras, who
were its promulgators in Greece. Herodotus upon this occasion says, that the
whole romance of the soul and its transmigrations was invented by the Egyptians,
and propagated in Greece by men, who pretended to be its authors. I know their
names, adds he, but shall not mention them (lib. 2). Cicero, however, has positively informed us, that it was Pherecydes, master of Pythagoras. *Tuscul.* lib. 1,
sect. 16. Now admitting that this system was at that period a novelty, it accounts
for Solomon's treating it as a fable, who lived 130 years before Pherecydes.
"Who knoweth," said he, "the spirit of a man that it goeth upwards? I said in
my heart concerning the estate of the sons of men, that God might manifest them

" Hence, also its transmigrations, known by the name of metempsychosis, that is, the passage of the vital principle from one body to another ; an idea which arose from the real transmigration of the material elements. And behold, ye Indians, ye Boudhists, ye Christians, ye Mussulmans! whence are derived all your opinions on the spirituality of the soul ; behold what was the source of the dreams of Pythagoras and Plato, your masters, who were themselves but the echoes of another, the last sect of visionary philosophers, which we will proceed to examine.

VIII. *Eighth system. The* WORLD-MACHINE : *Worship of the Demi-Ourgos, or Grand Artificer.*

" Hitherto the theologians, employing themselves in examining the fine and subtile substances of ether or the generating fire, had not, however, ceased to treat of beings palpable and perceptible to the senses ; and theology continued to be the theory of physical powers, placed sometimes exclusively in the stars, and sometimes disseminated through the universe ; but at this period, certain superficial minds, losing the chain of ideas which had directed them in their profound studies, or ignorant of the facts on which they were founded, distorted all the conclusions that flowed from them by the introduction of a strange and novel chimera. They pretended that this universe, these heavens, these stars, this sun, differed in no respect from an ordinary machine ; and applying to this first hypothesis a comparison drawn from the works of art, they raised an edifice of the most whimsical sophisms. A machine, said they, does not make itself ; it has had an anterior workman ; its very existence proves it. The world is a machine ; therefore it had an artificer.*

and that they might see that they themselves are beasts. For that which befalleth the sons of men, befalleth beasts ; even one thing befalleth them : as the one dieth, so dieth the other ; yea they have all one breath, so that a man hath no pre-eminence above a beast : for all is vanity." *Eccles.* c. iii : v. 18.

And such had been the opinion of Moses, as a translator of Herodotus (M. Archer of the Academy of Inscriptions) justly observes in note 389 of the second book ; where he says also that the immortality of the soul was not introduced among the Hebrews till their intercourse with the Assyrians. In other respects, the whole Pythagorean system, properly analysed, appears to be merely a system of physics badly understood.

*All the arguments of the spiritualists are founded on this. See *Macrobius*, at the end of the second book, and *Plato*, with the comments of *Marcilius Ficinus*.

" Here, then, is the Demi-Ourgos or grand artificer, constituted God autocratical and supreme. In vain the ancient
philosophy objected to this by saying that the artificer himself
must have had parents and progenitors ; and that they only
added another step to the ladder by taking eternity from the
world, and giving it to its supposed author. The innovators,
not content with this first paradox, passed on to a second ;
and, applying to their artificer the theory of the human understanding, they pretended that the Demi-Ourgos had framed
his machine on a plan already existing in his understanding.
Now, as their masters, the naturalists, had placed in the regions of the fixed stars the great *primum mobile*, under the
name of intelligence and reason, so their mimics, the spiritualists, seizing this idea, applied it to their Demi-Ourgos, and
making it a substance distinct and self-existent, they called it
mens or *logos* (reason or word). And, as they likewise admitted the existence of the soul of the world, or solar principle,
they found themselves obliged to compose three grades of
divine beings, which were : first, the Demi-Ourgos, or working
god ; secondly, the logos, word or reason ; thirdly, the spirit or
soul (of the world).* And here, Christians ! is the romance on
which you have founded your trinity ; here is the system
which, born a heretic in the temples of Egypt, transported a
pagan into the schools of Greece and Italy, is now found to
be good, catholic, and orthodox, by the conversion of its partisans, the disciples of Pythagoras and Plato, to Christianity.
" It is thus that God, after having been, *First*, The visible and
various action of the meteors and the elements ;
" *Secondly*, The combined powers of the stars, considered
in their relations to terrestrial beings ;
" *Thirdly*, These terrestrial beings themselves, by confounding the symbols with their archetypes ;
" *Fourthly*, The double power of nature in its two principal
operations of producing and destroying ;
" *Fifthly*, The animated world, with distinction of agent and
patient, of effect and cause ;
" *Sixthly*, The solar principle, or the element of fire con-
sidered as the only mover ;
" Has thus become, finally, in the last resort, a chimerical

* These are the real types of the Christian Trinity.

and abstract being, a scholastic subtilty, of substance without form, a body without a figure, a very delirium of the mind, beyond the power of reason to comprehend. But vainly does it seek in this last transformation to elude the senses; the seal of its origin is imprinted upon it too deep to be effaced; and its attributes, all borrowed from the physical attributes of the universe, such as immensity, eternity, indivisibility, incomprehensibility; or on the moral affections of man, such as goodness, justice, majesty; its names* even, all derived from the physical beings which were its types, and especially from the sun, from the planets, and from the world, constantly bring to mind, in spite of its corrupters, indelible marks of its real nature.

* In our last analysis we found all the names of the Deity to be derived from some material object in which it was supposed to reside. We have given a considerable number of instances; let us add one more relative to our word *God*. This is known to be the *Deus* of the Latins, and the *Theos* of the Greeks. Now by the confession of Plato (in *Cratylo*), of Macrobius (*Saturn*, lib. 1, c. 24,) and of Plutarch (*Isis and Osiris*) its root is *théin*, which signifies to wander, like *planéin*, that is to say, it is synonymous with planets; because, add our authors, both the ancient Greeks and Barbarians particularly worshipped the planets. I know that such enquiries into etymologies have been much decried: but if, as is the case, words are the representative signs of ideas, the genealogy of the one becomes that of the other, and a good etymological dictionary would be the most perfect history of the human understanding. It would only be necessary in this enquiry to observe certain precautions, which have hitherto been neglected, and particularly to make an exact comparison of the value of the letters of the different alphabets. But, to continue our subject, we shall add, that in the Phœnician language, the word *thah* (with *ain*) signifies also to wander, and appears to be the derivation of *théin*. If we suppose *Deus* to be derived from the Greek *Zeus*, a proper name of *You-piter*, having *zaw*, I live, for its root, its sense will be precisely that of *you*, and will mean *soul* of the world, *igneous* principle. (See note p. 143). *Div-us*, which only signifies Genius, God of the second order, appears to me to come from the oriental word *div* substituted for *dib*, wolf and chacal, one of the emblems of the sun. At Thebes, says Macrobius, the sun was painted under the form of a wolf or chacal, for there are no wolves in Egypt. The reason of this emblem, doubtless, is that the chacal, like the cock announces by its cries the sun's rising; and this reason is confirmed by the analogy of the words *lykos*, wolf, and *lyké*, light of the morning, whence comes *lux*.

Dius, which is to be understood also of the sun, must be derived from *dih*, a hawk. "The Egyptians," says Porphyry (*Euseb. Præcep. Evang.* p. 92,) "represent the sun under the emblem of a hawk, because this bird soars to the highest regions of air where light abounds." And in reality we continually see at Cairo large flights of these birds, hovering in the air, from whence they descend not but to stun us with their shrieks, which are like the monosyllable dih: and here, as in the preceding example, we find an analogy between the word *dies*, day, light, and *dius*, god, sun.

"Such is the chain of ideas which the human mind had already run through at an epoch previous to the records of history ; and since their continuity proves that they were the produce of the same series of studies and labors, we have every reason to place their origin in Egypt, the cradle of their first elements. This progress there may have been rapid ; because the physical priests had no other food, in the retirement of the temples, but the enigma of the universe, always present to their minds ; and because in the political districts into which that country was for a long time divided, every state had its college of priests, who, being by turns auxiliaries or rivals, hastened by their disputes the progress of science and discovery.*

* One of the proofs that all these systems were invented in Egypt, is that this is the only country where we see a complete body of doctrine formed from the remotest antiquity.

Clemens Alexandrinus has transmitted to us (*Stromat.* lib. 6,) a curious detail of the forty-two volumes which were borne in the procession of Isis. "The priest," says he, "or chanter, carries one of the symbolic instruments of music, and two of the books of Mercury ; one containing hymns of the gods, the other the list of kings. Next to him the *horoscope* (the regulator of time,) carries a palm and a dial, symbols of astrology ; he must know by heart the four books of Mercury which treat of astrology : the first on the order of the planets, the second on the risings of the sun and moon, and the two last on the rising and aspect of the stars. Then comes the sacred author, with feathers on his head (like *Kneph*) and a book in his hand, together with ink, and a reed to write with, (as is still the practice among the Arabs). He must be versed in hieroglyphics, must understand the description of the universe, the course of the sun, moon, stars, and planets, be acquainted with the division of Egypt into thirty-six *nomes*, with the course of the Nile, with instruments, measures, sacred ornaments, and sacred places. Next comes the stole bearer, who carries the cubit of justice, or measure of the Nile, and a cup for the libations ; he bears also in the procession ten volumes on the subject of sacrifices, hymns, prayers, offerings, ceremonies, festivals. Lastly arrives the prophet, bearing in his bosom a pitcher, so as to be exposed to view ; he is followed by persons carrying bread (as at the marriage of Cana.) This prophet, as president of the mysteries, learns ten other sacred volumes, which treat of the laws, the gods, and the discipline of the priests. Now there are in all forty-two volumes, thirty-six of which are studied and got by heart by these personages, and the remaining six are set apart to be consulted by the *pastophores;* they treat of medicine, the construction of the human body (anatomy), diseases, remedies, instruments, etc., etc."

We leave the reader to deduce all the consequences of an Encyclopedia. It is ascribed to Mercury ; but Jamblicus tells us that each book, composed by priests, was dedicated to that god, who, on account of his title of genius or *decan* opening the zodiac, presided over every enterprise. He is the *Yanus* of the Romans, and the *Guianesa* of the Indians, and it is remarkable that *Yanus* and *Guianes* are homonymous. In short it appears that these books are the source of all that

" There happened early on the borders of the Nile, what has since been repeated in every country ; as soon as a new system was formed its novelty excited quarrels and schisms ; then, gaining credit by persecution itself, sometimes it effaced antecedent ideas, sometimes it modified and incorporated them ; then, by the intervention of political revolutions, the aggregation of states and the mixture of nations confused all opinions ; and the filiation of ideas being lost, theology fell into a chaos, and became a mere logogriph of old traditions no longer understood. Religion, having strayed from its object was now nothing more than a political engine to conduct the credulous vulgar ; and it was used for this purpose, sometimes by men credulous themselves and dupes of their own visions, and sometimes by bold and energetic spirits in pursuit of great objects of ambition.

IX. *Religion of Moses, or Worship of the Soul of the World* (*You-piter*).

" Such was the legislator of the Hebrews ; who, wishing to separate his nation from all others, and to form a distinct and solitary empire, conceived the design of establishing its basis on religious prejudices, and of raising around it a sacred rampart of opinions and of rites. But in vain did he prescribe the worship of the symbols which prevailed in lower Egypt and in Phœnicia ; * for his god was nevertheless an Egyptian god, invented by those priests of whom Moses had been the disciple ; and *Yahouh*,† betrayed by its very name, *essence* (of

has been transmitted to us by the Greeks and Latins in every science, even in alchymy, necromancy, etc. What is most to be regretted in their loss is that part which related to the principles of medicine and diet, in which the Egyptians appear to have made a considerable progress, and to have delivered many useful observations.

* " At a certain period," says Plutarch (*de Iside*) " all the Egyptians have their animal gods painted. The Thebans are the only people who do not employ painters, because they worship a god whose form comes not under the senses, and cannot be represented." And this is the god whom Moses, educated at Heliopolis, adopted ; but the idea was not of his invention.

† Such is the true pronunciation of the Jehovah of the moderns, who violate, in this respect, every rule of criticism ; since it is evident that the ancients, particularly the eastern Syrians and Phœnicians, were acquainted neither with the *J* nor the *V*, which are of Tartar origin. The subsisting usage of the Arabs, which we have re-established here, is confirmed by Diodorus, who calls the god

beings), and by its symbol, the *burning bush*, is only the *soul
of the world*, the moving principle which the Greeks soon

of Moses *Iaw*, (lib. 1), and *Iaw* and *Yahouh* are manifestly the same word : the
identity continues in that of *You-piter;* but in order to render it more complete,
we shall demonstrate the signification to be the same.

In Hebrew, that is to say, in one of the dialects of the common language of
lower Asia, *Yahouh* is the participle of the verb *hih*, to exist, to be, and signifies
existing; in other words, the principle of life, the mover or even motion (the
universal soul of beings). Now what is Jupiter? Let us hear the Greeks and
Latins explain their theology. " The Egyptians," says Diodorus, after Manatho,
priest of Memphis, "in giving names to the five elements, called *spirit*, or ether,
You-piter, on account of the true meaning of that word : for *spirit* is the source
of life, author of the vital principle in animals ; and for this reason they considered
him as the father, the generator of beings." For the same reason Homer says,
father, and king of men and gods. (*Diod.* lib. 1, sect 1).

" Theologians," says Macrobius, " consider *You-piter* as the soul of the world."
Hence the words of Virgil : " Muses let us begin with You-piter ; the world is
full of You-piter." (*Somn. Scrip.*, ch. 17). And in the Saturnalia, he says,
"Jupiter is the sun himself." It was this also which made Virgil say, " The
spirit nourishes the life (of beings), and the soul diffused through the vast members (of the universe), agitates the whole mass, and forms but one immense
body."

" Ioupiter," says the ancient verses of the Orphic sect, which originated in
Egypt; verses collected by Onomacritus in the days of Pisistratus, " Ioupiter,
represented with the thunder in his hand, is the beginning, origin, end, and
middle of all things : a single and universal power, he governs every thing ;
heaven, earth, fire, water, the elements, day, and night. These are what constitute his immense body : his eyes are the sun and moon : he is space and eternity :
in fine," adds Porphyry, " Jupiter is the world, the universe, that which constitutes the essence and life of all beings. Now," continues the same author, " as
philosophers differed in opinion respecting the nature and constituent parts of
this god, and as they could invent no figure that should represent all his attributes,
they painted him in the form of a man. He is in a sitting posture, in allusion
to his immutable essence ; the upper part of his body is uncovered, because it is
in the upper regions of the universe (the stars) that he most conspicuously dis-
plays himself. He is covered from the waist downwards, because respecting terrestrial things he is more secret and concealed. He holds a scepter in his left
hand, because on the left side is the heart, and the heart is the seat of the understanding, which, (in human beings) regulates every action." *Euseb. Præper.
Evang.*, p. 100.

The following passage of the geographer and philosopher, Strabo, removes
every doubt as to the identity of the ideas of Moses and those of the heathen
theologians.

" Moses, who was one of the Egyptian priests, taught his followers that it was
an egregious error to represent the Deity under the form of animals, as the
Egyptians did, or in the shape of man, as was the practice of the Greeks and
Africans. That alone is the Deity, said he, which constitutes heaven, earth, and
every living thing ; that which we call the *world*, the *sum of all things, nature ;*
and no reasonable person will think of representing such a being by the image of
any one of the objects around us. It is for this reason, that, rejecting every

after adopted under the same denomination in their *you-piter*, regenerating being, and under that of *Ei*, existence,* which the Thebans consecrated by the name of *Kneph*, which Sais worshipped under the emblem of Isis veiled, with this inscription : *I am all that has been, all that is, and all that is to come, and no mortal has raised my veil;* which Pythagoras honored under the name of Vesta, and which the stoic philosophy defined precisely by calling it the principle of fire. In vain did Moses wish to blot from his religion every thing which had relation to the stars ; many traits call them to mind in spite of all he has done. The seven planetary luminaries of the great candlestick ; the twelve stones, or signs in the Urim of the high priests ; the feast of the two equinoxes, (entrances and gates of the two hemispheres); the ceremony of the lamb, (the celestial ram then in his fifteenth degree) ; lastly, the name even of Osiris preserved in his song,† and the ark, or coffer, an imitation of the tomb in which that God was laid, all remain as so many witnesses of the filiation of his ideas, and of their extraction from the common source.

species of images or idols, Moses wished the Deity to be worshipped without emblems, and according to his proper nature ; and he accordingly ordered a temple worthy of him to be erected, etc. *Geograph.* lib. 16, p. 1104, edition of 1707.

The theology of Moses has, then, differed in no respect from that of his followers, that is to say, from that of the Stoics and Epicureans, who consider the Deity as the soul of the world. This philosophy appears to have taken birth, or to have been disseminated when Abraham came into Egypt (200 years before Moses), since he quitted his system of idols for that of the god *Yahouh;* so that we may place its promulgation about the seventeenth or eighteenth century before Christ ; which corresponds with what we have said before.

As to the history of Moses, Diodorus properly represents it when he says, lib. 34 and 40. " That the Jews were driven out of Egypt at a time of dearth, when the country was full of foreigners, and that Moses, a man of extraordinary prudence seized this opportunity of establishing his religion in the mountains of Judea." It will seem paradoxical to assert, that the 600,000 armed men whom he conducted thither ought to be reduced to 6,000 ; but I can confirm the assertion by so many proofs drawn from the books themselves, that it will be necessary to correct an error which appears to have arisen from the mistake of the transcribers.

* This was the monosyllable written on the gates of the temple of Delphos. Plutarch has made it the subject of a dissertation.

† These are the literal expressions of the book of *Deuteronomy*, chap. XXXII. " The works of *Tsour* are perfect." Now *Tsour* has been translated by the word creator ; its proper signification is to give *forms*, and this is one of the definitions of Osiris in Plutarch.

X. *Religion of Zoroaster.*

" Such also was Zoroaster ; who, five centuries after Moses,
and in the time of David, revived and moralized among the
Medes and Bactrians, the whole Egyptian system of Osiris
and Typhon, under the names Ormuzd and Ahrimanes ; who
called the reign of summer, virtue and good ; the reign of
winter, sin and evil ; the renewal of nature in spring, creation
of the world ; the conjunction of the spheres at secular periods,
resurrection ; and the Tartarus and Elysium of the astrologers
and geographers were named future life, hell and paradise.
In a word, he did nothing but consecrate the existing dreams
of the mystical system.

XI. *Budsoism, or Religion of the Samaneans.*

" Such again are the propagators of the dismal doctrine of
the Samaneans ; who, on the basis of the Metempsychosis,
have erected the misanthropic system of self-denial, and of
privations ; who, laying it down as a principle that the body
is only a prison where the soul lives in an impure confinement,
that life is only a dream, an illusion, and the world only a passage to another country, to a life without end, placed virtue
and perfection in absolute immobility, in the destruction of
all sentiment, in the abnegation of physical organs, in the
annihilation of all our being ; whence resulted fasts, penances,
macerations, solitude, contemplations, and all the practices of
the deplorable delirium of the Anchorites.

XII. *Brahmism, or Indian System.*

" And such, too, were the founders of the Indian System ;
who, refining after Zoroaster on the two principles of creation
and destruction, introduced an intermediary principle, that of
preservation, and on their trinity in unity, of Brama, Chiven,
and Vichenou, accumulated the allegories of their ancient traditions, and the alembicated subtilities of their metaphysics.

" These are the materials which existed in a scattered state
for many centuries in Asia ; when a fortuitous concourse of
events and circumstances, on the borders of the Euphrates
and the Mediterranean, served to form them into new combinations.

XIII. *Christianity, or the Allegorical Worship of the Sun, under the cabalistical names of Chrish-en, or Christ, and Ye-sus or Jesus.*

" In constituting a separate nation, Moses strove in vain to defend it against the invasion of foreign ideas. An invisible inclination, founded on the affinity of their origin, had constantly brought back the Hebrews towards the worship of the neighboring nations; and the commercial and political relations which necessarily existed between them, strengthened this propensity from day to day. As long as the constitution of the state remained entire, the coercive force of the government and the laws opposed these innovations, and retarded their progress ; nevertheless the high places were full of idols; and the god Sun had his chariot and horses painted in the palaces of the kings, and even in the temples of Yahouh; but when the conquests of the sultans of Nineveh and Babylon had dissolved the bands of civil power, the people, left to themselves and solicited by their conquerors, restrained no longer their inclination for profane opinions, and they were publicly established in Judea. First, the Assyrian colonies, which came and occupied the lands of the tribes, filled the kingdom of Samaria with dogmas of the Magi, which very soon penetrated into the kingdom of Judea. Afterwards, Jerusalem being subjugated, the Egyptians, the Syrians, the Arabs, entering this defenceless country, introduced their opinions ; and the religion of Moses was doubly mutilated. Besides the priests and great men, being transported to Babylon and educated in the sciences of the Chaldeans, imbibed, during a residence of seventy years, the whole of their theology; and from that moment the dogmas of the hostile Genius (Satan), the archangel Michael,* the ancient of days (Ormuzd), the rebel angels, the battles in heaven, the immortality of the soul, and the resurrection, all

* " The names of the angels and of the months, such as Gabriel, Michael, Yar, Nisan, etc., came from Babylon with the Jews :" says expressly the *Talmud* of Jerusalem. See *Beausob. Hist. du Manich.* Vol. II, p. 624, where he proves that the saints of the *Almanac* are an imitation of the 365 angels of the Persians ; and Jamblicus in his *Egyptian Mysteries*, sect. 2, c. 3, speaks of angels, archangels, seraphims, etc., like a true Christian.

unknown to Moses, or rejected by his total silence respecting them, were introduced and naturalized among the Jews.

"The emigrants returned to their country with these ideas; and their innovation at first excited disputes between their partisans the Pharisees, and their opponents the Saducees, who maintained the ancient national worship; but the former, aided by the propensities of the people and their habits already contracted, and supported by the Persians, their deliverers and masters, gained the ascendant over the latter; and the sons of Moses consecrated the theology of Zoroaster.*

"A fortuitous analogy between two leading ideas was highly favorable to this coalition, and became the basis of a last system, not less surprising in the fortune it has had in the world, than in the causes of its formation.

"After the Assyrians had destroyed the kingdom of Samaria, some judicious men foresaw the same destiny for Jerusalem, which they did not fail to predict and publish; and their predictions had the particular turn of being terminated by prayers for a reëstablishment and regeneration, uttered in the form of prophecies. The Hierophants, in their enthusiasm, had painted a king as a deliverer, who was to reëstablish the nation in its ancient glory; the Hebrews were to become once more a powerful, a conquering nation, and Jerusalem the capital of an empire extended over the whole earth.

"Events having realized the first part of these predictions, the ruin of Jerusalem, the people adhered to the second with a firmness of belief in proportion to their misfortunes; and the afflicted Jews expected, with the impatience of want and desire, this victorious king and deliverer, who was to come and save the nation of Moses, and restore the empire of David.

"On the other hand, the sacred and mythological traditions of preceding times had spread through all Asia a dogma perfectly analogous. The cry there was a great mediator, a final judge, a future saviour, a king, god, conqueror and legislator,

---

* "The whole philosophy of the gymnosophists," says Diogenes Laertius on the authority of an ancient writer, "is derived from that of the Magi, and many assert that of the Jews to have the same origin." Lib. i. c. 9. Megasthenes, an historian of repute in the days of Seleucus Nicanor, and who wrote particularly upon India, speaking of the philosophy of the ancients respecting natural things, puts the Brachmans and the Jews precisely on the same footing.

who was to restore the golden age upon earth,* to deliver it from the dominion of evil, and restore men to the empire of good, peace, and happiness. The people seized and cherished these ideas with so much the more avidity, as they found in them a consolation under that deplorable state of suffering into which they had been plunged by the devastations of successive conquests, and the barbarous despotism of their governments. This conformity between the oracles of different nations, and those of the prophets, excited the attention of the Jews ; and doubtless the prophets had the art to compose their descriptions after the style and genius of the sacred books employed in the Pagan mysteries. There was therefore a general expectation in Judea of a great ambassador, a final Saviour ; when a singular circumstance determined the epoch of his coming.

" It is found in the sacred books of the Persians and Chaldeans, that the world, composed of a total revolution of twelve thousand, was divided into two partial revolutions ; one of which, the age and reign of good, terminated in six thousand ; the other, the age and reign of evil, was to terminate in six thousand more.

" By these records, the first authors had understood the annual revolution of the great celestial orb called the world, (a revolution composed of twelve months or signs, divided each into a thousand parts), and the two systematic periods, of winter and summer, composed each of six thousand. These expressions, wholly equivocal and badly explained, having received an absolute and moral, instead of a physical and astrological sense, it happened that the annual world was taken for the secular world, the thousand of the zodiacal divisions, for a thousand of years ; and supposing, from the state of things, that they lived in the age of evil, they inferred that it would end with the six thousand pretended years.†

* This is the reason of the application of the many Pagan oracles to Jesus, and particularly the fourth eclogue of Virgil, and the Sybilline verses so celebrated among the ancients.

† We have already seen this tradition current among the Tuscans ; it was disseminated through most nations, and shows us what we ought to think of all the pretended creations and terminations of the world, which are merely the beginnings and endings of astronomical periods invented by astrologers. That of the year or solar revolution, being the most simple and perceptible, served as a model

" Now, according to calculations admitted by the Jews, they began to reckon near six thousand years since the supposed creation of the world.* This coincidence caused a fermenta-
to the rest, and its comparison gave rise to the most whimsical ideas. Of this description is the idea of the four ages of the world among the Indians. Originally these four ages were merely the four seasons; and as each season was under the supposed influence of a planet, it bore the name of the metal appropriated to that planet ; thus spring was the age of the sun, or of gold ; summer the age of the moon, or of silver ; autumn the age of Venus, or of brass ; and winter the age of Mars, or of iron. Afterwards when astronomers invented the great year of 25 and 36 thousand common years, which had for its object the bringing back all the stars to one point of departure and a general conjunction, the ambiguity of the terms introduced a similar ambiguity of ideas ; and the myriads of celestial signs and periods of duration which were thus measured were easily converted into so many revolutions of the sun. Thus the different periods of creation which have been so great a source of difficulty and misapprehension to curious enquirers, were in reality nothing more than hypothetical calculations of astronomical periods. In the same manner the creation of the world has been attributed to different seasons of the year, just as these different seasons have served for the fictitious period of these conjunctions ; and of consequence has been adopted by different nations for the commencement of an ordinary year. Among the Egyptians this period fell upon the summer solstice, which was the commencement of their year ; and the departure of the spheres, according to their conjectures, fell in like manner upon the period when the sun enters Cancer. Among the Persians the year commenced at first in the spring, or when the sun enters Aries ; and from thence the first Christians were led to suppose that God created the world in the spring : this opinion is also favored by the book of Genesis ; and it is farther remarkable, that the world is not there said to be created by the God of Moses (*Yahouh*), but by the *Elohim* or gods in the plural, that is by the *angels* or *genii*, for so the word constantly means in the Hebrew books. If we farther observe that the root of the word *Elohim* signifies strong or powerful, and that the Egyptians called their *decans* strong and powerful leaders, attributing to them the creation of the world, we shall presently perceive that the book of Genesis affirms neither more nor less than that the world was created by the *decans*, by those very genii whom, according to Sanchoniathon, Mercury excited against Saturn, and who were called *Elohim*. It may be farther asked why the plural substantive *Elohim* is made to agree with the singular verb *bara* (the Elohim creates). The reason is that after the Babylonish captivity the unity of the Supreme Being was the prevailing opinion of the Jews ; it was therefore thought proper to introduce a pious solecism in language, which it is evident had no existence before Moses ; thus in the names of the children of Jacob many of them are compounded of a plural verb, to which Elohim is the nominative case understood, as *Raouben* (Reuben), *they have looked upon me*, and *Samaonni* (Simeon), *they have granted me my prayer ;* to wit, the Elohim. The reason of this etymology is to be found in the religious creeds of the wives of Jacob, whose gods were the *taraphim* of Laban, that is, the angels of the Persians, and Egyptian decans.

* According to the computation of the Seventy, the period elapsed consisted of about 5,600 years, and this computation was principally followed. It is well known how much, in the first ages of the church, this opinion of the end of the world agitated the minds of men. In the sequel, the general councils encouraged

tion in the public mind. Nothing was thought of but the approaching end. They consulted the hierophants and the mystical books, which differed as to the term ; the great mediator, the final judge, was expected and desired, to put an end to so many calamities. This being was so much spoken of, that some person finally was said to have seen him ; and a first rumor of this sort was sufficient to establish a general certainty. Popular report became an established fact: the imaginary being was realized ; and all the circumstances of mythological tradition, being assembled around this phantom, produced a regular history, of which it was no longer permitted to doubt.

" These mythological traditions recounted that, in the beginning, a woman and a man had by their fall introduced sin and misery into the world. (Consult plate of the *Astrological Heaven of the Ancients.*)

" By this was denoted the astronomical fact, that the celestial virgin and the herdsman (Bootes), by setting heliacally at the autumnal equinox, delivered the world to the wintry constellations, and seemed, on falling below the horizon, to introduce into the world the genius of evil, Ahrimanes, represented by the constellation of the Serpent.*

These traditions related that the woman had decoyed and seduced the man.†

" And in fact, the virgin, setting first, seems to draw the herdsman after her.

" *That the woman tempted him by offering him fruit fair to the sight and good to eat, which gave the knowledge of good and evil.*

" And in fact, the Virgin holds in her hand a branch of

by finding that the general conflagration did not come, pronounced the expectation that prevailed heretical, and its believers were called Millenarians ; a circumstance curious enough, since it is evident from the history of the gospels that Jesus Christ was a Millenarian, and of consequence a heretic.

* " The Persians," says Chardin, " call the constellation of the serpent *Ophiucus*, serpent of Eve: and this serpent *Ophiucus* or *Ophioneus* plays a similar part in the theology of the Phœnicians," for Pherecydes, their disciple and the master of Pythagoras, said " that *Ophioneus Serpentinus* had been chief of the rebels against Jupiter." See Mars. Ficin. Apol. Socrat. p. m. 797, col. 2. I shall add that *ephah* (with *ain*) signifies in Hebrew, serpent.

† In a physical sense to seduce, *seducere*, means only to attract, to draw after us

fruit, which she seems to offer to the Herdsman ; and the branch, emblem of autumn, placed in the picture of Mithra* between winter and summer, seems to open the door and give knowledge, the key of good and evil.

" *That this couple had been driven from the celestial garden, and that a cherub with a flaming sword had been placed at the gate to guard it.*

" And in fact, when the virgin and the herdsman fall beneath the horizon, Perseus rises on the other side ; † and this Genius, with a sword in his hand, seems to drive them from the sum- mer heaven, the garden and dominion of fruits and flowers.

" *That of this virgin should be born, spring up, an offspring, a child, who should bruise the head of the serpent, and deliver the world from sin.*

" This denotes the son, which, at the moment of the winter solstice, precisely when the Persian Magi drew the horoscope of the new year, was placed on the bosom of the Virgin, rising heliacally in the eastern horizon ; on this account he was figured in their astrological pictures under the form of a child suckled by a chaste virgin,‡ and became afterwards, at the

---

* See this picture in Hyde, page 111, edition of 1760.

† Rather the head of Medusa ; that head of a woman once so beautiful, which Perseus cut off and which he holds in his hand, is only that of the virgin, whose head sinks below the horizon at the very moment that Perseus rises ; and the serpents which surround it are Orphiucus and the Polar Dragon, who then occupy the zenith. This shows us in what manner the ancients composed all their figures and fables. They took such constellations as they found at the same time on the circle of the horizon, and collecting the different parts, they formed groups which served them as an almanac in hieroglyphic characters. Such is the secret of all their pictures, and the solution of all their mythological monsters. The virgin is also Andromeda, delivered by Perseus from the whale that *pursues* her (*pro-sequitor*).

‡ Such was the picture of the Persian sphere, cited by Aben Ezra in the *Cælum Poeticum* of Blaeu, p. 71. " The picture of the first decan of the Virgin," says that writer, "represents a beautiful virgin with flowing hair ; sitting in a chair, with two ears of corn in her hand, and suckling an infant, called Jesus by some nations, and Christ in Greek."
In the library of the king of France is a manuscript in Arabic, marked 1165, in which is a picture of the twelve signs ; and that of the Virgin represents a young woman with an infant by her side : the whole scene indeed of the birth of Jesus is to be found in the adjacent part of the heavens. The stable is the constellation of the charioteer and the goat, formerly Capricorn : a constellation called *præsepe Jovis Heniochi, stable of Iou ;* and the word *Iou* is found in the name Iou-seph (Joseph). At no great distance is the ass of Typhon (the great she-bear), and the ox or bull, the ancient attendants of the manger. Peter the porter, is Janus

vernal equinox, the ram, or the lamb, triumphant over the constellation of the Serpent, which disappeared from the skies.

" *That, in his infancy, this restorer of divine and celestial nature would live abased, humble, obscure and indigent.*

"And this, because the winter sun is abased below the horizon ; and that this first period of his four ages or seasons, is a time of obscurity, scarcity, fasting, and want.

" *That, being put to death by the wicked, he had risen gloriously ; that he had reascended from hell to heaven, where he would reign forever.*

" This is a sketch of the life of the sun ; who, finishing his career at the winter solstice, when Typhon and the rebel angels gain the dominion, seems to be put to death by them ; but who soon after is born again, and rises* into the vault of heaven, where he reigns.

" Finally, these traditions went so far as to mention even his astrological and mythological names, and inform us that he was called sometimes Chris, that is to say, preserver,† and

with his keys and bald forehead : the twelve apostles are the genii of the twelve months, etc. This Virgin has acted very different parts in the various systems of mythology : she has been the Isis of the Egyptians, who said of her in one of their inscriptions cited by Julian, *the fruit I have brought forth is the sun.* The majority of traits drawn by Plutarch apply to her, in the same manner as those of Osiris apply to Bootes : also the seven principal stars of the she-bear, called David's chariot, were called the chariot of Osiris (*See Kirker*) *;* and the crown that is situated behind, formed of ivy, was called *Chen-Osiris,* the tree of Osiris. The Virgin has likewise been Ceres, whose mysteries were the same with those of Isis and Mithra ; she has been the Diana of the Ephesians ; the great goddess of Syria, Cybele, drawn by lions ; Minerva, the mother of Bacchus ; Astræa, a chaste virgin taken up into heaven at the end of a golden age ; Themis, at whose feet is the balance that was put in her hands ; the Sybil of Virgil, who descends into hell, or sinks below the hemisphere with a branch in her hand, etc.

Resurgere, to rise a second time, cannot signify to return to life, but in a metaphorical sense ; but we see continually mistakes of this kind result from the ambiguous meaning of the words made use of in ancient tradition.

† The Greeks used to express by X, or Spanish iota, the aspirated *ha* of the Orientals, who said *haris.* In Hebrew *heres* signifies the sun, but in Arabic the meaning of the radical word is, to guard, to preserve, and of *haris,* guardian, preserver. It is the proper epithet of Vichenou, which demonstrates at once the identity of the Indian and Christian Trinities, and their common origin. It is manifestly but one system, which, divided into two branches, one extending to the east, and the other to the west, assumed two different forms : Its principal trunk is the Pythagorean system of the soul of the world, or *Iou-piter.* The epithet *piter,* or father, having been applied to the demi-ourgos of Plato, gave rise to an ambiguity which caused an enquiry to be made respecting the son of this father. In the opinion of the philosophers the son was understanding, *Nous* and

from that, ye Indians, you have made your god Chrish-en or
Chrish-na ; and, ye Greek and Western Christians, your
Chris-tos, son of Mary, is the same ; sometimes he is called
Yes, by the union of three letters, which by their numerical
value form the number 608, one of the solar periods.* And
this, Europeans, is the name which, with the Latin termina-
tion, is become your Yes-us or Jesus, the ancient and cabal-
istic name attributed to young Bacchus, the clandestine son
(nocturnal) of the Virgin Minerva, who, in the history of his
whole life, and even of his death, brings to mind the history
of the god of the Christians, that is, of the star of day, of
which they are each of them the emblems. "

Here a great murmur having arisen among all the Christian
groups, the Lamas, the Mussulmans and the Indians called
them to order, and the orator went on to finish his discourse :

" You know at present," said he, " how the rest of this system was composed in the chaos and anarchy of the three first
centuries ; what a multitude of singular opinions divided the
minds of men, and armed them with an enthusiasm and a
reciprocal obstinacy ; because, being equally founded on ancient tradition, they were equally sacred. You know how
the government, after three centuries, having embraced one
of these sects, made it the orthodox, that is to say, the pre-

---

Logos, from which the *Latins* made their *Verbum*. And thus we clearly perceive
the origin of the *eternal father* and of the *Verbum* his son, proceeding from him
(*Mens Ex Deo nata*, says Macrobius) : the *œnima* or *spiritus mundi*, was the
Holy Ghost ; and it is for this reason that Manes, Pasilides, Valentinius, and
other pretended heretics of the first ages, who traced things to their source, said,
that God the Father was the supreme inaccessible light (that of the heaven, the
primum mobile, or the *aplanes*) ; the Son the secondary light resident in the sun,
and the Holy Ghost the atmosphere of the earth (See *Beausob.* vol. ii, p. 586) :
hence, among the Syrians, the representation of the Holy Ghost by a dove, the
bird of Venus Urania, that is of the air. The Syrians (says *Nigidius de Germaico*)
assert that a dove sat for a certain number of days on the egg of a fish, and that
from this incubation Venus was born : Sextus Empiricus also observes (*Inst.
Pyrrh.* lib. 3, c. 23) that the Syrians abstain from eating doves ; which intimates to
us a period commencing in the sign *Pisces*, in the winter solstice. We may farther observe, that if *Chris* comes from *Harisch* by a *chin*, it will signify *artificer*,
an epithet belonging to the sun. These variations, which must have embarrassed
the ancients, prove it to be the real type of Jesus, as had been already remarked
in the time of Tertullian. " Many, says this writer, suppose with greater probability that the sun is our God, and they refer us to the religion of the Persians."
Apologet. c. 16.

* See a curious ode to the sun, by Martianus Capella, translated by Gebelin.

dominant religion, to the exclusion of the rest; which, being less in number, became heretics; you know how and by what means of violence and seduction this religion was propagated, extended, divided, and enfeebled; how, six hundred years after the Christian innovation, another system was formed from it and from that of the Jews; and how Mahomet found the means of composing a political and theological empire at the expense of those of Moses and the vicars of Jesus.

"Now, if you take a review of the whole history of. the spirit of all religion, you will see that in its origin it has had no other author than the sensations and wants of man; that the idea of God has had no other type and model than those of physical powers, material beings, producing either good or evil, by impressions of pleasure or pain on sensitive beings; that in the formation of all these systems the spirit of religion has always followed the same course, and been uniform in its proceedings; that in all of them the dogma has never failed to represent, under the name of gods, the operations of nature, and passions and prejudices of men; that the moral of them all has had for its object the desire of happiness and the aversion to pain; but that the people, and the greater part of legislators, not knowing the route to be pursued, have formed false, and therefore discordant, ideas of virtue and vice, of good and evil, that is to say, of what renders man happy or miserable; that in every instance, the means and the causes of propagating and establishing systems have exhibited the same scenes of passion and the same events; everywhere disputes about words, pretexts for zeal, revolutions and wars excited by the ambition of princes, the knavery of apostles, the credulity of proselytes, the ignorance of the vulgar, the exclusive cupidity and intolerant arrogance of all. Indeed, you will see that the whole history of the spirit of religion is only the history of the errors of the human mind, which, placed in a world that it does not comprehend, endeavors nevertheless to solve the enigma; and which, beholding with astonishment this mysterious and visible prodigy, imagines causes, supposes reasons, builds systems; then, finding one defective, destroys it for another not less so; hates the error that it abandons, misconceives the one that it embraces, rejects the truth that it is seeking, composes chimeras of discordant beings ; and thus, while always dreaming of wisdom and happiness, wanders blindly in a labyrinth of illusion and doubt."

———

CHAPTER XXIII.

ALL RELIGIONS HAVE THE SAME OBJECT.

THUS spoke the orator in the name of those men who had studied the origin and succession of religious ideas.

The theologians of various systems, reasoning on this discourse: " It is an impious representation," said some, " whose tendency is nothing less than to overturn all belief, to destroy subordination in the minds of men, and annihilate our ministry and power." " It is a romance," said others, " a tissue of conjectures, composed with art, but without foundation." The moderate and prudent men added: " Supposing all this to be true, why reveal these mysteries ? Doubtless our opinions are full of errors ; but these errors are a necessary restraint on the multitude. The world has gone thus for two thousand years ; why change it now ? "

A murmur of disapprobation, which never fails to rise at every innovation, now began to increase ; when a numerous group of the common classes of people, and of untaught men of all countries and of every nation, without prophets, without doctors, and without doctrine, advancing in the circle, drew the attention of the whole assembly ; and one of them, in the name of all, thus addressed the multitude :

" Mediators and arbiters of nations ! the strange relations which have occupied the present debate were unknown to us until this day. Our understanding, confounded and amazed at so many statements, some of them learned, others absurd and all incomprehensible, remains in uncertainty and doubt. One only reflection has struck us : on reviewing so many prodigious facts, so many contradictory assertions, we ask ourselves : What are all these discussions to us ? What need

have we of knowing what passed five or six thousand years
ago, in countries we never heard of, and among men who
will ever be unknown to us? True or false, what interest
have we in knowing whether the world has existed six thousand, or twenty-five thousand years? Whether it was made
of nothing, or of something; by itself, or by a maker, who
in his turn would require another maker? What! we are not
sure of what happens near us, and shall we answer for what
happens in the sun, in the moon, or in imaginary regions of
space? We have forgotten our own infancy, and shall we
know the infancy of the world? And who will attest what
no one has seen? who will certify what no man com-
prehends?

"Besides, what addition or diminution will it make to our
existence, to answer yes or no to all these chimeras? Hitherto neither our fathers nor ourselves have had the least
knowledge or notion of them, and we do not perceive that we
have had on this account either more or less of the sun, more
or less of subsistence, more or less of good or of evil.

"If the knowledge of these things is so necessary, why
have we lived as well without it as those who have taken so
much trouble concerning it? If this knowledge is superfluous,
why should we burden ourselves with it to-day?"

Then addressing himself to the doctors and theologians:

"What!" said he, "is it necessary that we, poor and ignorant men, whose every moment is scarcely sufficient for the
cares of life, and the labors of which you take the profit,—is
it necessary for us to learn the numberless histories that you
have recounted, to read the quantity of books that you have
cited, and to study the various languages in which they are
composed! A thousand years of life would not suffice —"

"It is not necessary," replied the doctors, "that you should
acquire all this science; we have it for you —"

"But even you," replied the simple men, "with all your
science, you are not agreed; of what advantage, then, is your
science? Besides, how can you answer for us? If the faith
of one man is applicable to many, what need have even you
to believe? your fathers may have believed for you; and this
would be reasonable, since they have seen for you.

"Farther, what is believing, if believing influences no action? And what action is influenced by believing, for instance, that the world is or is not eternal?"

"The latter would be offensive to God," said the doctors.

"How prove you that?" replied the simple men.

"In our books," answered the doctors.

"We do not understand them," returned the simple men.

"We understand them for you," said the doctors.

"That is the difficulty," replied the simple men. "By what right do you constitute yourselves mediators between God and us?"

"By his orders," said the doctors.

"Where is the proof of these orders?" said the simple men.

"In our books," said the doctors.

"We understand them not," said the simple men; "and how came this just God to give you this privilege over us? Why did this common father oblige us to believe on a less degree of evidence than you? He has spoken to you; be it so; he is infallible, and deceives you not. But it is you who speak to us! And who shall assure us that you are not in error yourselves, or that you will not lead us into error? And if we should be deceived, how will that just God save us contrary to law, or condemn us on a law which we have not known?"

"He has given you the natural law," said the doctors.

"And what is the natural law?" replied the simple men. "If that law is sufficient, why has he given any other? If it is not sufficient, why did he make it imperfect?"

"His judgments are mysteries," said the doctors, "and his justice is not like that of men."

"If his justice," replied the simple men, "is not like ours, by what rule are we to judge of it? And, moreover, why all these laws, and what is the object proposed by them?"

"To render you more happy," replied a doctor, "by rendering you better and more virtuous. It is to teach man to enjoy his benefits, and not injure his fellows, that God has manifested himself by so many oracles and prodigies."

"In that case," said the simple men, "there is no necessity for so many studies, nor of such a variety of arguments; only tell us which is the religion that best answers the end which they all propose."

Immediately, on this, every group, extolling its own morality above that of all others, there arose among the different
sects a new and most violent dispute.

" It is we," said the Mussulmans, " who possess the most
excellent morals, who teach all the virtues useful to men and
agreeable to God. We profess justice, disinterestedness, resignation to providence, charity to our brethren, alms-giving,
and devotion ; we torment not the soul with superstitious
fears ; we live without alarm, and die without remorse."

" How dare you speak of morals," answered the Christian
priests, " you, whose chief lived in licentiousness and preached
impurity ? You, whose first precept is homicide and war ?
For this we appeal to experience : for these twelve hundred
years your fanatical zeal has not ceased to spread commotion
and carnage among the nations. If Asia, so flourishing in
former times, is now languishing in barbarity and depopula-
tion, it is in your doctrine that we find the cause ; in that doctrine, the enemy of all instruction, which sanctifies ignorance,
which consecrates the most absolute despotism in the governors, imposes the most blind and passive obedience in the
people, that has stupified the faculties of man, and brutalized
the nations.

" It is not so with our sublime and celestial morals ; it was
they which raised the world from its primitive barbarity, from
the senseless and cruel superstitions of idolatry, from human
sacrifices,* from the shameful orgies of pagan mysteries ; they
it was that purified manners, proscribed incest and adultery,
polished savage nations, banished slavery, and introduced
new and unknown virtues, charity for men, their equality in
the sight of God, forgiveness and forgetfulness of injuries, the
restraint of all the passions, the contempt of worldly greatness, a life completely spiritual and completely holy ! "

" We admire," said the Mussulmans, " the ease with which
you reconcile that evangelical meekness, of which you are so
ostentatious, with the injuries and outrages with which you

*Read the cold declaration of Eusebius (*Præp. Evang.* lib. 1, p. 11,), who pretends that, since the coming of Christ, there have been neither wars, nor tyrants,
nor cannibals, nor sodomites, nor persons committing incest, nor savages destroying their parents, etc. When we read these fathers of the church we are astonished at their insincerity or infatuation.

are constantly galling your neighbors. When you criminate
so severely the great man whom we revere, we might fairly
retort on the conduct of him whom you adore ; but we scorn
such advantages, and confining ourselves to the real object in
question, we maintain that the morals of your gospel have by
no means that perfection which you ascribe to them ; it is not
true that they have introduced into the world new and unknown virtues : for example, the equality of men in the sight
of God,— that fraternity and that benevolence which follow
from it, were formal doctrines of the sect of the Hermatics or
Samaneans,* from whom you descend. As to the forgiveness
of injuries, the Pagans themselves had taught it ; but in the
extent that you give it, far from being a virtue, it becomes an
immorality, a vice. Your so much boasted precept of turning
one cheek after the other, is not only contrary to every sentiment of man, but is opposed to all ideas of justice. It
emboldens the wicked by impunity, debases the virtuous by
servility, delivers up the world to despotism and tyranny, and
dissolves all society. Such is the true spirit of your doctrines.
Your gospels in their precepts and their parables, never represent God but as a despot without any rules of equity ; a
partial father treating a debauched and prodigal son with
more favor than his respectful and virtuous children ; a capricious master, who gives the same wages to workmen who
had wrought but one hour, as to those who had labored
through the whole day ; one who prefers the last comers to
the first. The moral is everywhere misanthropic and anti-
social ; it disgusts men with life and with society ; and tends
only to encourage hermitism and celibacy.

  "As to the manner in which you have practised these
morals, we appeal in our turn to the testimony of facts. We
ask whether it is this evangelical meekness which has excited
your interminable wars between your sects, your atrocious
persecutions of pretended heretics, your crusades against
Arianism, Manicheism, Protestantism, without speaking of
your crusades against us, and of those sacrilegious associations, still subsisting, of men who take an oath to continue

---

* The equality of mankind in a state of nature and in the eyes of God was one
of the principal tenets of the Samaneans, and they appear to be the only ancients
that entertained this opinion.

them ? * We ask you whether it be gospel charity which has made you exterminate whole nations in America, to annihilate the empires of Mexico and Peru; which makes you continue to dispeople Africa and sell its inhabitants like cattle, notwithstanding your abolition of slavery ; which makes you ravage India and usurp its dominions ; and whether it be the same charity which, for three centuries past, has led you to harrass the habitations of the people of three continents, of whom the most prudent, the Chinese and Japanese, were constrained to drive you off, that they might escape your chains and recover their internal peace ? "

Here the Bramins, the Rabbins, the Bonzes, the Chamans, the Priests of the Molucca islands, and the coasts of Guinea, loading the Christian doctors with reproaches: "Yes !" cried they, "these men are robbers and hypocrites, who preach simplicity, to surprise confidence ; humility, to enslave with more ease ; poverty, to appropriate all riches to themselves. They promise another world, the better to usurp the present ; and while they speak to you of tolerance and charity, they burn, in the name of God, the men who do not worship him in their manner."

"Lying priests," retorted the missionaries, "it is you who abuse the credulity of ignorant nations to subjugate them. It is you who have made of your ministry an art of cheating and imposture ; you have converted religion into a traffic of cupidity and avarice. You pretend to hold communications with spirits, and they give for oracles nothing but your wills. You feign to read the stars, and destiny decrees only your desires. You cause idols to speak, and the gods are but the instruments of your passions. You have invented sacrifices and libations, to collect for your own profit the milk of flocks, and the flesh and fat of victims ; and under the cloak of piety you devour the offerings of the gods, who cannot eat, and the substance of the people who are forced to labor."

"And you," replied the Bramins, the Bonzes, the Chamans, "you sell to the credulous living, your vain prayers for the souls of the dead. With your indulgences and your absolutions you have usurped the power of God himself ; and

* The oath taken by the knights of the Order of Malta, is to kill, or make the Mahometans prisoners, for the glory of God.

making a traffic of his favors and pardons, you have put
heaven at auction; and by your system of expiations you
have formed a tariff of crimes, which has perverted all
consciences." *

"Add to this," said the Imans, "that these men have invented the most insidious of all systems of wickedness,— the
absurd and impious obligation of recounting to them the
most intimate secrets of actions and of thoughts (confessions);
so their insolent curiosity has carried their inquisition even
into the sanctuary of the marriage bed,† and the inviolable
recesses of the heart."

Thus by mutual reproaches the doctors of the different sects
began to reveal all the crimes of their ministry—all the vices
of their craft; and it was found that among all nations the
spirit of the priesthood, their system of conduct, their actions,
their morals, were absolutely the same:

That they had everywhere formed secret associations and
corporations at enmity with the rest of society :‡

---

* As long as it shall be possible to obtain purification from crimes and exemp-
tion from punishment by means of money or other frivolous practices; as long as
kings and great men shall suppose that building temples or instituting foundations, will absolve them from the guilt of oppression and homicide; as long as individuals shall imagine that they may rob and cheat, provided they observe fast
during Lent, go to confession, and receive extreme unction, it is impossible there
should exist in society any morality or virtue; and it is from a deep conviction
of truth, that a modern philosopher has called the doctrine of expiations *la vérola
des sociétés.*

† Confession is a very ancient invention of the priests, who did not fail to avail
themselves of that means of governing. It was practised in the Egyptian, Greek,
Phrygian, Persian mysteries, etc. Plutarch has transmitted us the remarkable
answer of a Spartan whom a priest wanted to confess. "Is it to you or to God
I am to confess?" "To God," answered the priest: "In that case," replied the
Spartan, "man, begone!" (*Remarkable Sayings of the Lacedemonians.*) The first
Christians confessed their faults publicly, like the Essenians. Afterwards, priests
began to be established, with power of absolution from the sin of idolatry. In the
time of Theodosius, a woman having publicly confessed an intrigue with a deacon,
bishop Necterius, and his successor Chrysostom, granted communion without
confession. It was not until the seventh century that the abbots of convents ex-
acted from monks and nuns confession twice a year; and it was at a still later
period that bishops of Rome generalized it.

The Mussulmen, who suppose women to have no souls, are shocked at the
idea of confession; and say ; How can an honest man think of listening to the
recital of the actions or the secret thoughts of a woman? May we not also ask,
on the other hand, how can an honest woman consent to reveal them?

‡ That we may understand the general feelings of priests respecting the rest of
mankind, whom they always call by the name of the people, let us hear one of the

That they had everywhere attributed to themselves prerog-
atives and immunities, by means of which they lived exempt
from the burdens of other classes :

That they everywhere avoided the toils of the laborer, the
dangers of the soldier, and the disappointments of the merchant :

That they lived everywhere in celibacy, to shun even the
cares of a family :

That, under the cloak of poverty, they found everywhere
the secret of procuring wealth and all sorts of enjoyments :

That under the name of mendicity they raised taxes to a
greater amount than princes :

That in the form of gifts and offerings they had established
fixed and certain revenues exempt from charges :

That under pretence of retirement and devotion they lived
in idleness and licentiousness :

That they had made a virtue of alms-giving, to live quietly
on the labors of others :

doctors of the church. "The people," says Bishop Synnesius, *in Calvit.* page 315,
"are desirous of being deceived, we cannot act otherwise respecting them. The
case was similar with the ancient priests of Egypt, and for this reason they shut
themselves up in their temples, and there composed their mysteries, out of the
reach of the eye of the people." And forgetting what he has before just said, he
adds: "for had the people been in the secret they might have been offended at
the deception played upon them. In the mean time how is it possible to conduct
one's self otherwise with the people so long as they are people? For my own
part, to myself I shall always be a philosopher, but in dealing with the mass of
mankind, I shall be a priest."

"A little jargon," says Geogory Nazianzen to St. Jerome (*Hieron. ad. Nep.*)
"is all that is necessary to impose on the people. The less they comprehend, the
more they admire. Our forefathers and doctors of the church have often said,
not what they thought, but what circumstances and necessity dictated to them.'

"We endeavor," says Sanchoniaton, "to excite admiration by means of the
marvellous." (*Præp. Evang.* lib. 3.)

Such was the conduct of all the priests of antiquity, and is still that of the Bramins and Lamas who are the exact counterpart of the Egyptian priests. Such
was the practice of the Jesuits, who marched with hasty strides in the same career. It is useless to point out the whole depravity of such a doctrine. In general every association which has mystery for its basis, or an oath of secrecy, is a
league of robbers against society, a league divided in its very bosom into knaves
and dupes, or in other words agents and instruments. It is thus we ought to
judge of those modern clubs, which, under the name of Illuminatists, Martinists,
Cagliostronists, and Mesmerites, infest Europe. These societies are the follies
and deceptions of the ancient Cabalists, Magicians, Orphies, etc., "who," says
Plutarch, "led into errors of considerable magnitude, not only individuals, but
kings and nations."

That they had invented the ceremonies of worship, as a means of attracting the reverence of the people, while they were playing the parts of gods, of whom they styled themselves the interpreters and mediators, to assume all their powers; that, with this design, they had (according to the degree of ignorance or information of their people) assumed by turns the character of astrologers, drawers of horoscopes, fortune-tellers, magicians,* necromancers, quacks, physicians, courtiers, confessors of princes, always aiming at the great object to govern for their own advantage :

That sometimes they had exalted the power of kings and consecrated their persons, to monopolize their favors, or participate their sway :

That sometimes they had preached up the murder of tyrants (reserving it to themselves to define tyranny), to avenge themselves of their contempt or their disobedience:

And that they always stigmatised with impiety whatever crossed their interests ; that they hindered all public instruction, to exercise the monopoly of science ; that finally, at all times and in all places, they had found the secret of living in peace in the midst of the anarchy they created, in safety under the despotism that they favored, in idleness amidst the industry they preached, and in abundance while surrounded with scarcity; and all this by carrying on the singular trade of selling words and gestures to credulous people, who purchase them as commodities of the greatest value.†

*What is a magician, in the sense in which people understand the word? A man who by words and gestures pretends to act on supernatural beings, and compel them to descend at his call and obey his orders. Such was the conduct of the ancient priests, and such is still that of all priests in idolatrous nations ; for which reason we have given them the denomination of Magicians.

And when a Christian priest pretends to make God descend from heaven, to fix him to a morsel of leaven, and render, by means of this talisman, souls pure and in a state of grace, what is this but a trick of magic ? And where is the difference between a Chaman of Tartary who invokes the Genii, or an Indian Bramin, who makes Vichenou descend in a vessel of water to drive away evil spirits ? Yes, the identity of the spirit of priests in every age and country is fully established! Every where it is the assumption of an exclusive privilege, the pretended faculty of moving at will the powers of nature ; and this assumption is so direct a violation of the right of equality, that whenever the people shall regain their importance, they will forever abolish this sacrilegious kind of nobility, which has been the type and parent stock of the other species of nobility.

†A curious work would be the comparative history of the *agnuses* of the pope and the *pastils* of the grand Lama. It would be worth while to extend this idea

Then the different nations, in a transport of fury, were going to tear in pieces the men who had thus abused them; but the legislator, arresting this movement of violence, addressed the chiefs and doctors:

"What!" said he, "instructors of nations, is it thus that you have deceived them?"

And the terrified priests replied.

"O legislator! we are men. The people are so superstitious! they have themselves encouraged these errors." *

And the kings said:

"O legislator! the people are so servile and so ignorant! they prostrated themselves before the yoke, which we scarcely dared to show them."†

Then the legislator, turning to the people — "People!" said he, "remember what you have just heard; they are two indelible truths. Yes, you yourselves cause the evils of which you complain; yourselves encourage the tyrants, by a base adulation of their power, by an imprudent admiration of their false beneficence, by servility in obedience, by licentiousness in liberty, and by a credulous reception of every imposition. On whom shall you wreak vengeance for the faults committed by your own ignorance and cupidity?"

And the people, struck with confusion, remained in mournful silence.

to religious ceremonies in general, and to confront, column by column, the analogous or contrasting points of faith and superstitious practices in all nations. There is one more species of superstition which it would be equally salutary to cure, blind veneration for the great; and for this purpose it would be alone sufficient to write a minute detail of the private life of kings and princes. No work could be so philosophical as this; and accordingly we have seen what a general outcry was excited among kings and the panders of kings, when the *Anecdotes of the Court of Berlin* first appeared. What would be the alarm were the public put in possession of the sequel of this work? Were the people fairly acquainted with all the absurdities of this species of idol, they would no longer be exposed to covet their specious pleasures, of which the plausible and hollow appearance disturbs their peace, and hinders them from enjoying the much more solid happiness of their own condition.

* Consider in this veiw the Brabanters.

† The inhabitants of Vienna, for example, who harnessed themselves like cattle, and drew the chariot of Leopold.

CHAPTER XXIV.

SOLUTION OF THE PROBLEM OF CONTRADICTIONS.

THE legislator then resumed his discourse: " O nations!" said he, " we have heard the discussion of your opinions. The different sentiments which divide you have given rise to many reflections, and furnished several questions which we shall propose to you to solve.

" *First*, considering the diversity and opposition of the creeds to which you are attached, we ask on what motives you found your persuasion? Is it from a deliberate choice that you follow the standard of one prophet rather than another? Before adopting this doctrine, rather than that, did you first compare? did you carefully examine them? Or have you received them only from the chance of birth, from the empire of education and habit? Are you not born Christians on the borders of the Tiber, Mussulmans on those of the Euphrates, Idolaters on the Indus, just as you are born fair in cold climates, and sable under the scorching sun of Africa? And if your opinions are the effect of your fortuitous position on the earth, of consanguinity, of imitation, how is it that such a hazard should be a ground of conviction, an argument of truth?

" *Secondly*, when we reflect on the mutual proscriptions and arbitrary intolerance of your pretensions, we are frightened at the consequences that flow from your own principles. Nations! who reciprocally devote each other to the bolts of heavenly wrath, suppose that the universal Being, whom you revere, should this moment descend from heaven on this multitude; and, clothed with all his power, should sit on this throne to judge you; suppose that he should say to you: Mortals! it is your own justice that I am going to exercise upon you. Yes, of all the religious systems that divide you, one alone shall this day be preferred; all the others, all this multitude of standards, of nations, of prophets, shall be condemned to eternal destruction. This is not enough: among the particular sects of the chosen system, one only can be favored; all the others must be condemned: neither is this enough;—from this little remnant of a group I must exclude all those who have not fulfilled the conditions enjoined by its precepts. O men! to what a small number of elect have you limited your race! to what a penury of beneficence do you reduce the immensity of my goodness! to what a solitude of beholders do you condemn my greatness and my glory!

"But," said the legislator rising, "no matter; you have willed it so. Nations! here is an urn in which all your names are placed: one only is a prize: approach, and draw this tremendous lottery!" And the nations, seized with terror, cried: "No, no; we are all brothers, all equal; we cannot condemn each other."

"Then," said the legislator, resuming his seat: "O men! who dispute on so many subjects, lend an attentive ear to one problem which you exhibit, and which you ought to decide yourselves."

And the people, giving great attention, he lifted an arm towards heaven, and, pointing to the sun, said:

"Nations, does that sun, which enlightens you, appear square or triangular?"

"No," answered they with one voice, "it is round."

Then, taking the golden balance that was on the altar:

"This gold," said the legislator, "that you handle every day, is it heavier than the same volume of copper?"

"Yes," answered all the people, "gold is heavier than copper."

Then, taking the sword:

"Is this iron," said the legislator, "softer than lead?"

"No," said the people.

"Is sugar sweet, and gall bitter?"

"Yes."

"Do you love pleasure and hate pain?"

"Yes."

"Thus, then, you are agreed in these points, and many others of the same nature.

"Now, tell us, is there a cavern in the centre of the earth, or inhabitants in the moon?"

This question caused a universal murmur. Every one answered differently — some yes, others no; one said it was probable, another said it was an idle and ridiculous question; some, that it was worth knowing. And the discord was universal.

After some time the legislator, having obtained silence, said:

"Explain to us, O Nations! this problem: we have put to you several questions which you have answered with one voice, without distinction of race or of sect: white men, black men, followers of Mahomet and of Moses, worshippers of Boudha and of Jesus, all have returned the same answer. We then proposed another question, and you have all disagreed! Why this unanimity in one case, and this discordance in the other?"

And the group of simple men and savages answered and said: "The reason of this is plain. In the first case we see and feel the objects, and we speak from sensation; in the second, they are beyond the reach of our senses — we speak of them only from conjecture."

"You have resolved the problem," said the legislator; "and your own consent has established this first truth:

"That whenever objects can be examined and judged of by your senses, you are agreed in opinion; and that you only differ when the objects are absent and beyond your reach.

"From this first truth flows another equally clear and worthy of notice. Since you agree on things which you know with certainty, it follows that you disagree only on those which you know not with certainty, and about which you are not sure; that is to say, you dispute, you quarrel, you fight, for that which is uncertain, that of which you doubt. O men! is this wisdom?

"Is it not, then, demonstrated that truth is not the object of your contests? that it is not her cause which you defend, but that of your affections, and your prejudices? that it is not the object, as it really is in itself, that you would verify, but the object as you would have it; that is to say, it is not the evidence of the thing that you would enforce, but your own personal opinion, your particular manner of seeing and judging? It is a power that you wish to exercise, an interest that you wish to satisfy, a prerogative that you arrogate to yourself; it is a contest of vanity. Now, as each of you, on comparing himself to every other, finds himself his equal and his fellow, he resists by a feeling of the same right. And your disputes, your combats, your intolerance, are the effect of this right which you deny each other, and of the intimate conviction of your equality.

" Now, the only means of establishing harmony is to return to nature, and to take for a guide and regulator the order of things which she has founded; and then your accord will prove this other truth :

" That real beings have in themselves an identical, constant and uniform mode of existence; and that there is in your organs a like mode of being affected by them.

" But at the same time, by reason of the mobility of these organs as subject to your will, you may conceive different affections, and find yourselves in different relations with the same objects; so that you are to them like a mirror, capable of reflecting them truly as they are, or of distorting and disfiguring them.

" Hence it follows, that whenever you perceive objects as they are, you agree among yourselves, and with the objects ; and this similitude between your sensations and their manner of existence, is what constitutes their truth with respect to you ; and, on the contrary, whenever you differ in opinion, your disagreement is a proof that you do not represent them such as they are,— that you change them.

" Hence, also, it follows, that the causes of your disagreement exist not in the objects themselves, but in your minds, in your manner of perceiving or judging.

" To establish, therefore, a uniformity of opinion, it is necessary first to establish the certainty, completely verified, that the portraits which the mind forms are perfectly like the originals ; that it reflects the objects correctly as they exist. Now, this result cannot be obtained but in those cases where the objects can be brought to the test, and submitted to the examination of the senses. Everything which cannot be brought to this trial is, for that reason alone, impossible to be determined ; there exists no rule, no term of comparison, no means of certainty, respecting it.

" From this we conclude, that, to live in harmony and peace, we must agree never to decide on such subjects, and to attach to them no importance ; in a word, we must trace a line of distinction between those that are capable of verification, and those that are not; and separate by an inviolable barrier the world of fantastical beings from the world of realities ; that is to say, all civil effect must be taken away from theological and religious opinions.

"This, O ye people of the earth! is the object proposed by a great nation freed from her fetters and her prejudices ; this is the work which, under her eye and by her orders, we had undertaken, when your kings and your priests came to inter-rupt it. O kings and priests! you may suspend, yet for a while, the solemn publication of the laws of nature ; but it is no longer in your power to annihilate or to subvert them."

A general shout then arose from every part of the assembly ; and the nations universally, and with one voice, testified their assent to the proposals of the delegates : "Resume," said they, "your holy and sublime labors, and bring them to perfection. Investigate the laws which nature, for our guidance, has im-planted in our breasts, and collect from them an authentic and immutable code ; nor let this code be any longer for one fam-ily only, but for us all without exception. Be the legislators of the whole human race, as you are the interpreters of nature herself.   Show us the line of partition between the world of chimeras and that of realities ; and teach us, after so many religions of error and delusion, the religion of evidence and truth ! "

Then the delegates, having resumed their enquiries into the physical and constituent attributes of man, and examined the motives and affections which govern him in his individual and social state, unfolded in these words the laws on which nature herself has founded his happiness.

THE LAW OF NATURE.

———

CHAPTER I

OF THE LAW OF NATURE.

Q. WHAT is the law of nature?

A. It is the constant and regular order of events, by which God governs the universe; an order which his wisdom presents to the senses and reason of men, as an equal and common rule for their actions, to guide them, without distinction of country or sect, towards perfection and happiness.

Q. Give a clear definition of the word law.

A. The word law, taken literary, signifies lecture,* because, originally, ordinances and regulations were the lectures, preferably to all others, made to the people, in order that they might observe them, and not incur the penalties attached to their infraction: whence follows the original custom explaining the true idea.

The definition of law is, " An order or prohibition to act, with the express clause of a penalty attached to the infraction, or of a recompense attached to the observance of that order."

Q. Do such orders exist in nature?

A. Yes.

Q. What does the word nature signify?

A. The word nature bears three different significations.

1. It signifies the universe, the material world: in this first sense we say the beauties of nature, the riches of nature, that is to say, the objects in the heavens and on the earth exposed to our sight;

2. It signifies the power that animates, that moves the universe, considering it as a distinct being, such as the soul is to

———

* From the Latin word lex, lectio. Alcoran likewise signifies lecture and is only a literal translation of the word law.

the body; in this second sense we say, "The intentions of nature, the incomprehensible secrets of nature."

3. It signifies the partial operations of that power on each being, or on each class of beings; and in this third sense we say, "The nature of man is an enigma; every being acts according to its nature."

Wherefore, as the actions of each being, or of each species of beings, are subjected to constant and general rules, which cannot be infringed without interrupting and troubling the general or particular order, those rules of action and of motion are called natural laws, or laws of nature.

Q. Give me examples of those laws.

A. It is a law of nature, that the sun illuminates successively the surface of the terrestrial globe; — that its presence causes both light and heat; — that heat acting upon water, produces vapors; — that those vapors rising in clouds into the regions of the air, dissolve into rain or snow, and renew incessantly the waters of fountains and rivers.

It is a law of nature, that water flows downwards; that it endeavors to find its level; that it is heavier than air; that all bodies tend towards the earth; that flame ascends towards the heavens; — that it disorganizes vegetables and animals; that air is essential to the life of certain animals; that, in certain circumstances, water suffocates and kills them; that certain juices of plants, certain minerals attack their organs, and destroy their life, and so on in a multitude of other instances.

Wherefore, as all those and similar facts are immutable, constant, and regular, so many real orders result from them for man to conform himself to, with the express clause of punishment attending the infraction of them, or of welfare attending their observance. So that if man pretends to see clear in darkness, if he goes in contradiction to the course of the seasons, or the action of the elements; if he pretends to remain under water without being drowned, to touch fire without burning himself, to deprive himself of air without being suffocated, to swallow poison without destroying himself, he receives from each of those infractions of the laws of nature a corporeal punishment proportionate to his fault; but if on the contrary, he observes and practises each of those laws according to the regular and exact relations they have to him, he preserves his existence, and renders it as happy as it can be: and as the only and common end of all those laws, considered relatively to mankind, is to preserve, and render them happy, it has been agreed upon to reduce the idea to one simple expression, and to call them collectively the *law of nature*.

CHAPTER II.

CHARACTERS OF THE LAW OF NATURE.

Q. WHAT are the characters of the law of nature?

A. There can be assigned ten principal ones.

Q. Which is the first?

A. To be inherent to the existence of things, and, consequently, primitive and anterior to every other law : so that all those which man has received, are only imitations of it, and their perfection is ascertained by the resemblance they bear to this primordial model.

Q. Which is the second?

A. To be derived immediately from God, and presented by him to each man, whereas all other laws are presented to us by men, who may be either deceived or deceivers.

Q. Which is the third?

A. To be common to all times, and to all countries, that is to say, one and universal.

Q. Is no other law universal?

A. No: for no other is agreeable or applicable to all the people of the earth ; they are all local and accidental, originating from circumstances of places and of persons ; so that if such a man had not existed, or such an event happened, such a law would never have been enacted.

Q. Which is the fourth character?

A. To be uniform and invariable.

Q. Is no other law uniform and invariable?

A. No : for what is good and virtue according to one, is evil and vice according to another ; and what one and the same law approves of at one time, it often condemns at another.

Q. Which is the fifth character?

A. To be evident and palpable, because it consists entirely of facts incessantly present to the senses, and to demonstration.

Q. Are not other laws evident?

A. No: for they are founded on past and doubtful facts, on equivocal and suspicious testimonies, and on proofs inaccessible to the senses.

Q. Which is the sixth character?

A. To be reasonable, because its precepts and entire doctrine are conformable to reason, and to the human understanding.

Q. Is no other law reasonable?

A. No: for all are in contradiction to the reason and the understanding of men, and tyrannically impose on him a blind and impracticable belief.

Q. Which is the seventh character?

A. To be just, because in that law, the penalties are proportionate to the infractions.

Q. Are not other laws just?

A. No: for they often exceed bounds, either in rewarding deserts, or in punishing delinquencies, and consider as meritorious or criminal, null or indifferent actions.

Q. Which is the eighth character?

A. To be pacific and tolerant, because in the law of nature, all men being brothers and equal in rights, it recommends to them only peace and toleration, even for errors.

Q. Are not other laws pacific?

A. No: for all preach dissension, discord, and war, and divide mankind by exclusive pretensions of truth and domination.

Q. Which is the ninth character?

A. To be equally beneficent to all men, in teaching them the true means of becoming better and happier.

Q. Are not other laws beneficent likewise?

A. No: for none of them teach the real means of attaining happiness; all are confined to pernicious or futile practices; and this is evident from facts, since after so many laws, so many religions, so many legislators and prophets, men are still as unhappy and ignorant, as they were six thousand years ago.

Q. Which is the last character of the law of nature?

A. That it is alone sufficient to render men happier and better, because it comprises all that is good and useful in other laws, either civil or religious, that is to say, it constitutes essentially the moral part of them; so that if other laws were divested of it, they would be reduced to chimerical and imaginary opinions devoid of any practical utility.

Q. Recapitulate all those characters.

A. We have said that the law of nature is,

1. Primitive;	6. Reasonable;
2. Immediate;	7. Just;
3. Universal;	8. Pacific;
4. Invariable;	9. Beneficent: and
5. Evident;	10. Alone sufficient.

And such is the power of all these attributes of perfection and truth, that when in their disputes the theologians can agree upon no article of belief, they recur to the law of nature, the neglect of which, say they, forced God to send from time to time prophets to proclaim new laws; as if God enacted laws for particular circumstances, as men do; especially when the first subsists in such force, that we may assert it to have been at all times and in all countries the rule of conscience for every man of sense or understanding.

Q. If, as you say, it emanates immediately from God, does it teach his existence?

A. Yes, most positively: for, to any man whatever, who observes with reflection the astonishing spectacle of the universe, the more he meditates on the properties and attributes of each being, on the admirable order and harmony of their motions, the more it is demonstrated that there exists a supreme agent, a universal and identic mover, designated by the appellation of God; and so true it is that the law of nature suffices to elevate him to the knowledge of God, that all-which men have pretended to know by supernatural means, has constantly turned out ridiculous and absurd, and that they have ever been obliged to recur to the immutable conceptions of natural reason.

Q. Then it is not true that the followers of the law of nature are atheists?

A. No; it is not true; on the contrary, they entertain stronger and nobler ideas of the Divinity than most other men; for they do not sully him with the foul ingredients of all the weaknesses and passions entailed on humanity.

Q. What worship do they pay to him?

A. A worship wholly of action; the practice and observance of all the rules which the supreme wisdom has imposed on the motion of each being; eternal and unalterable rules, by which it maintains the order and harmony of the universe, and which, in their relations to man, constitute the law of nature.

Q. Was the law of nature known before this period:

A. It has been at all times spoken of: most legislators pretend to adopt it as the basis of their laws; but they only quote some of its precepts, and have only vague ideas of its totality.

Q. Why.

A. Because, though simple in its basis, it forms in its developements and consequences, a complicated whole which requires an extensive knowledge of facts, joined to all the sagacity of reasoning.

Q. Does not instinct alone teach the law of nature?

A. No; for by instinct is meant nothing more than that blind sentiment by which we are actuated indiscriminately towards everything that flatters the senses.

Q. Why, then, is it said that the law of nature is engraved in the hearts of all men.

A. It is said for two reasons: first, because it has been remarked, that there are acts and sentiments common to all men, and this proceeds from their common organization; secondly, because the first philosophers believed that men were born with ideas already formed, which is now demonstrated to be erroneous.

Q. Philosophers, then, are fallible?

A. Yes, sometimes.

Q. Why so?

A. First, because they are men; secondly, because the ignorant call all those who reason, right or wrong, philosophers; thirdly, because those who reason on many subjects, and who are the first to reason on them, are liable to be deceived.

Q. If the law of nature be not written, must it not become arbitrary and ideal?

A. No: because it consists entirely in facts, the demonstration of which can be incessantly renewed to the senses,

and constitutes a science as accurate and precise as geometry and mathematics; and it is because the law of nature
forms an exact science, that men, born ignorant and living
inattentive and heedless, have had hitherto only a superficial
knowledge of it.

CHAPTER III.

PRINCIPLES OF THE LAW OF NATURE RELATING TO MAN.

Q. EXPLAIN the principles of the law of nature with relation
to man.

A. They are simple; all of them are comprised in one fundamental and single precept.

Q. What is that precept?

A. It is self-preservation.

Q. Is not happiness also a precept of the law of nature?

A. Yes: but as happiness is an accidental state, resulting
only from the development of man's faculties and his social
system, it is not the immediate and direct object of nature; it
is in some measure, a superfluity annexed to the necessary
and fundamental object of preservation.

Q. How does nature order man to preserve himself?

A. By two powerful and involuntary sensations, which it
has attached, as two guides, two guardian Geniuses to all his
actions: the one a sensation of pain, by which it admonishes
him of, and deters him from, everything that tends to destroy
him; the other, a sensation of pleasure, by which it attracts
and carries him towards everything that tends to his preservation and the development of his existence.

Q. Pleasure, then, is not an evil, a sin, as casuists pretend?

A. No, only inasmuch as it tends to destroy life and health,
which, by the avowal of those same casuists, we derive from
God himself.

Q. Is pleasure the principal object of our existence, as some
philosophers have asserted?

A. No; not more than pain; pleasure is an incitement to
live as pain is a repulsion from death.

Q. How do you prove this assertion?

A. By two palpable facts : One, that pleasure, when taken immoderately, leads to destruction ; for instance, a man who abuses the pleasure of eating or drinking, attacks his health, and injures his life. The other, that pain sometimes leads to self-preservation ; for instance, a man who permits a mortified member to be cut off, suffers pain in order not to perish totally.

Q. But does not even this prove that our sensations can deceive us respecting the end of our preservation ?

A. Yes ; they can momentarily.

Q. How do our sensations deceive us ?

A. In two ways : by ignorance, and by passion.

Q. When do they deceive us by ignorance ?

A. When we act without knowing the action and effect of objects on our senses : for example, when a man touches nettles without knowing their stinging quality, or when he swallows opium without knowing its soporiferous effects.

Q. When do they deceive us by passion ?

A. When, conscious of the pernicious action of objects, we abandon ourselves, nevertheless, to the impetuosity of our desires and appetites : for example, when a man who knows that wine intoxicates, does nevertheless drink it to excess.

Q. What is the result ?

A. That the ignorance in which we are born, and the unbridled appetites to which we abandon ourselves, are contrary to our preservation ; that, therefore, the instruction of our minds and the moderation of our passions are two obligations, two laws, which spring directly from the first law of preservation.

Q. But being born ignorant, is not ignorance a law of nature?

A. No more than to remain in the naked and feeble state of infancy. Far from being a law of nature, ignorance is an obstacle to the practice of all its laws. It is the real original sin.

Q. Why, then, have there been moralists who have looked upon it as a virtue and perfection ?

A. Because, from a strange or perverted disposition, they confounded the abuse of knowledge with knowledge itself ; as if, because men abuse the power of speech, their tongues should be cut out ; as if perfection and virtue consisted in the nullity, and not in the proper development of our faculties.

Q. Instruction, then, is indispensable to man's existence ?

A. Yes, so indispensable, that without it he is every instant assailed and wounded by all that surrounds him ; for if he does not know the effects of fire, he burns himself; those of water he drowns himself; those of opium, he poisons himself; if, in the savage state, he does not know the wiles of animals, and the art of seizing game, he perishes through hunger; if in the social state, he does not know the course of the seasons, he can neither cultivate the ground, nor procure nourishment ; and so on, of all his actions, respecting all his wants.

Q. But can man individually acquire this knowledge necessary to his existence, and to the development of his faculties ?

A. No ; not without the assistance of his fellow men, and by living in society.

Q. But is not society to man a state against nature ?

A. No : it is on the contrary a necessity, a law that nature imposed on him by the very act of his organization ; for, first, nature has so constituted man, that he cannot see his species of another sex without feeling emotions and an attraction, which induce him to live in a family, which is already a state of society ; secondly, by endowing him with sensibility, she organized him so that the sensations of others reflect within him, and excite reciprocal sentiments of pleasure and of grief, which are attractions, and indissoluble ties of society ; thirdly, and finally, the state of society, founded on the wants of man, is only a further means of fulfilling the law of preservation : and to pretend that this state is out of nature, because it is more perfect, is the same as to say, that a bitter and wild fruit of the forest, is no longer the production of nature, when rendered sweet and delicious by cultivation in our gardens.

Q. Why, then, have philosophers called the savage state the state of perfection ?

A. Because, as I have told you, the vulgar have often given the name of philosophers to whimsical geniuses, who, from moroseness, from wounded vanity, or from a disgust to the vices of society, have conceived chimerical ideas of the savage state, in contradiction with their own system of a perfect man.

Q. What is the true meaning of the word philosopher ?

A. The word philosopher signifies a lover of wisdom ; and as wisdom consists in the practice of the laws of nature, the true philosopher is he who knows those laws, and conforms the whole tenor of his conduct to them.

Q. What is man in the savage state?

A. A brutal, ignorant animal, a wicked and ferocious beast.

Q. Is he happy in that state?

A. No; for he only feels momentary sensations, which are habitually of violent wants which he cannot satisfy, since he is ignorant by nature, and weak by being isolated from his race.

Q. Is he free?

A. No; he is the most abject slave that exists; for his life depends on everything that surrounds him: he is not free to eat when hungry, to rest when tired, to warm himself when cold; he is every instant in danger of perishing; wherefore nature offers but fortuitous examples of such beings; and we see that all the efforts of the human species, since its origin, sorely tends to emerge from that violent state by the pressing necessity of self-preservation.

Q. But does not this necessity of preservation engender in individuals egotism, that is to say self-love? and is not egotism contrary to the social state?

A. No; for if by egotism you mean a propensity to hurt our neighbor, it is no longer self-love, but the hatred of others. Self-love, taken in its true sense, not only is not contrary to society, but is its firmest support, by the necessity we lie under of not injuring others, lest in return they should injure us.

Thus man's preservation, and the unfolding of his faculties, directed towards this end, teach the true law of nature in the production of the human being; and it is from this essential principle that are derived, are referred, and in its scale are weighed, all ideas of good and evil, of vice and virtue, of just and unjust, of truth or error, of lawful or forbidden, on which is founded the morality of individual, or of social man.

CHAPTER IV.

BASIS OF MORALITY; OF GOOD, OF EVIL, OF SIN, OF CRIME, OF VICE AND OF VIRTUE.

Q. WHAT is good, according to the law of nature?

A. It is everything that tends to preserve and perfect man.

Q. What is evil?

A. That which tends to man's destruction or deterioration.

Q. What is meant by physical good and evil, and by moral good and evil ?

A. By the word physical is understood, whatever acts immediately on the body. Health is a physical good; and sickness a physical evil. By moral, is meant what acts by consequences more or less remote. Calumny is a moral evil; a fair reputation is a moral good, because both one and the other occasion towards us, on the part of other men, dispositions and habitudes,* which are useful or hurtful to our preservation, and which attack or favor our means of existence.

Q. Everything that tends to preserve, or to produce is therefore a good ?

A. Yes; and it is for that reason that certain legislators have classed among the works agreeable to the divinity, the cultivation of a field and the fecundity of a woman.

Q. Whatever tends to cause death is, therefore, an evil ?

A. Yes; and it is for that reason some legislators have extended the idea of evil and of sin even to the killing of animals.

Q. The murdering of a man is, therefore, a crime in the law of nature ?

A. Yes, and the greatest that can be committed; for every other evil can be repaired, but murder alone is irreparable.

Q. What is a sin in the law of nature ?

A. Whatever tends to disturb the order established by nature for the preservation and perfection of man and of society.

Q. Can intention be a merit or a crime ?

A. No, for it is only an idea void of reality: but it is a commencement of sin and evil, by the impulse it gives to action.

Q. What is virtue according to the law of nature ?

A. It is the practice of actions useful to the individual and to society.

Q. What is meant by the word individual ?

A. It means a man considered separately from every other.

Q. What is vice according to the law of nature ?

A. It is the practice of actions prejudicial to the individual and to society.

Q. Have not virtue and vice an object purely spiritual and abstracted from the senses ?

* It is from this word habitudes, (reiterated actions,) in Latin *mores*, that the word moral, and all its family, are derived.

A. No; it is always to a physical end that they finally relate, and that end is always to destroy or preserve the body.

Q. Have vice and virtue degrees of strength and intensity?

A. Yes: according to the importance of the faculties, which they attack or which they favor; and according to the number of persons in whom those faculties are favored or injured.

Q. Give me some examples?

A. The action of saving a man's life is more virtuous than that of saving his property; the action of saving the lives of ten men, than that of saving only the life of one, and an action useful to the whole human race is more virtuous than an action that is only useful to one single nation.

Q. How does the law of nature prescribe the practice of good and virtue, and forbid that of evil and vice?

A. By the advantages resulting from the practice of good and virtue for the preservation of our body, and by the losses which result to our existence from the practice of evil and vice.

Q. Its precepts are then in action?

A. Yes: they are action itself, considered in its present effect and in its future consequences.

Q. How do you divide the virtues?

A. We divide them in three classes, first, individual virtues, as relative to man alone; secondly, domestic virtues, as relative to a family; thirdly, social virtues, as relative to society.

CHAPTER V.

OF INDIVIDUAL VIRTUES.

Q. WHICH are the individual virtues?

A. There are five principal ones, to wit: first, science, which comprises prudence and wisdom; secondly, temperance, comprising sobriety and chastity; thirdly, courage, or strength of body and mind; fourthly, activity, that is to say, love of labor and employment of time; fifthly, and finally, cleanliness, or purity of body, as well in dress as in habitation.

Q. How does the law of nature prescribe science?

A. Because the man acquainted with the causes and effects of things attends in a careful and sure manner to his preservation, and to the development of his faculties. Science is to him the eye and the light, which enable him to discern clearly and accurately all the objects with which he is conversant, and hence by an enlightened man is meant a learned and well-informed man. With science and instruction a man never wants for resources and means of subsistence ; and upon this principle a philosopher, who had been shipwrecked, said to his companions, that were inconsolable for the loss of their wealth : " For my part, I carry all my wealth within me."

Q. Which is the vice contrary to science?

A. It is ignorance.

Q. How does the law of nature forbid ignorance ?

A. By the grievous detriments resulting from it to our existence ; for the ignorant man who knows neither causes nor effects, commits every instant errors most pernicious to himself and to others ; he resembles a blind man groping his way at random, and who, at every step, jostles or is jostled by every one he meets.

Q. What difference is there between an ignorant and a silly man ?

A. The same difference as between him who frankly avows his blindness and the blind man who pretends to sight; silliness is the reality of ignorance, to which is superadded the vanity of knowledge.

Q. Are ignorance and silliness common ?

A. Yes, very common ; they are the usual and general distempers of mankind : more than three thousand years ago the wisest of men said : " The number of fools is infinite ; " and the world has not changed.

Q. What is the reason of it ?

A. Because much labor and time are necessary to acquire instruction, and because men, born ignorant and indolent, find it more convenient to remain blind, and pretend to see clear.

Q. What difference is there between a learned and a wise man ?

A. The learned knows, and the wise man practices.

Q. What is prudence ?

A. It is the anticipated perception, the foresight of the effects and consequences of every action ; by means of which foresight, man avoids the dangers which threaten him, while he seizes on and creates opportunities favorable to him: he thereby provides for his present and future safety in a certain and secure manner, whereas the imprudent man, who calculates neither his steps nor his conduct, nor efforts, nor resistance, falls every instant into difficulties and dangers, which sooner or later impair his faculties and destroy his existence.

Q. When the Gospel says, "Happy are the poor of spirit," does it mean the ignorant and imprudent?

A. No; for, at the same time that it recommends the simplicity of doves, it adds the prudent cunning of serpents. By simplicity of mind is meant uprightness, and the precept of the Gospel is that of nature.

CHAPTER VI.

ON TEMPERANCE.

Q. WHAT is temperance?

A. It is a regular use of our faculties, which makes us never exceed in our sensations the end of nature to preserve us; it is the moderation of the passions.

Q. Which is the vice contrary to temperance?

A. The disorder of the passions, the avidity of all kind of enjoyments, in a word, cupidity.

Q. Which are the principal branches of temperance?

A. Sobriety, and continence or chastity.

Q. How does the law of nature prescribe sobriety?

A. By its powerful influence over our health. The sober man digests with comfort; he is not overpowered by the weight of aliments; his ideas are clear and easy; he fulfills all his functions properly; he conducts his business with intelligence; his old age is exempt from infirmity; he does not spend his money in remedies, and he enjoys, in mirth and gladness, the wealth which chance and his own prudence have procured him. Thus, from one virtue alone, generous nature derives innumerable recompenses.

Q. How does it prohibit gluttony?

A. By the numerous evils that are attached to it. The glutton, oppressed with aliments, digests with anxiety; his head, troubled by the fumes of indigestion, is incapable of conceiving clear and distinct ideas; he abandons himself with violence to the disorderly impulse of lust and anger, which impair his health ; his body becomes bloated, heavy, and unfit for labor; he endures painful and expensive distempers; he seldom lives to be old; and his age is replete with infirmities and sorrow.

Q. Should abstinence and fasting be considered as virtuous actions ?

A. Yes, when one has eaten too much; for then abstinence and fasting are simple and efficacious remedies ; but when the body is in want of aliment, to refuse it any, and let it suffer from hunger or thirst, is delirium and a real sin against the law of nature.

Q. How is drunkenness considered in the law of nature?

A. As a most vile and pernicious vice. The drunkard, deprived of the sense and reason given us by God, profanes the donations of the divinity: he debases himself to the condition of brutes ; unable even to guide his steps, he staggers and falls as if he were epileptic; he hurts and even risks killing himself; his debility in this state exposes him to the ridicule and contempt of every person that sees him ; he makes in his drunkenness, prejudicial and ruinous bargains, and injures his fortune ; he makes use of opprobrious language, which creates him enemies and repentance; he fills his house with trouble and sorrow, and ends by a premature death or by a cacochymical old age.

Q. Does the law of nature interdict absolutely the use of wine ?

A. No ; it only forbids the abuse; but as the transition from the use to the abuse is easy and prompt among the generality of men, perhaps the legislators, who have proscribed the use of wine, have rendered a service to humanity.

Q. Does the law of nature forbid the use of certain kinds of meat, or of certain vegetables, on particular days, during certain seasons ?

A. No ; it absolutely forbids only whatever is injurious to health ; its precepts, in this respect, vary according to persons, and even constitute a very delicate and important science ; for the quality, the quantity, and the combination of aliments have the greatest influence, not only over the momentary affections of the soul, but even over its habitual disposition. A man is not the same when fasting as after a meal, even if he were sober. A glass of spirituous liquor, or a dish of coffee, gives degrees of vivacity, of mobility, of disposition to anger, sadness, or gaiety ; such a meat, because it lies heavy on the stomach, engenders moroseness and melancholy ; such another, because it facilitates digestion, creates sprightliness, and an inclination to oblige and to love. The use of vegetables, because they have little nourishment, enfeebles the body, and gives a disposition to repose, indolence, and ease ; the use of meat, because it is full of nourishment, and of spirituous liquors, because they stimulate the nerves, creates vivacity, uneasiness, and audacity. Now from those habitudes of aliment result habits of constitution and of the organs, which form afterwards different kinds of temperaments, each of which is distinguished by a peculiar characteristic. And it is for this reason that, in hot countries especially, legislators have made laws respecting regimen or food. The ancients were taught by long experience that the dietetic science constituted a considerable part of morality ; among the Egyptians, the ancient Persians, and even among the Greeks, at the Areopagus, important affairs were examined fasting ; and it has been remarked that, among those people, where public affairs were discussed during the heat of meals, and the fumes of digestion, deliberations were hasty and violent, and the results of them frequently unreasonable, and productive of turbulence and confusion.

CHAPTER VII.

ON CONTINENCE.

Q. DOES the law of nature prescribe continence ?

A. Yes : because a moderate use of the most lively of pleasures is not only useful, but indispensable, to the support of strength and health : and because a simple calculation proves that, for some minutes of privation, you increase the number of your days, both in vigor of body and of mind.

Q. How does it forbid libertinism ?

A. By the numerous evils which result from it to the physical and the moral existence. He who carries it to an excess enervates and pines away; he can no longer attend to study or labor; he contracts idle and expensive habits, which destroy his means of existence, his public consideration, and his credit; his intrigues occasion continual embarrassment, cares, quarrels and lawsuits, without mentioning the grievous deep-rooted distempers, and the loss of his strength by an inward and slow poison; the stupid dullness of his mind, by the exhaustion of the nervous sytem; and, in fine, a premature and infirm old age.

Q. Does the law of nature look on that absolute chastity so recommeded in monastical institutions, as a virtue?

A. No: for that chastity is of no use either to the society that witnesses, or the individual who practises it; it is even prejudicial to both. First, it injures society by depriving it of population, which is one of its principal sources of wealth and power; and as bachelors confine all their views and affections to the term of their lives, they have in general an egotism unfavorable to the interests of society.

In the second place, it injures the individuals who practise it, because it deprives them of a number of affections and relations which are the springs of most domestic and social virtues; and besides, it often happens, from circumstances of age, regimen, or temperament, that absolute continence injures the constitution and causes severe diseases, because it is contrary to the physical laws on which nature has founded the system of the reproduction of beings; and they who recommend so strongly chastity, even supposing them to be sincere, are in contradiction with their own doctrine, which consecrates the law of nature by the well known commandment: increase and multiply.

Q. Why is chastity considered a greater virtue in women than in men?

A. Because a want of chastity in women is attended with inconveniences much more serious and dangerous for them and for society; for, without taking into account the pains and diseases they have in common with men, they are further exposed to all the disadvantages and perils that precede, attend, and follow child-birth. When pregnant contrary to law, they

become an object of public scandal and contempt, and spend
the remainder of their lives in bitterness and misery. Moreover, all the expense of maintaining and educating their
fatherless children falls on them : which expense impover-
ishes them, and is every way prejudicial to their physical and
moral existence. In this situation, deprived of the freshness
and health that constitute their charm, carrying with them
an extraneous and expensive burden, they are less prized by
men, they find no solid establishment, they fall into poverty,
misery, and wretchedness, and thus drag on in sorrow their
unhappy existence.

Q. Does the law of nature extend so far as the scruples of
desires and thoughts.

A. Yes ; because, in the physical laws of the human body,
thoughts and desires inflame the senses, and soon provoke to
action : now, by another law of nature in the organization of
our body, those actions become mechanical wants which recur
at certain periods of days or of weeks, so that, at such a time,
the want is renewed of such an action and such a secretion ;
if this action and this secretion be injurious to health, the
habitude of them becomes destructive of life itself. Thus
thoughts and desires have a true and natural importance.

Q. Should modesty be considered as a virtue ?

A. Yes ; because modesty, inasmuch as it is a shame of certain actions, maintains the soul and body in all those habits
useful to good order, and to self-preservation. The modest
woman is esteemed, courted, and established, with advantages
of fortune which ensure her existence, and render it agreeable
to her, while the immodest and prostitute are despised, re-
pulsed, and abandoned to misery and infamy.

CHAPTER VIII.

ON COURAGE AND ACTIVITY.

Q. ARE courage and strength of body and mind virtues in
the law of nature ?

A. Yes, and most important virtues ; for they are the efficacious and indispensable means of attending to our preservation and welfare. The courageous and strong man repulses
oppression, defends his life, his liberty, and his property ; by

his labor he procures himself an adundant subsistence, which he enjoys in tranquillity and peace of mind. If he falls into misfortunes, from which his prudence could not protect him, he supports them with fortitude and resignation; and it is for this reason that the ancient moralists have reckoned strength and courage among the four principal virtues.

Q. Should weakness and cowardice be considered as vices?

A. Yes, since it is certain that they produce innumerable calamities. The weak or cowardly man lives in perpetual cares and agonies; he undermines his health by the dread, oftentimes ill founded, of attacks and dangers: and this dread which is an evil, is not a remedy; it renders him, on the contrary, the slave of him who wishes to oppress him; and by the servitude and debasement of all his faculties, it degrades and diminishes his means of existence, so far as the seeing his life depend on the will and caprice of another man.

Q. But, after what you have said on the influence of aliments, are not courage and force, as well as many other virtues, in a great measure the effect of our physical constitution and temperament?

A. Yes, it is true; and so far, that those qualities are transmitted by generation and blood, with the elements on which they depend: the most reiterated and constant facts prove that in the breed of animals of every kind, we see certain physical and moral qualities, attached to the individuals of those species, increase or decay according to the combinations and mixtures they make with other breeds.

Q. But, then, as our will is not sufficient to procure us those qualities, is it a crime to be destitute of them?

A. No, it is not a crime, but a misfortune; it is what the ancients call an unlucky fatality; but even then we have it yet in our power to acquire them; for, as soon as we know on what physical elements such or such a quality is founded, we can promote its growth, and hasten its developments, by a skillful management of those elements; and in this consists the science of education, which, according as it is directed, meliorates or degrades individuals, or the whole race, to such a pitch as totally to change their nature and inclinations; for which reason it is of the greatest importance to be acquainted with the laws of nature by which those operations and changes are certainly and necessarily effected.

Q. Why do you say that activity is a virtue according to the law of nature ?

A. Because the man who works and employs his time usefully, derives from it a thousand precious advantages to his existence. If he is born poor, his labor furnishes him with subsistence ; and still more so, if he is sober, continent, and prudent, for he soon acquires a competency, and enjoys the sweets of life ; his very labor gives him virtues ; for, while he occupies his body and mind, he is not affected with unruly desires, time does not lie heavy on him, he contracts mild habits, he augments his strength and health, and attains a peaceful and happy old age.

Q. Are idleness and sloth vices in the law of nature ?

A. Yes, and the most pernicious of all vices, for they lead to all the others. By idleness and sloth man remains ignorant, he forgets even the science he had acquired, and falls into all the misfortunes which accompany ignorance and folly ; by idleness and sloth man, devoured with disquietude, in order to dissipate it, abandons himself to all the desires of his senses, which, becoming every day more inordinate, render him intemperate, gluttonous, lascivious, enervated, cowardly, vile, and contemptible. By the certain effect of all those vices, he ruins his fortune, consumes his health, and terminates his life in all the agonies of sickness and of poverty,

Q. From what you say, one would think that poverty was a vice ?

A. No, it is not a vice ; but it is still less a virtue, for it is by far more ready to injure than to be useful ; it is even commonly the result, or the beginning of vice, for the effect of all individual vices is to lead to indigence, and to the privation of the necessaries of life ; and when a man is in want of necessaries, he is tempted to procure them by vicious means, that is to say, by means injurious to society. All the individual virtues tend, on the contrary, to procure to a man an abundant subsistence ; and when he has more than he can consume, it is much easier for him to give to others, and to practice the actions useful to society.

Q. Do you look upon opulence as a virtue ?

A. No ; but still less as a vice : it is the use alone of wealth that can be called virtuous or vicious, according as it is serviceable or prejudicial to man and to society. Wealth is an instrument, the use and employment alone of which determine its virtue or vice.

CHAPTER IX.

ON CLEANLINESS.

Q. WHY is cleanliness included among the virtues ?

A. Because it is, in reality, one of the most important among them, on account of its powerful influence over the health and preservation of the body. Cleanliness, as well in dress as in residence, obviates the pernicious effects of the humidity, baneful odors, and contagious exhalations, proceeding from all things abandoned to putrefaction. Cleanliness, maintains free transpiration ; it renews the air, refreshes the blood, and disposes even the mind to cheerfulness.

From this it appears that persons attentive to the cleanliness of their bodies and habitations are, in general, more healthy, and less subject to disease, than those who live in filth and nastiness ; and it is further remarked, that cleanliness carries with it, throughout all the branches of domestic administration, habits of order and arrangement, which are the chief means and first elements of happiness.

Q. Uncleanliness or filthiness is, then, a real vice?

A. Yes, as real a one as drunkenness, or as idleness, from which in a great measure it is derived. Uncleanliness is the second, and often the first, cause of many inconveniences, and even of grievous disorders ; it is a fact in medicine, that it brings on the itch, the scurf, tetters, leprosies, as much as the use of tainted or sour aliments ; that it favors the contagious influence of the plague and malignant fevers, that it even produces them in hospitals and prisons ; that it occasions rheumatisms, by incrusting the skin with dirt, and thereby preventing transpiration ; without reckoning the shameful inconvenience of being devoured by vermin—the foul appendage of misery and depravity.

Most ancient legislators, therefore, considered cleanliness, which they called purity, as one of the essential dogmas of their religions. It was for this reason that they expelled from society, and even punished corporeally those who were infected with distempers produced by uncleanliness ; that they instituted and consecrated ceremonies of ablutions, baths, baptisms, and of purifications, even by fire and the aromatic fumes of incense, myrrh, benjamin, etc., so that the entire system of pollutions, all those rites of clean and unclean things, degenerated since into abuses and prejudices, were only founded originally on the judicious observation, which wise and learned men had made, of the extreme influence that cleanliness in dress and abode exercises over the health of the body, and by an immediate consequence over that of the mind and moral faculties.

Thus all the individual virtues have for their object, more or less direct, more or less near, the preservation of the man who practises them ; and by the preservation of each man, they lead to that of families and society, which are composed of the united sum of individuals.

CHAPTER X.

ON DOMESTIC VIRTUES.

Q. WHAT do you mean be domestic virtues ?

A. I mean the practice of actions useful to a family, supposed to live in the same house.*

Q. What are those virtues ?

A. They are economy, paternal love, filial love, conjugal love, fraternal love, and the accomplishment of the duties of master and servant.

Q. What is economy ?

A. It is, according to the most extensive meaning of the word, the proper administration of every thing that concerns the existence of the family or house ; and as subsistence holds the first rank, the word economy in confined to the employment of money for the wants of life.

* Domestic is derived from the Latin word *domus*, a house.

Q. Why is economy a virtue?

A. Because a man who makes no useless expenses acquires a superabundancy, which is true wealth, and by means of which he procures for himself and his family everything that is really convenient and useful ; without mentioning his securing thereby resources against accidental and unforeseen losses, so that he and his family enjoy an agreeable and undisturbed competency, which is the basis of human felicity.

Q. Dissipation and prodigality, therefore, are vices?

A. Yes, for by them man, in the end, is deprived of the necessaries of life ; he falls into poverty and wretchedness ; and his very friends, fearing to be obliged to restore to him what he has spent with or for them, avoid him as a debtor does his creditor, and he remains abandoned by the whole world.

Q. What is paternal love?

A. It is the assiduous care taken by parents to make their children contract the habit of every action useful to themselves and to society.

Q. Why is paternal tenderness a virtue in parents?

A. Because parents, who rear their children in those habits, procure for themselves, during the course of their lives, enjoyments and helps that give a sensible satisfaction at every instant, and which assure to them, when advanced in years, supports and consolations against the wants and calamities of all kinds with which old age is beset.

Q. Is paternal love a common virtue?

A. No ; notwithstanding the ostentation made of it by parents, it is a rare virtue. They do not love their children, they caress and spoil them. In them they love only the agents of their will, the instruments of their power, the trophies of their vanity, the pastime of their idleness. It is not so much the welfare of their children that they propose to themselves, as their submission and obedience ; and if among children so many are seen ungrateful for benefits received, it is because there are among parents as many despotic and ignorant benefactors.

Q. Why do you say that conjugal love is a virtue?

A. Because the concord and union resulting from the love of the married, establish in the heart of the family a multitude of habits useful to its prosperity and preservation. The united pair are attached to, and seldom quit their home ; they superintend each particular direction of it ; they attend to the education of their children ; they maintain the respect and fidelity of domestics ; they prevent all disorder and dissipation ; and from the whole of their good conduct, they live in ease and consideration ; while married persons who do not love one another, fill their house with quarrels and troubles, create dissension between their children and the servants, leaving both indiscriminately to all kinds of vicious habits ; every one in turn spoils, robs, and plunders the house : the revenues are absorbed without profit ; debts accumulate ; the married pair avoid each other, or contend in lawsuits ; and the whole family falls into disorder, ruin, disgrace and want.

Q. Is adultery an offence in the law of nature ?

A. Yes ; for it is attended with a number of habits injurious to the married and to their families. The wife or husband, whose affections are estranged, neglect their house, avoid it, and deprive it, as much as they can, of its revenues or income, to expend them with the object of their affections ; hence arise quarrels, scandal, lawsuits, the neglect of their children and servants, and at last the plundering and ruin of the whole family ; without reckoning that the adulterous woman commits a most grievous theft, in giving to her husband heirs of foreign blood, who deprive his real children of their legitimate portion.

Q. What is filial love ?

A. It is, on the side of children, the practice of those actions useful to themselves and to their parents.

Q. How does the law of nature prescribe filial love ?

A. By three principal motives :

1. By sentiment ; for the affectionate care of parents inspires from the most tender age, mild habits of attachment.

2. By justice ; for children owe to their parents a return and indemnity for the cares, and even for the expenses, they have caused them.

3. By personal interest ; for, if they use them ill, they give to their own children examples of revolt and ingratitude, which authorize them, at a future day, to behave to themselves in a similar manner.

Q. Are we to understand by filial love a passive and blind submission ?

A. No ; but a reasonable submission, founded on the knowledge of the mutual rights and duties of parents and children ; rights and duties, without the observance of which their mutual conduct is nothing but disorder.

Q. Why is fraternal love a virtue ?

A. Because the concord and union, which result from the love of brothers, establish the strength, security, and conservation of the family : brothers united defend themselves against all oppression, they aid one another in their wants, they help one another in their misfortunes, and thus secure their common existence ; while brothers disunited, abandoned each to his own personal strength, fall into all the inconveniences attendant on an insulated state and individual weakness. This is what a certain Scythian king ingeniously expressed when, on his death-bed, calling his children to him, he ordered them to break a bundle of arrows. The young men, though strong, being unable to effect it, he took them in his turn, and untieing them, broke each of the arrows separately with his fingers. " Behold," said he, " the effects of union ; united together, you will be invincible ; taken separately, you will be broken like reeds."

Q. What are the reciprocal duties of masters and of servants ?

A. They consist in the practice of the actions which are respectively and justly useful to them ; and here begin the relations of society ; for the rule and measure of those respective actions is the equilibrium or equality between the service and the recompense, between what the one returns and the other gives ; which is the fundamental basis of all society.

Thus all the domestic and individual virtues refer, more or less mediately, but always with certitude, to the physical object of the amelioration and preservation of man, and are thereby precepts resulting from the fundamental law of nature in his formation.

CHAPTER XI.

THE SOCIAL VIRTUES ; JUSTICE.

Q. WHAT is society ?

A. It is every reunion of men living together under the clauses of an expressed or tacit contract, which has for its end their common preservation.

Q. Are the social virtues numerous ?

A. Yes ; they are in as great number as the kinds of actions useful to society ; but all may be reduced to one principle.

Q. What is that fundamental principle ?

A. It is justice, which alone comprises all the virtues of society.

Q. Why do you say that justice is the fundamental and almost only virtue of society ?

A. Because it alone embraces the practice of all the actions useful to it ; and because all the other virtues, under the denominations of charity, humanity, probity, love of one's country, sincerity, generosity, simplicity of manners, and modesty, are only varied forms and diversified applications of the axiom, " Do not to another what you do not wish to be done to yourself," which is the definition of justice.

Q. How does the law of nature prescribe justice ?

A. By three physical attributes, inherent in the organization of man.

Q. What are those attributes ?

A. They are equality, liberty, and property.

Q. How is equality a physical attribute of man ?

A. Because all men, having equally eyes, hands, mouths, ears, and the necessity of making use of them, in order to live, have, by this reason alone, an equal right to life, and to the use of the aliments which maintain it ; they are all equal before God.

Q. Do you suppose that all men hear equally, see equally, feel equally, have equal wants, and equal passions ?

A. No ; for it is evident, and daily demonstrated, that one is short, and another long-sighted ; that one eats much, another little ; that one has mild, another violent passions ; in a word, that one is weak in body and mind, while another is strong in both.

Q. They are, therefore, really unequal ?

A. Yes, in the development of their means, but not in the nature and essence of those means. They are made of the same stuff, but not in the same dimensions ; nor are the weight and value equal. Our language possesses no one word capable of expressing the identity of nature, and the diversity of its form and employment. It is a proportional equality ; and it is for this reason I have said, equal before God, and in the order of nature.

Q. How is liberty a physical attribute of man ?

A. Because all men having senses sufficient for their preservation — no one wanting the eye of another to see, his ear to hear, his mouth to eat, his feet to walk — they are all, by this very reason, constituted naturally independent and free ; no man is necessarily subjected to another, nor has he a right to dominate over him.

Q. But if a man is born strong, has he a natural right to master the weak man ?

A. No ; for it is neither a necessity for him, nor a convention between them ; it is an abusive extension of his strength ; and here an abuse is made of the word right, which in its true meaning implies, justice or reciprocal faculty.

Q. How is property a physical attribute of man ?

A. Inasmuch as all men being constituted equal or similar to one another, and consequently independent and free, each is the absolute master, the full proprietor of his body and of the produce of his labor.

Q. How is justice derived from these three attributes ?

A. In this, that men being equal and free, owing nothing to each other, have no right to require anything from one another only inasmuch as they return an equal value for it; or inasmuch as the balance of what is given is in equilibrium with what is returned: and it is this equality, this equilibrium which is called justice, equity ;* that is to say that equality and justice are but one and the same word, the same law of nature, of which the social virtues are only applications and derivatives.

* Æquitas, æquilibrium, æqualitas, are all of the same family.

CHAPTER XII.

DEVELOPMENT OF THE SOCIAL VIRTUES.

Q. EXPLAIN how the social virtues are derived from the law of nature. How is charity or the love of one's neighbor a precept and application of it?

A. By reason of equality and reciprocity; for when we injure another, we give him a right to injure us in return; thus, by attacking the existence of our neighbor, we endanger our own, from the effect of reciprocity; on the other hand, by doing good to others, we have room and right to expect an equivalent exchange; and such is the character of all social virtues, that they are useful to the man who practises them, by the right of reciprocity which they give him over those who are benefited by them.

Q. Charity is then nothing but justice?

A. No: it is only justice; with this slight difference, that strict justice confines itself to saying, " Do not to another the harm you would not wish he should do to you;" and that charity, or the love of one's neighbor, extends so far as to say, " Do to another the good which you would wish to receive from him." Thus when the gospel said, that this precept contained the whole of the law and the prophets, it announced nothing more than the precept of the law of nature.

Q. Does it enjoin forgiveness of injuries?

A. Yes, when that forgiveness implies self-preservation.

Q. Does it prescribe to us, after having received a blow on one cheek, to hold out the other?

A. No; for it is, in the first place, contrary to the precept of loving our neighbor as ourselves, since thereby we should love, more than ourselves, him who makes an attack on our preservation. Secondly, such a precept in its literal sense, encourages the wicked to oppression and injustice. The law of nature has been more wise in prescribing a calculated proportion of courage and moderation, which induces us to forget a first or unpremediated injury, but which punishes every act tending to oppression.

Q. Does the law of nature prescribe to do good to others beyond the bounds of reason and measure?

A. No ; for it is a sure way of leading them to ingratitude. Such is the force of sentiment and justice implanted in the heart of man, that he is not even grateful for benefits conferred without discretion. There is only one measure with them, and that is to be just.

Q. Is alms-giving a virtuous action ?

A. Yes, when it is practised according to the rule first mentioned ; without which it degenerates into imprudence and vice, inasmuch as it encourages laziness, which is hurtful to the beggar and to society ; no one has a right to partake of the property and fruits of another's labor, without rendering an equivalent of his own industry.

Q. Does the law of nature consider as virtues faith and hope, which are often joined with charity ?

A. No ; for they are ideas without reality ; and if any effects result from them, they turn rather to the profit of those who have not those ideas, than of those who have them ; so that faith and hope may be called the virtues of dupes for the benefit of knaves.

Q. Does the law of nature prescribe probity ?

A. Yes, for probity is nothing more than respect for one's own rights in those of another ; a respect founded on a prudent and well combined calculation of our interests compared to those of others.

Q. But does not this calculation, which embraces the complicated interests and rights of the social state, require an enlightened understanding and knowledge, which make it a difficult science ?

A. Yes, and a science so much the more delicate as the honest man pronounces in his own cause.

Q. Probity, then, shows an extension and justice in the mind?

A. Yes, for an honest man almost always neglects a present interest, in order not to destroy a future one ; whereas the knave does the contrary, and loses a great future interest for a present smaller one.

Q. Improbity, therefore, is a sign of false judgment and a narrow mind?

A. Yes, and rogues may be defined ignorant and silly calculators ; for they do not understand their true interest, and they pretend to cunning : nevertheless, their cunning only ends in

making known what they are — in losing all confidence and
esteem, and the good services resulting from them ·for their
physical and social existence. They neither live in peace
with others, nor with themselves; and incessantly menaced by
their conscience and their enemies, they enjoy no other real
happiness but that of not being hanged.

Q. Does the law of nature forbid robbery?

A. Yes, for the man who robs another gives him a right to
rob him; from that moment there is no security in his property, nor in his means of preservation : thus, in injuring others,
he, by a counterblow, injures himself.

Q. Does it interdict even an inclination to rob?

A. Yes; for that inclination leads naturally to action, and it
is for this reason that envy is considered a sin?

Q. How does it forbid murder?

A. By the most powerful motives of self-preservation ; for,
first, the man who attacks exposes himself to the risk of being
killed, by the right of defence ; secondly, if he kills, he gives
to the relations and friends of the deceased, and to society at
large, an equal right of killing him; so that his life is no
longer in safety.

Q. How can we, by the law of nature, repair the evil we
have done?

A. By rendering a proportionate good to those whom we
have injured.

Q. Does it allow us to repair it by prayers, vows, offerings
to God, fasting and mortifications?

A. No : for all those things are foreign to the action we wish
to repair : they neither restore the ox to him from whom it has
been stolen, honor to him whom we have deprived of it, nor
life to him from whom it has been taken away ; consequently
they miss the end of justice ; they are only perverse contracts
by which a man sells to another goods which do not belong
to him ; they are a real depravation of morality, inasmuch as
they embolden to commit crimes through the hope of expi-
ating them ; wherefore, they have been the real cause of all
the evils by which the people among whom those expiatory
practices were used, have been continually tormented.

Q. Does the law of nature order sincerity?

A. Yes ; for lying, perfidy, and perjury create distrust, quarrels, hatred, revenge, and a crowd of evils among men, which tend to their common destruction; while sincerity and fidelity establish confidence, concord, and peace, besides the infinite good resulting from such a state of things to society.

Q. Does it prescribe mildness and modesty?

A. Yes; for harshness and obduracy, by alienating from us the hearts of other men, give them an inclination to hurt us; ostentation and vanity, by wounding their self-love and jealousy, occasion us to miss the end of a real utility.

Q. Does it prescribe humility as a virtue?

A. No; for it is a propensity in the human heart to despise secretly everything that presents to it the idea of weakness; and self-debasement encourages pride and oppression in others; the balance must be kept in equipoise.

Q. You have reckoned simplicity of manners among the social virtues; what do you understand by that word?

A. I mean the restricting our wants and desires to what is truly useful to the existence of the citizen and his family; that is to say, the man of simple manners has but few wants, and lives content with a little.

Q. How is this virtue prescribed to us?

A. By the numerous advantages which the practice of it procures to the individual and to society; for the man whose wants are few, is free at once from a crowd of cares, perplexities, and labors; he avoids many quarrels and contests arising from avidity and a desire of gain; he spares himself the anxiety of ambition, the inquietudes of possession, and the uneasiness of losses; finding superfluity everywhere, he is the real rich man; always content with what he has, he is happy at little expense; and other men, not fearing any competition from him, leave him in quiet, and are disposed to render him the services he should stand in need of. And if this virtue of simplicity extends to a whole people, they insure to themselves abundance; rich in everything they do not consume, they acquire immense means of exchange and commerce; they work, fabricate, and sell at a lower price than others, and attain to all kinds of prosperity, both at home and abroad.

Q. What is the vice contrary to this virtue?

A. It is cupidity and luxury.

Q. Is luxury a vice in the individual and in society?

A. Yes, and to that degree, that it may be said to include all the others; for the man who stands in need of many things, imposes thereby on himself all the anxiety, and submits to all the means just or unjust of acquiring them. Does he possess an enjoyment, he covets another; and in the bosom of superfluity, he is never rich; a commodious dwelling is not sufficient for him, he must have a beautiful hotel; not content with a plenteous table, he must have rare and costly viands: he must have splendid furniture, expensive clothes, a train of attendants, horses, carriages, women, theatrical representations and games. Now, to supply so many expenses, much money must be had; and he looks on every method of procuring it as good and even necessary; at first he borrows, afterwards he steals, robs, plunders, turns bankrupt, is at war with every one, ruins and is ruined.

Should a nation be involved in luxury, it occasions on a larger scale the same devastations; by reason that it consumes its entire produce, it finds itself poor even with abundance; it has nothing to sell to foreigners; its manufactures are carried on at a great expense, and are sold too dear; it becomes tributary for everything it imports; it attacks externally its consideration, power, strength, and means of defence and preservation, while internally it undermines and falls into the dissolution of its members. All its citizens being covetous of enjoyments, are engaged in a perpetual struggle to obtain them; all injure or are near injuring themselves; and hence arise those habits and actions of usurpation, which constitute what is denominated moral corruption, intestine war between citizen and citizen. From luxury arises avidity, from avidity, invasion by violence and perfidy; from luxury arises the iniquity of the judge, the venality of the witness, the improbity of the husband, the prostitution of the wife, the obduracy of parents, the ingratitude of children, the avarice of the master, the dishonesty of the servant, the dilapidation of the administrator, the perversity of the legislator, lying, perfidy, perjury, assassination, and all the disorders of the social state; so that it was with a profound sense of truth, that ancient moralists have laid the basis of the social virtues on simplicity of manners, restriction of wants, and contentment with a little; and a sure way of knowing the extent of a man's virtues and vices is, to find out if his expenses are proportionate to his fortune, and calculate, from his want of money, his probity, his integrity in fulfilling his engagements, his devotion to the public weal, and his sincere or pretended love of his country.

Q. What do you mean by the word country?

A. I mean the community of citizens who, united by fraternal sentiments, and reciprocal wants, make of their respective strength one common force, the reaction of which on each of them assumes the noble and beneficent character of paternity. In society, citizens form a bank of interest; in our country we form a family of endearing attachments; it is charity, the love of one's neighbor extended to a whole nation. Now as charity cannot be separated from justice, no member of the family can pretend to the enjoyment of its advantages, except in proportion to his labor; if he consumes more than it produces, he necessarily encroaches on his fellow-citizens; and it is only by consuming less than what he produces or possesses, that he can acquire the means of making sacrifices and being generous.

Q. What do you conclude from all this?

A. I conclude from it that all the social virtues are only the habitude of actions useful to society and to the individual who practices them; That they refer to the physical object of man's preservation; That nature having implanted in us the want of that preservation, has made a law to us of all its consequences, and a crime of everything that deviates from it; That we carry in us the seed of every virtue, and of every perfection; That it only requires to be developed; That we are only happy inasmuch as we observe the rules established by nature for the end of our preservation; And that all wisdom, all perfection, all law, all virtue, all philosophy, consist in the practice of these axioms founded on our own organization:

Preserve thyself; Instruct thyself; Moderate thyself; Live for thy fellow citizens, that they may live for thee.

VOLNEY'S ANSWER TO DR. PRIESTLY.*

SIR.—I received in due time your pamphlet on the increase of infidelity, together with the note without date which accompanied it.† My answer has been delayed by the incidents of business, and even by ill health, which you will surely excuse: this delay has, besides, no inconvenience in it. The question between us is not of a very urgent nature: the world would not go on less well with or without my answer as with or without your book. I might, indeed, have dispensed with returning you any answer at all; and I should have been warranted in so doing, by the manner in which you have stated the debate, and by the opinion pretty generally received that, on certain occasions, and with certain persons, the most noble reply is silence. You seem to have been aware of this yourself, considering the extreme precautions you have taken to deprive me of this resource; but as according to our French customs, any answer is an act of civility, I am not willing to concede the advantage of politeness—besides, although silence is sometimes very significant, its eloquence is not understood by every one, and the public which has not leisure to analyze disputes (often of little interest) has a reasonable right to require at least some preliminary explanations; reserving to itself, should the discussion degenerate into the recriminative clamors of an irritated self-love, to allow the right of silence to him in whom it becomes the virtue of moderation.

I have read, therefore, your animadversions on my *Ruins*, which you are pleased to class among the writings of modern

---

* In 1797, Dr. Priestly published a pamphlet, entitled, "*Observation on the increase of infidelity, with animadversions upon the writings of several modern unbelievers, and especially the Ruins of Mr. Volney.*" The motto to this tract was:

"Minds of little penetration rest naturally on the surface of things. They do not like to pierce deep into them, for fear of labor and trouble; sometimes still more for fear of truth."

This Letter is an answer from Volney, taken from the *Anti-Jacobin Review* of March and April, 1799.

† Dr. Priestly sent his pamphlet to Volney, desiring his answer to the strictures on his opinions in his *Ruins of Empires.*

unbelievers, and since you absolutely insist on my expressing my opinion before the public, I shall now fulfill this rather disagreeable task with all possible brevity, for the sake of economizing the time of our readers. In the first place, sir, it appears evidently, from your pamphlet, that your design is less to attack my book than my personal and moral character; and in order that the public may pronounce with accuracy on this point, I submit several passages fitted to throw light on the subject.

You say, in the preface of your discourses, p. 12, " There are, however, unbelievers more ignorant than Mr. Paine, Mr. Volney, Lequino, and others in France say," &c.

Also in the preface of your present observations, p. 20. " I can truly say that in the writings of Hume, Mr. Gibbon, Voltaire, Mr. Volney — there is nothing of solid argument : all abound in gross mistakes and misrepresentations." Idem, p. 38 — " Whereas had he (Mr. Volney) given attention to the history of the times in which Christianity was promulgated . . . . he could have no more doubt . . . &c., it is as much in vain to argue with such a person as this, as with a Chinese or even a Hottentot."

Idem, p. 119 — " Mr. Volney, if we may judge from his numerous quotations of ancient writers in all the learned languages, oriental as well as occidental, must be acquainted with all ; for he makes no mention of any translation, and yet if we judge from this specimen of his knowledge of them, he cannot have the smallest tincture of that of the Hebrew or even of the Greek."

And, at last, after having published and posted me in your very title page, as an unbeliever and an infidel ; after having pointed me out in your motto as one of those superficial spirits who know not how to find out, and are unwilling to encounter, truth ; you add, p. 124, immediately after an article in which you speak of me under all these denominations —

" The progress of infidelity, in the present age, is attended with a circumstance which did not so frequently accompany it in any former period, at least, in England, which is, that unbelievers in revelation generally proceed to the disbelief of the being and providence of God so as to become properly Atheists." So that, according to you, I am a Chinese, a Hotten-

tot, an unbeliever, an Atheist, an ignoramus, a man of no
sincerity; whose writings are full of nothing but gross mistakes and misrepresentations.   Now I ask you, sir, What has
all this to do with the main question?   What has my book in
common with my person?   And how can you hold any con-
verse with a man of such bad connexions?   In the second
place, your invitation, or rather, your summons to me, to point
out the mistakes which *I think you have made with respect to
my opinions*, suggest to me several observations.

First.   You suppose that the public attaches a high importance to your mistakes and to my opinions: but I cannot act
upon a supposition.   Am I not an unbeliever?

Secondly.   You say, p. 18, that the public *will expect it from
me:* Where are the powers by which you make the public
speak and act?   Is this also a revelation?

Thirdly.   You require me to point out your mistakes.   I do
not know that I am under any such obligation: I have not re-
proached you with them; it is not, indeed, very correct to
ascribe to me, by selection or indiscriminately, as you have
done, all the opinions scattered through my book, since, having
introduced many different persons, I was under the necessity
of making them deliver different sentiments, according to their
different characters   The part which belongs to me is that of
a traveler, resting upon the ruins and meditating on the causes
of the misfortunes of the human race.   To be consistent with
yourself you ought to have assigned to me that of the Hottentot or Samoyde savage, who argues with the Doctors, chap.
xxiii, and I should have accepted it; you have preferred that
of the erudite historian, chap. xxii, nor do I look upon this as
a mistake; I discover on the contrary, an insidious design to
engage me in a duel of self-love before the public, wherein you
would excite the exclusive interest of the spectators by supporting the cause which they approve; while the task which
you would impose on me, would only, in the event of success,
be attended with sentiments of disapprobation.   Such is your
artful purpose, that, in attacking me as doubting the existence
of Jesus, you might secure to yourself, by surprise, the favor
of every Christian sect, although your own incredulity in his
divine nature is not less subversive of Christianity than the
profane opinion, which does not find in history the proof

required by the English law to establish a fact : to say nothing
of the extraordinary kind of pride assumed in the silent, but
palpable, comparison of yourself to Paul and to Christ, by
likening your labors to theirs as tending to the same object,
p. 10, preface. Nevertheless, as the first impression of an
attack always confers an advantage, you have some ground
for expecting you may obtain the apostolic crown ; unfortunately for your purpose I entertain no disposition to that
of martyrdom : and however glorious it might be to me to fall
under the arm of him who has overcome Hume, Gibbon,
Voltaire and even Frederick II., I find myself under the necessity of declining your theological challenge, for a number
of substantial reasons.

1. Because, to religious quarrels there is no end, since the
prejudices of infancy and education almost unavoidably exclude impartial reasoning, and besides, the vanity of the
champions becomes committed by the very publicity of the
contest, never to give up a first assertion, whence result a
spirit of sectarism and faction.

2. Because no one has a right to ask of me an account of my
religious opinions. Every inquisition of this kind is a pretension to sovereignty, a first step towards persecution ; and
the tolerant spirit of this country, which you invoke, has much
less in view to engage men to speak, than to invite them to
be silent.

3. Because, supposing I do hold the opinions you attribute
to me, I wish not to engage my vanity so as never to retract,
nor to deprive myself of the resource of a conversion on
some furture day after more ample information.

4. And because, reverend sir, if, in the support of your own
thesis, you should happen to be discomfited before the
Christian audience, it would be a dreadful scandal ; and I will
not be a cause for scandal, even for the sake of good.

5. Because in this metaphysical contest our arms are too
unequal ; you speaking in your mother tongue, which I
scarcely lisp, might bring forth huge volumes, while I could
hardly oppose pages ; and the public, who would read neither
production, might take the weight of the books for that of
reasoning.

6. And because, being endowed with the gift of faith in a

pretty sufficient quantity, you might swallow in a quarter of an hour more articles than my logic would digest in a week.

7. Because again, if you were to oblige me to attend your sermons, as you have compelled me to read your pamphlet, the congregation would never believe that a man powdered and adorned like any worldling, could be in the right against a man dressed out in a large hat, *with straight hair*,* and a mortified countenance, although the gospel, speaking of the pharisees of other times, who were unpowdered, says that when one fasts he must anoint his head and wash his face.†

8. Because, finally, a dispute to one having nothing else to do would be a gratification, while to me, who can employ my time better, it would be an absolute loss.

I shall not then, reverend sir, make you my confessor in matters of religion, but I will disclose to you my opinion, as a man of letters, on the composition of your book. Having in former days, read many works of theology, I was curious to learn whether by any chemical process you had discovered real beings in that world of invisibles. Unfortunately, I am obliged to declare to the public, which, according to your expression, p. 19, "hopes to be instructed, to be led into truth, and not into error by me," that I have not found in your book a single new argument, but the mere repetition of what is told over and over in thousands of volumes, the whole fruit of which has been to procure for their authors a cursory mention in the dictionary of heresies. You everywhere lay down that as proved which remains to be proved; with this peculiarity, that, as Gibbon says, firing away your double battery against those who believe too much, and those who believe too little, you hold out your own peculiar sensations, as to the precise criterion of truth; so that we must all be just of your size in order to pass the gate of that New Jerusalem which you are building. After this, your reputation as a divine might have become problematical with me; but recollecting the principle of the association of ideas so well developed by Locke, whom you hold in estimation, and whom, for that reason I am happy to cite to you, although to him I owe that pernicious use of my

---

* Dr. Priestly has discarded his wig since he went to America, and wears his own hair. Editor A. J. Reveiw.

† St. Matthew, Chapter VI. verses 16 and 17.

understanding which makes me disbelieve what I do not comprehend — I perceive why the public having originally attached the idea of talents to the name of Mr. Priestly, doctor in chemistry, continued by habit to associate it with the name of Mr. Priestly, doctor in divinity ; which, however, is not the same thing : an association of ideas the more vicious as it is liable to be moved inversely.* Happily you have yourself raised a bar of separation between your admirers, by advising us in the first page of your preface, that your present book is especially destined for believers. To coöperate, however, with you, sir, in this judicious design, I must observe that it is necessary to retrench two passages, seeing they afford the greatest support to the arguments of unbelievers.

You say, p. 15, "What is manifestly contrary to natural reason cannot be received by it ;"— and p. 62, "With respect to intellect, men and brute animals are born in the same state, having the same external senses, which are the only inlets to all ideas, and consequently the source of all the knowledge and of all the mental habits they ever acquire."

Now if you admit, with Locke, and with us infidels, that every one has the right of rejecting whatever is contrary to his natural reason, and that all our ideas and all our knowledge are acquired only by the inlets of our external senses ; What becomes of the system of revelation, and of that order of things in times past, which is so contradictory to that of the time present ? unless we consider it as a dream of the human brain during the state of superstitious ignorance.

With these two single phrases, I could overturn the whole edifice of your faith. Dread not, however, sir, in me such overflowing zeal. For the same reason that I have not the frenzy of martyrdom, I have not that of making proselytes. It becomes those ardent, or rather acrimonious tempers, who mistake the violence of their sentiments for the enthusiasm of truth ; the ambition of noise and rumor, for the love of

---

* Mr. Blair, doctor of divinity, and Mr. Black, doctor in chemistry, met at the coffee house in Edinburg : a new theological pamphlet written by doctor Priestly was thown upon the table, "Really," said Dr. Blair, "this man had better confine himself to chemistry, for he is absolutely ignorant in theology:"—"I beg your pardon," answered Dr. Black, "he is in the right, he is a minister of the gospel, he ought to adhere to his profession, for in truth he knows nothing of chemistry."

glory ; and for the love of their neighbor, the detestation of his opinions, and the secret desire of dominion.

As for me, who have not received from nature the turbulent qualities of an apostle, and never sustained in Europe the character of a dissenter, I am come to America neither to agitate the conscience of men, nor to form a sect, nor to establish a colony, in which, under the pretext of religion, I might erect a little empire to myself. I have never been seen evangelizing my ideas, either in temples or in public meetings. I have never likewise practiced that quackery of beneficence, by which a certain divine, imposing a tax upon the generosity of the public, procures for himself the honors of a more numerous audience, and the merit of distributing at his pleasure a bounty which costs him nothing, and for which he receives grateful thanks dexterously stolen from the original donors.

Either in the capacity of a stranger, or in that of a citizen, a sincere friend to peace, I carry into society neither the spirit of dissension, nor the desire of commotion ; and because I respect in every one what I wish him to respect in me, the name of liberty is in my mind nothing else but the synonyma of justice.

As a man, whether from moderation or indolence, a spectator of the world rather than an actor in it, I am every day less tempted to take on me the management of the minds or bodies of men : it is sufficient for an individual to govern his own passions and caprices.

If by one of these caprices, I am induced to think it may be useful, sometimes, to publish my reflections, I do it without obstinacy or pretension to that implicit faith, the ridicule of which you desire to impart to me, p. 123. My whole book of the *Ruins* which you treat so ungratefully, since you thought it amusing, p. 122, evidently bears this character. By means of the contrasted opinions I have scattered through it, it breathes that spirit of doubt and uncertainty which appears to me the best suited to the weakness of the human mind, and the most adapted to its improvement, inasmuch as it always leaves a door open to new truths ; while the spirit of dogmatism and immovable belief, limiting our progress to a first received opinion, binds us at hazard, and without resource, to the yoke

of error or falsehood, and occasions the most serious mis-
chiefs to society ; since by combining with the passions, it
engenders fanaticism, which, sometimes misled and sometimes
misleading, though always intolerant and despotic, attacks
whatever is not of its own nature; drawing upon itself persecution when it is weak, and practising persecution when it is
powerful; establishing a religion of terror, which annihilates
the faculties, and vitiates the conscience: so that, whether
under a political or a religious aspect, the spirit of doubt is
friendly to all ideas of liberty, truth, or genius, while a spirit
of confidence is connected with the ideas of tyranny, servility,
and ignorance.

If, as is the fact, our own experience and that of others daily
teaches us that what at one time appeared true, afterwards
appeared demonstrably false, how can we connect with our
judgments that blind and presumptuous confidence which
pursues those of others with so much hatred ?

No doubt it is reasonable, and even honest, to act according
to our present feelings and conviction : but if these feelings
and their causes do vary by the very nature of things, how
dare we impose upon ourselves or others an invariable conviction ?   How, above all, dare we require this conviction in
cases where there is really no sensation, as happens in purely
speculative questions, in which no palpable fact can be presented ?

Therefore, when opening the book of nature, (a more authentic one and more easy to be read than leaves of paper
blackened over with Greek or Hebrew,) and when I reflected
that the slightest change in the material world has not been
in times past, nor is at present effected by the difference of so
many religions and sects which have appeared and still exist
on the globe, and that the course of the seasons, the path of
the sun, the return of rain and drought, are the same for the
inhabitants of each country, whether Christians, Mussulmans,
Idolaters, Catholics, Protestants, etc., I am induced to believe
that the universe is governed by laws of wisdom and justice,
very different from those which human ignorance and intolerance would enact.

And as in living with men of very opposite religious persuasions, I have had occasion to remark that their manners

were, nevertheless, very analagous ; that is to say, among the different Christian sects, among the Mahometans, and even among those people who were of no sect, I have found men who practise all the virtues, public and private, and that too without affectation ; while others, who were incessantly declaiming of God and religion, abandoned themselves to every vicious habit which their belief condemned, I thereby became convinced that Ethics, the doctrines of morality, are the only essential, as they are only demonstrable, part of religion. And as, by your own avowal, the only end of religion is to render men better, in order to add to their happiness, p. 62, I have concluded that there are but two great systems of religion in the world, that of good sense and beneficence, and that of malice and hypocrisy.

In closing this letter, I find myself embarrassed by the nature of the sentiment which I ought to express to you, for in declaring as you have done, p. 123, that you do not care for the contempt of such as me * (ignorant as you were of my opinion), you tell me plainly that you do not care for their esteem. I leave, therefore, to your discernment and taste to determine the sentiment most congenial to my situation and your desert.

C. F. VOLNEY.

Philadelphia, March 10, 1797.

P. S. I do not accompany this public letter with a private note to Dr. Priestly, because communications of that nature carry an appearance of bravado, which, even in exercising the right of a necessary defence, appear to me imcompatible with decency and politeness.

---

* "And what does it do for me here, except, perhaps, expose me to the contempt of such men as Mr. Volney, which, however, I feel myself pretty well able to bear?" p. 124. This language is the more surprising, as Dr. Priestly never received anything from me but civilities. In the year 1791 I sent him a dissertation of mine on the *Chronology of the Ancients*, in consequence of some charts which he had himself published. His only answer was to abuse me in a pamphlet in 1792. After this first abuse, on meeting me here last winter, he procured me an invitation to dine with his friend Mr. Russell, at whose house he lodged ; after having shown me polite attention at that dinner, he abuses me in his new pamphlet. After this second abuse he meets me in Spruce Street, and takes me by the hand as a friend, and speaks of me in a large company under that denomination. Now I ask the public, what kind of a man is Dr. Priestly ?

THE ZODIACAL SIGNS AND CONSTELLATIONS.

(Compiled by the publisher from recognized authorities.)

———

THE Zodiac is an imaginary girdle or belt in the celestial sphere, which extends about eight degrees on each side of the Ecliptic. It is divided into twelve portions, called the *signs of the Zodiac*, within which all the planets make their revolutions. The Zodiac is so called from the animals represented upon it, and is supposed to have originated in remote ages and in latitudes where the camel and elephant were comparatively unknown. This pictorial representation of the zodiac was probably the origin, as M. Dupuis suggests, of the Arabian and Egyptian adoration of animals and birds, and has led in the natural progress of events to the adoration of images by both christians and pagans.

"The Signs of the Zodiac, (says Godfrey Higgins in *The Anacalypsis*,) with the exception of the Scorpion, which was exchanged by Dan for the Eagle, were carried by the different tribes of the Israelites on their standards; and Taurus, Leo, Aquarius, and Scorpio or the Eagle—the four signs of Reuben, Judah, Ephriam, and Dan—were placed at the four corners, (the four cardinal points), of their encampment, evidently in allusion to the cardinal points of the sphere, the equinoxes and solstices, when the equinox was in *Taurus*. (See Parkhust's Lexicon.) These coincidences prove that this religious system had its origin before the bull ceased to be an equinoctial sign, and prove also, that the religion of Moses was originally the same in its secret mysteries as that of the Heathen, or, if my reader likes it better, that the Heathen secret mysteries were the same as those of Moses."

The Ecliptic, a great circle of the sphere, (shown on the preceding map by two parallel lines), is supposed to be drawn through the middle of the Zodiac, cutting the Equator at two points, (called the Equinoctial points), at an angle with the equinoctial of 23° 28', (the sun's greatest declination), and is the path which the earth is supposed to describe amidst the fixed stars in performing its annual circuit around the sun. It is called the Ecliptic because the eclipses of the sun and moon always occur under it.

The Signs are each the twelfth part of the Ecliptic or Zodiac, (30°,) and are reckoned from the point of intersection of the ecliptic and equator at the vernal equinox. They are named respectively Aries, Taurus, Gemini, Cancer, Leo, Virgo, Libra, Scorpio, Sagittarius, Capricornus, Aquarius, Pisces. These names are borrowed from the constellations of the zodiac of the same denomination, which corresponded when these divisions were originally made; but in consequence of the precession, recession, or retrocession of the equinoxes, (about 50⅒" yearly, at the rate of about 72 years to a degree, displacing an entire sign in about 2152 years, and making an entire revolution of the equinoctial in about 25,868 years), the positions of these constellations in the heavens no longer correspond with the divisions of the ecliptic of the same name, but are in advance of them. Thus, the constellation Aries is now in that part of the ecliptic called Taurus, and the stars of Taurus are in Gemini, those of Gemini in Cancer, and so on throughout the ecliptic.

The relative positions of the signs and constellations in the zodiac and ecliptic seem thus to have gradually changed with the revolving years; and the worship

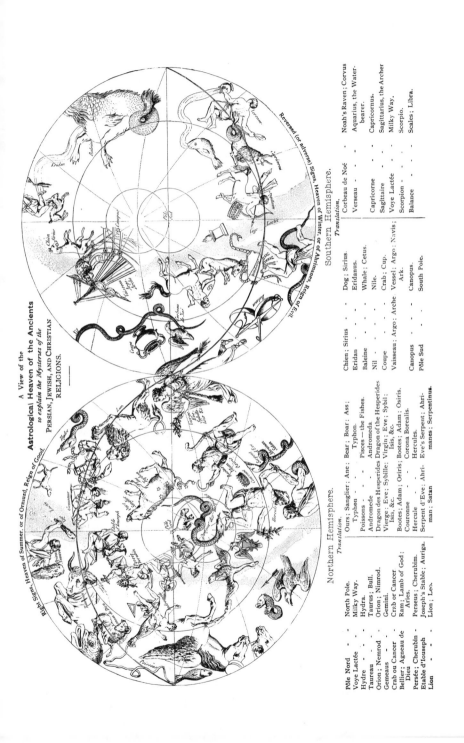

A View of the
Astrological Heaven of the Ancients
to explain the Mysteries of the
PERSIAN, JEWISH, AND CHRISTIAN RELIGIONS.

Right Signs, Heaven of Summer, or of Ormuzd, Reign of Good.

Reversed (or adverse) Signs, Heaven of Winter, or of Ahrimanes, Reign of Evil.

Northern Hemisphere.

Translation.

Pôle Nord	North Pole.
Voye Lactée	Milky Way.
Hydre	Hydra.
Taureau	Taurus; Bull.
Orion; Nemrod	Orion; Nimrod.
Gemeaux	Gemini.
Crab ou Cancer	Crab or Cancer.
Bellier; Agneau de Dieu	Ram; Lamb of God; Aries.
Persée; Cherubin	Perseus; Cherubim.
Etable d'Iouseph	Joseph's Stable; Auriga.
Lion	Lion; Leo.
Ours; Sanglier; Ane; Typhon	Bear; Boar; Ass; Typhon.
Poissons	Pisces — the Fishes.
Andromede	Andromeda.
Dragon des Hesperides	Dragon of the Hesperides
Vierge; Eve; Sybille; Isis, &c.	Virgin; Eve; Sybil; Isis, &c.
Bootes; Adam; Osiris	Bootes; Adam; Osiris.
Couronne	Corona Borealis.
Hercule	Hercules.
Serpent d'Eve; Ahriman; Satan	Eve's Serpent; Ahrimanes; Serpentinus.

Southern Hemisphere.

Translation.

Chien; Sirius	Dog; Sirius.
Eridan	Eridanus.
Baleine	Whale; Cetus.
Nil	Nile.
Coupe	Crab; Cup.
Vaisseau; Argo; Arche	Vessel; Argo; Navis; Ark.
Canopus	Canopus.
Pôle Sud	South Pole.
Corbeau de Noé	Noah's Raven; Corvus
Verseau	Aquarius, the Water-bearer.
Capricorne	Capricornus.
Sagittaire	Sagittarius, the Archer
Voye Lactée	Milky Way.
Scorpion	Scorpio.
Balance	Scales; Libra.

APPENDIX.

of the three constellations, Taurus, Aries, and Pisces, with which christianity is so intimately connected, seems to have changed in a corresponding degree. The worship of the bull of Egypt — the celestial *Taurus* —has given place to that of the lamb of Palestine — the celestial *Aries*; and under the astronomical emblem *Pisces* — the twelfth sign of the zodiac — the dominant faith of to-day was appropriately taught by the twelve apostolic fishermen.

It is from one of these chosen fishermen, St. Peter, that the Pope of Rome claims to have derived his arbitrary power for binding and loosing on earth those who are to be bound and loosed in heaven. (Matt. xvi, 19.) The grave responsibility of wielding with justice and equity this tremendous power over the future destiny of mankind, seems never to have disconcerted any of the successors of St. Peter. They have all proved to be equally arrogant and intolerant, zealous for both temporal and spiritual domination, and merciless to those who have opposed their pretensions. The present incumbent of the papal chair, who modestly claims the attribute of infallibility, seems proud of his inherited title, *The Great Fisherman!* and hopes in the progress of time, with the assistance of his monks, bishops, and cardinals, to entangle all nations in his net of faith, and to dictate with unquestioned authority the religious worship of the entire human race.

As the precession of the equinoxes still continues as of yore, and as the masses still continue credulous and devout, they may in succeeding ages be again called upon to worship the god Apis, when the sign of *Taurus* shall again coincide in the zodiac and the ecliptic ; and Aries, " the lamb of God," may again be offered in the " fullness of time" as a sacrifice for mankind, again be crucified, and again shed his redeeming blood to wash away the sins of a believing world.

M. Dupuis has satisfactorily shown in *The History of all Religions* that the twelve labors of the god and saviour Hercules were astronomical allegories— the history of the passage of the sun through the twelve signs of the zodiac — and these labors are so similar to the sufferings of Jesus, that the Rev. Mr. Parkhurst has been obliged, much against his inclination, to acknowledge that they " were types of what the real Saviour was to do and suffer." (Parkhurst, p. 47.) An intimate connection, if not identity, is thus shown between ancient and modern belief—between the paganism of the past and the orthodoxy of the present.

The Zodiacal Signs.

Aries, *the Ram:* (marked ♈.) —A northern constellation, usually named as the first sign in the zodiac, into which, when the sun enters at the vernal equinox in March, the days and nights are of equal length. Aries has been regarded by the devout during many ages as the celestial representative, visible in the heavens, of " the Lamb of God that taketh away the sins of the world."

Taurus, *the Bull:* (marked thus, ♉.) — The second sign in the zodiac, which by the Arabians is called *Ataur*. This constellation was worshipped for ages by the idolatrous Egyptians as the heavenly representative of their god Osiris ; and derives its name, according to Grecian fable, from the bull into which Jupiter transformed himself in order to carry Europa over into Crete; but the constellation was probably so named by the Egyptians to designate that period of the year, (April), in which cows mostly bring forth their young.

" The Rev. Mr. Maurice in his work on the antiquities of India, has shown that the May-day festival and the May-pole of Great Britain with its garlands, etc., are the remains of an ancient festival of Egypt and India, and probably of Phœnicia, when these nations, in countries very distant, and from times very remote, have all, with one consent, celebrated the entrance of the sun into the sign of Taurus at the vernal equinox."

APPENDIX.

GEMINI, *the Twins:* (marked thus, ♊.)—A zodiacal constellation, visible in May, containing the two bright stars Castor and Pollux, the fabled sons of Leda and Jupiter, who during their lives had cleared the Hellespont and neighboring seas of pirates, and were therefore deemed the protectors of navigators and sailors.

CANCER, *the Crab:* (marked thus, ♋.)— Is the fourth sign of the zodiac, which the sun enters on the 21st day of June, and is thence called the summer solstice. According to Grecian fable, the crab was transported to heaven at the request of Juno, after it had been slain by Hercules during his battle with the serpent Python, but the evident design of the name is to represent the apparent backward motion of the sun in June, which is said to resemble the motions of a crab.

LEO, *the Lion:* (♌). — Is the fifth sign in the zodiac, and contains one star of the first magnitude, called *Regulus,* or *Cor Leonis—* the *Lion's Heart.* The fervid heat of July, when the sun has attained its greatest power, is now symbolized in our almanacs by the figure of an enraged lion ; and the feasts or sacrifices formerly celebrated among the ancients during this month, in honor of the sun, (which they also represented under the form of a lion,) were called *Leonitica.* The priests who performed the sacred rites were called *Leones.* This feast was sometimes called *Mithriaca,* because Mithra was the name of the sun among the Persians. The sacred writings abound with references to the " king of beasts ; " among the most interesting of which is the story of the battle between the lion and Samson, the Jewish Hercules ; while the most wonderful example of animal evolution on record is found in the sixty-fifth chapter of Isaiah, where we are gravely informed that " the lion shall eat straw like the bullock."

VIRGO, *Virgin Mother, Venus, Eve, Isis, &c.*—(♍). — Is the sixth sign of the zodiac, which the sun enters about the 21st of August. The myths and fables regarding the virgin which abound among all nations and all religions, are both various and voluminous, and we may add somewhat improbable. They all agree, however, in this, that the female, shown on the preceding diagram, holding in her right hand a branch of ripened fruit,— the apples of Paradise,— was intended to represent the reproductive powers of nature,— the abundance, satisfaction and contentment which mortals enjoy during the happy period of harvest.

LIBRA, *the Balance.* — The seventh sign of the zodiac, directly opposite to Aries, from which it is distant 180°. It is marked thus ♎, after the manner of a pair of scales ; to denote, probably, that when the sun arrives at this part of the ecliptic, the days and nights are equal, as if weighed in a balance. Hence the period when the sun enters Libra, (about September 21st,) is called the *Autumnal* equinox. On the 25th of September was born John the Baptist, the forerunner of his cousin Jesus, who came to his exaltation of glory on the 25th of March, the *Vernal* equinox. "The equinoxes and solstices," says Higgins, " equally marked the births and deaths of John and Jesus." The one preceded and prepared the way for the other, who receded. One advanced, the other declined. Jesus ascended, John descended. Astrologically speaking, " *He must increase, but I must decrease.* " (John iii, 30.)

SCORPIO, *the Scorpion.* — The eighth sign of the zodiac, which the sun enters on the 23d of October, is marked thus ♏. Scorpio is fabled to have killed the great hunter Orion, and for that exploit to have been placed among the constellations. For this reason it is also said that when Scorpio rises Orion sets.

SAGITTARIUS, *the Archer:* (marked thus, ♐,) is the ninth zodiacal sign, and corresponds with the month of November. This sign is represented like a centaur and was fabled to be Crotus, the son of Eupheme, the nurse of the Muses.

CAPRICORNUS, *the Goat.* (♑)—The tenth sign of the zodiac, which the sun enters the 21st of December, (the longest night in the year,) called the winter solstice.

APPENDIX.

This sign is drawn to represent the horns of a goat, and is fabled to have been Pan, who in the war of the giants was taken to heaven in the shape of a goat. Others claim that it was the goat of Amalthæa, which fed Jupiter with her milk. Macrobius, who calls Cancer and Capricorn the gates of the sun, makes the latter sign to represent his motion, after the manner of a goat climbing the mountains.

AQUARIUS, *the Water Bearer.*—A constellation in the heavens so called, because during its rising there is usually an abundance of rain. It is the eleventh sign in the zodiac, reckoned from Aries, and is marked thus, ♒. It rises in January and sets in February, and is supposed by the poets to be Ganymede.

PISCES, *the Fishes,* (♓).—The twelfth sign of the zodiac, rises in February and is represented by two fishes tied together by the tails. These fishes are fabled by the Greeks to be those into which Venus and Cupid were changed to escape from the giant Typhon. This fable may not be true, but that wonderful miracles were once performed with two small fishes is stated in the ninth chapter of the Gospel of St. Luke, where it is said that 5000 hungry mortals were cheaply, if not sumptuously regaled with two small fishes and five loaves of bread ; while a large surplus of this piscatory diet, larger indeed than the original stock, still remained intact.

In the vestibule or approaches to catholic churches is usually found a vase filled with water, (called *Piscina,*) and this water is considered holy. The Fish-days are observed as holy days, or fast days, in which Fish may be eaten and meat is forbidden ; and learned writers have asserted that in the worship of *Pisces* may be found the true secret of the origin of the rite of baptism. The Fish-god Oannes, is said to have come out of the Erythræan Sea and taught the Babylonians all kinds of useful knowledge. *Ionnes* or *Jonas* went headlong into the sea and into a fish, and has kindly recorded for our instruction his remarkable adventures. The miraculous draughts of fishes in the apostolic age still excite the emulation of modern fishermen, who cannot even hope to rival the wonders that have been recorded. St. Peter is said to have secured ready money from the mouth of a fish that he caught with a hook and line in the sea of Galilee. (Matthew xvii, 27.) His success was justly rewarded, and to him was delegated the power of ruling the infant church. *Pisces* thus displaced *Aries.* The fisherman succeeded the shepherd. The precession of the equinoxes produced a new avatar ; a new sign arose in the heavens ; and a new saviour was born to save mankind.

THE CONSTELLATIONS.

SIRIUS, *the Dog Star.* — A bright star of the first magnitude in the mouth of the constellation *Canis Major.* This is the brightest star that appears in our firmament, and is supposed by some to be the nearest.

LEPUS. — One of the southern constellations, placed near *Orion,* according to Grecian fable, because it was one of the animals which he hunted.

ERIDANUS. — A winding southern constellation, near the *Cetus,* containing the bright star *Achemar.*

CETUS, *the Whale.* — A southern constellation, and one of the forty-eight old asterisms. It is fabled to have been the sea monster sent by Neptune to devour Andromeda, which was killed by Perseus.

CRATER, *the Cup.* — A southern constellation, near Hydra. This is supposed by Hyainus to be the cup which Apollo gave to the *Corvus,* or Raven.

CORVUS. — One of the old constellations in the southern hemisphere, near Sagittarius. This bird is fabled to have been translated to heaven by Apollo for discovering to him the infidelity of the nymph Coronis.

ARGO NAVIS, *the Ship.* — A constellation near to the *Canis Major,* and the name of the ship which carried Jason and his fifty-four companions to Colchis in quest of the golden fleece, and was said to have been translated into the heavens.

APPENDIX.

CANOPUS. — The name formerly given to a star in the second bend of Eridanus. A bright star of the first magnitude in the rudder of the ship Argo, which, according to Pliny, was visible at Alexandria in Egypt.

CENTAURUS. — One of the forty-eight old constellations in the southern hemisphere, represented in the form of half man and half horse, who was fabled by the Greeks to have been Chiron, the tutor of Achilles.

AVA, or ALTAR. — One of the old constellations, and fabled to have been that at which the giants entered into their conspiracy against the gods; wherefore Jupiter, in commemoration of the event, transplanted the altar into the heavens.

PEGASUS. — One of the forty-eight old constellations of the northern hemisphere, figured in the form of a flying horse.

DELPHINUS, or DOLPHIN. — A northern constellation, near Pegasus. The Dolphin is fabled to have been translated to heaven by Neptune.

AQUILA, *the Eagle.* — In the Arabic *Altair,* but in the Persian tables the *Flying Vulture.* This is one of the old constellations, situated near Delphinus in the northern hemisphere. According to Grecian fable, Aquila represented Ganymede or Hebe, who was transported to heaven and made cup-bearer to Jupiter.

SAGITTA — *the Dart or Arrow,* called by the Arabians *Schahan.* One of the old constellations in the northern hemisphere, near Aquila and Delphinus. It is fabled to have been the arrow with which Hercules slew the vulture that was devouring the liver of Prometheus who was, like Jesus, crucified for loving mankind.

CYGNUS, *the Swan.* — An old constellation in the milky-way, between Equus and the Dragon. This is fabled to be the swan into which Jupiter transformed himself in order to deceive the virtuous Leda, wife of Tyndareus, king of Sparta. The Grecian matron, like the Jewish virgin, thus became the mother of a God.

LYRA. — A northern constellation between Hercules and Cygnus, containing a white star of the first magnitude.

MILKY-WAY. — *Galaxy,* or *Via Lactia.* — A broad luminous path or circle encompassing the heavens, which is easily discernible by its white appearance, from which it derives its name. It is supposed to be the blended light of innumerable fixed stars, which are not distinguishable with ordinary telescopes.

HYDRA, *the Serpent.* — A southern constellation of great length, which is drawn to represent a serpent. The Hydra is fabled to have been placed in the heavens by Apollo, to frighten the Raven from drinking.

ORION, *the Hunter.* — A constellation of the southern hemisphere with respect to the ecliptic, but half southern and half northern with respect to the equinoctial. It is placed near the feet of the bull, and is composed of seventeen stars in the form of a sword, which has given occasion to the poets to speak of Orion's sword. He was described by the Greeks as a "mighty hunter," who for his exploits was placed in the heavens by Jupiter, between the *Canis* and the *Lepus.* He is believed by many to have been the "mighty hunter" spoken of in the bible, under the name of Nimrod. (See Gen. x : 8, 9; 1 Chron. i : 10; Micha v : 6, Job ix, 9; Amos v, 8.)

PERSEUS. — This constellation is named from Perseus, the son of Jupiter by Danæ, who was translated into the heavens by the assistance of Minerva, for having released Andromeda from her confinement on the rock to which she was chained. He is represented in the preceding illustration holding a drawn sword in his right hand and in his left the head of Medusa, the Gorgon, whose terrifying appearance changed all who beheld her into stone, and whom he had destroyed with the assistance of the wings he had borrowed from Mercury, the helmet from Pluto, the sword from Vulcan, and the shield from Minerva.

APPENDIX.

JOSEPH'S STABLE ; AURIGA, *the Wagoner :*—A northern constellation between Perseus and Gemini, represented by the figure of an old man supporting a goat. He is said to have been taken to heaven by Jupiter after the invention of wagons.

URSA MAJOR, *the Bear.*—One of the prominent northern constellations, situated near the north pole. It contains the stars called the *Dipper*. *Ursa Minor* contains the pole-star, which is shown in the extremity of the tail of the bear.

ANDROMEDA.—A northern constellation, represented by a woman chained ; as, according to Grecian fable, Andromeda, the daughter of Cassiopia, was bound to a rock by the Nereides, and afterwards released by Perseus. Minerva changed her into a constellation after her death, and placed her in the heavens.

DRACO OR DRAGON. — A northern constellation, supposed to represent the Dragon that guarded the Hesperian fruit, and was killed by Hercules. It is said that Juno took it up to heaven and placed it among the constellations.

BOOTIS, *the Ox driver :* so called because this constellation seems to follow the Great Bear as the driver follows his oxen. Bootis is represented as grasping in his right hand a sickle and in his left a club, and is fabled to have been Icarius, who was transported to heaven because he was a great cultivator of the vine ; for when Bootes rises the works of ploughing and cultivation go forward.

CORONA BOREALIS. *Northern Crown.*—One of the old northern constellations, between Hercules and Bootes.

CORONA AUSTRALIS.—*Southern Crown.* — One of the old constellations in the southern hemisphere, between Sagittarius and Scorpio. The Corona were fabled to be Menippe and Metioche, two daughters of Orion, who sacrificed themselves at the suggestion of an oracle, to protect Bœotia, their native country, from the ravages of a pestilence : it being the belief of idolatrous nations that an angry god could be propitiated by human sacrifices, and that the death of the innocent might atone for the sins of the guilty. The deities of Hades were astonished, it is said, at the patriotism and devotion of these Grecian maidens, who had so generously and uselessly sacrificed their lives. After their death two stars were seen to issue from the altars that still smoked with their blood, and these stars were placed in the heavens in the form of a crown or coronet.

CEPHEUS AND CASSIOPIA. — One of the old asterism in the northern hemisphere, near the pole. According to Grecian fables, Cassiopia and her husband Cepheus, king of Etheopia, were placed among the constellations to witness the punishment inflicted on their daughter, Andromeda.

TRIANGULARIUM.—A name for both one of the old and new constellations in the northern hemisphere, between Andromeda and Aries.

SERPENTARIUS, called *Ophiucus,* is a constellation in the northern hemisphere, between Scorpio and Hercules.

HERCULES, one of the old northern constellations. In Grecian mythology it was taught and believed that Hercules, the *Theban,* was born of a human mother and an immortal father, like other so-called saviours of mankind. His mother, the fair Alcmena, wife of Amphitryon, having found favor in the eyes of the god Jupiter, soon fell an unwilling victim to his celestial wiles. The life of the infant Hercules, born of this unnatural union, was threatened by the jealous Juno, the same as the life of the infant Jesus was threatened by the tyrant Herod. Like Jesus, Hercules devoted his life to the benefit of the human race, and like Jesus he was also worshipped after his death as a God in heaven. He is shown in the astrological chart, enveloped in the skin of the lion he has slain, with his club upraised, and his foot placed threateningly above the head of the Dragon, as if about to fulfill the scriptural prophecy, that "the seed of the woman shall bruise the serpent's head."

East

North

South

West

EUROPE

TARTARY

CHINA

SINÆ

Baikal
CORI

Seric
CORI

Ganges

INDIA

Ceylon

Persia

ARABIA

AFRICA

Thebes

Palmyra

OCEAN

OCEAN

8 Babylon.
9 Nineveh.
10 Cassmere.
11 Crimea.
12 Constantinople.
13 Lassa.

1 Piramids
2 Gaza
3 R. Jordan.
4 Mt Sinai.
5 Bahara Islands
6 Persepolis
7 Ecbatana.